"It is worth our best effort to make this a livable society for every American, a society in which ignorance and disease and want will tyrannize no longer, a society in which every individual is of value."

—John W. Gardner

This volume is one in a series of reports prepared by the Joint Commission as part of a national mental health study which culminated in the publication of the Commission's Final Report, entitled *Crisis in Child Mental Health*. This present volume discusses the findings and recommendations reported by Task Force VI, which was concerned with the study, "Innovation and Social Progress in Relation to Mental Health of Children," as well as portions of the report of the Committee on Children of Minority Groups.

In considering the broad mental health needs of our nation's child population the Joint Commission offers a number of proposals designed to narrow the present gap between the poor and the more affluent and to eliminate the fragmentation and disconnection which characterize both our service institutions and our interpersonal relations. For all who believe that the major crisis of our time is a crisis in human relations and the devaluation of the individual, *Social Change and the Mental Health of Children* presents a vital and illuminating statement that is both timely and provocative.

SOCIAL CHANGE AND

THE MENTAL HEALTH OF CHILDREN

Volumes from the Joint Commission on Mental Health of Children

ADOLESCENCE, by Irene M. Josselyn, M.D.
CHILD MENTAL HEALTH IN INTERNATIONAL PERSPECTIVE,
  edited by Henry P. David
CRISIS IN CHILD MENTAL HEALTH: *Challenge for the 1970's*
MENTAL HEALTH: *From Infancy Through Adolescence*
THE MENTAL HEALTH OF CHILDREN: *Services, Research, and Manpower*
SOCIAL CHANGE AND THE MENTAL HEALTH OF CHILDREN

Forthcoming
THE MENTAL HEALTH OF CHILDREN: *A Reader*
  Selected Papers of the Joint Commission on Mental Health of Children

Social Change and
the Mental Health of Children

REPORT OF TASK FORCE VI AND EXCERPTS
FROM THE REPORT OF THE COMMITTEE
ON CHILDREN OF MINORITY GROUPS BY
THE JOINT COMMISSION ON MENTAL HEALTH
OF CHILDREN

HARPER & ROW, PUBLISHERS

NEW YORK, EVANSTON, SAN FRANCISCO, LONDON

1817

Official distribution of this book has been made possible through a grant from the Foundation for Child Mental Welfare, Inc.

Designed by Sidney Feinberg

ACKNOWLEDGEMENTS

This Task Force is indebted to Dr. Ronald Lippitt for the preparation of the chapter, Directions for Change and to Mrs. Barbara Sowder of the Commission staff for research, writing, and editorial work on this report. Throughout her work Mrs. Sowder has tried to reflect the thinking of Task Force VI. Thanks and appreciation should also be extended to Mrs. Rita Pennington and Mrs. Elizabeth Bogan for their assistance in the preparation of this report.

It is worth our best effort to make this a livable society for every American, a society in which ignorance and disease and want will tyrannize no longer, a society in which every individual is of value.

We have a long way to go before we reach that kind of society. The controversies of the day sometimes drown out the progress which is being made. But it is just this work—the liberation of the individual from all the conditions that afflict his body or stunt his mind or stifle his spirit—that gives meaning—that has always given meaning—to American life.

—JOHN W. GARDNER

Contents

Foreword

This is one in a series of reports prepared for the Joint Commission on Mental Health of Children, Inc., and is part of a national mental health study which culminated in the publication of a Final Report containing the findings and recommendations for a national mental health program for children and youth.

The present document constitutes the entire report of Task Force VI, which was concerned with the study "Innovation and Social Progress in Relation to Mental Health of Children" as well as portions of the report of the Committee on Children of Minority Groups.

Listed below are the titles of the present series:

CRISIS IN CHILD MENTAL HEALTH: *Challenge for the 1970's*

   This Final Report is based on an earlier version that was submitted in June, 1969, to members of the United States Senate and House of Representatives, to the governors of the fifty states, the National Institute of Mental Health, the Secretary of Health, Education and Welfare, and to participating agencies and members of the Joint Commission on Mental Health of childen.

ADOLESCENCE, by Irene M. Josselyn, M.D.

CHILD MENTAL HEALTH IN INTERNATIONAL PERSPECTIVE, edited by Henry P. David

MENTAL HEALTH: *From Infancy Through Adolescence*

   A volume combining reports of Task Forces I, II, and III and the Committees on Education and Religion.

THE MENTAL HEALTH OF CHILDREN: *Services, Research, and Manpower*
   A volume combining reports of Task Forces IV, V, and the Committee on Clinical Issues.

SOCIAL CHANGE AND THE MENTAL HEALTH OF CHILDREN
   A volume combining reports of Task Force VI and the Committee on Children of Minority Groups.

Forthcoming

MENTAL HEALTH OF CHILDREN: *A Reader*
  Selected Papers of the Joint Commission on Mental Health of Children

These reports contain much of the detailed information which formed the basis of the Commission's Final Report. The series is also a valuable source of recommendations, many of which could not be included in the final document because of the sheer limitations of space. In preparing these reports for publication, note has been made of any recommendations contained in the series which differ substantially from those formulated by the Commission in its final deliberations.

Participating organizations, members and officers of the Board of Directors of the Commission, and the headquarters staff are listed in the Appendix at the end of the book.

The Commission is a nongovernmental, multidisciplinary, nonprofit organization. Its study was authorized by Congress and largely funded through grants from the National Institute of Mental Health. Financial contributions were also made by the following organizations and individuals:

American Academy of Child Psychiatry
American Academy of Pediatrics
American Association for Children's Residential Centers
American Association of Psychiatric Clinics for Children
American Child Guidance Foundation
American Medical Association
American Nurses Association
American Orthopsychiatric Association
The Grant Foundation, Ind.
Milwaukee County Mental Health Association
    (Maurice Falk Medical Fund)
National Association for Retarded Children
National Association of Social Workers
National Foundation for Child Mental Welfare, Inc.
Pittsburg Brothers Fund
Smith Kline & French Laboratories
Dr. Viola Bernard
Dr. Joseph Bobbitt
Dr. Reginald Lourie
Charles Schlaifer, Esq.
Dr. Meyer Sonis
Mr. and Mrs. David J. Winton

—BARBARA SOWDER

I

INNOVATION AND SOCIAL PROGRESS IN RELATION TO MENTAL HEALTH OF CHILDREN

REPORT OF TASK FORCE VI

MEMBERS OF TASK FORCE VI

Chairman: ROBERT H. FELIX, M.D.,
Dean, School of Medicine
Saint Louis University
St. Louis, Missouri

Co-chairman: ROBERT H. ALWAY, M.D.,
Professor of Pediatrics, School of Medicine
Stanford University School of Medicine
Palo Alto, California

CONRAD M. ARENSBERG, Ph.D.
Professor of Anthropology
Columbia University
New York, New York

JOSEPH J. DOWNING, M.D.
Program Chief, Mental Health Services
Division
Dept. of Public Health and Welfare
San Mateo, California

MRS. FRED R. HARRIS
President, Oklahomans for Indian
Opportunity
Washington, D.C.

MATTHEW HUXLEY, M.S.
Director, Division of Educational
Development
Smithsonian Institution
Washington, D.C.

ROBERT L. LEON, M.D.
Professor and Chairman, Department
of Psychiatry
The University of Texas Medical
School
San Antonio, Texas

RONALD LIPPITT, Ph.D.
Program Director, Center for
Research on the Utilization
of Scientific Knowledge
University of Michigan
Institute for Social Research
Ann Arbor, Michigan

JOHN H. NIEMEYER
President, Bank Street College of
Education
New York, New York

JUSTINE WISE POLIER
Judge, Family Court of the State
of New York
New York, New York

M. BREWSTER SMITH, Ph.D.
Professor and Chairman
Department of Psychology
University of Chicago
Chicago, llinois

Preface

A RATIONALE FOR THE REPORT

Task Force VI faced a very complex and somewhat ill-defined job as the name of the group—"Innovation and Social Progress in Relation to Mental Health of Children"—indicates. As an approach to the problem, the group explored many parameters and reviewed a wide range of considerations with respect to the social milieu of the present times, social change, trends, and future potentials as they relate to the mental health of children and youth.

The Task Force found it necessary to give some preliminary consideration to trends affecting the mental health of children before they could talk sensibly about children's reactions to these trends. In this consideration "mental health" in the younger years is considered broadly and untheoretically to include psychological effectiveness and well-being in childhood as the basis for these attributes in adulthood.

In the initial stages of discussion, there was a high degree of frustration. It proved very difficult to define and state the social circumstances of the day and those changes which are in fact occurring and will be occurring that are of importance to the mental health of children. There was, of course, the strong conviction that the nature of the world and of this country has changed dramatically in the last 20 years; that the rate of change is, in fact, revolutionary. The welter of evidence made it difficult to separate transient, unimportant changes from those which are basic, continuing, and of great impact. It was finally decided, however, that it would be possible to document some of the matters of importance; and the group fastened upon the task of stating the evidences of what they called, for want of a better term, "our malaise." In other words, what are the present and developing conditions that are having a detrimental influence upon children and youth? It was recognized that many of the situations that are

5

having an adverse impact are not new. For instance, poverty and the slums have been with us for a long time; but they have a new importance today because people are admitting their existence, reacting to their detrimental influences, and trying to bring about change. The facts of poverty have become, therefore, much more salient causes of the malaise than they were when they were ignored. Hopes have been stirred, moreover, about the possibility of change where formerly fatalism prevailed. What before was taken for granted or regarded as "Acts of God" now is recognized as the fault of man. On the other hand, there are new patterns of relationships developing in all segments of the society, among the working class and the affluent as well as among the poor people of the ghetto. It appeared to the group that many of the new kinds of relationships between groups and generations were initiated by the young people; that many of the innovations in patterns of conduct, concepts of responsibilities, and the development of activist response to difficulties, are really the contributions of youth. Some of these developments cause many people anguish while other people are gratified. There are both constructive and destructive aspects to the complaints and activities of youth, but it is obvious that these activities are part of the present social scene and are likely to continue. In and of themselves, the protests represent problem-finding efforts. The things about which young people are complaining are, by definition, things that they do not like about our society, though we may need to look deeper for the sources of "malaise."

As a consequence of these considerations, the group decided to see if it could document the malaise and the problems affecting children and youth in our society, looking separately at children growing up in poverty, those living in the families of working-class members of our society, and those coming from the families of the affluent. This task required bibliographical scanning of scholarly research. It also involved the more difficult task of reading the record of the current scene, whether in reports such as that of the National Advisory Commission on Civil Disorders or the daily press as it reports riots, student rebellions, and an occasional successful accommodation between the many conflicting segments of our society. It was necessary to deal with current statistics about income, poverty, housing, and the multiplicity of factors associated with social circumstances in our society. This task has been tackled by the staff of the Commission and reviewed by members of the Task Force.

The first part of the report represents a documentation of such matters from the fairly complete references at hand. Only exemplary data are incorporated here. The report indicates where additional documentation is readily available, via the extensive bibliography. We have tried to draw a picture of the conditions under which children in this country live, as these conditions affect children and the way in which they grow up. Since it is a picture of the whole spectrum, it is not preoccupied with the poor people, or the rich people, or the working people. Whether or not there is equally adequate data in each section is another question. Probably the hardest part of the fact-collecting was faced in getting good data about the working-class families. Any imbalance is not due to lack of effort, but to lack of availability of data.

The Task Force, having thus defined what it wanted to know about our society, and having decided to put the analytic emphasis on negative influences, then faced the task of constructive contribution with respect to the problems. This part of the task was approached by first trying to analyze the factors associated with change in our society and the factors arrayed against change, the clash between which underlies the present confrontations between the old and young. Another task was the difficult one of trying to identify constructive innovations and ways in which change can be promoted on a selective and constructive basis. The Task Force found many kinds of change that it considered desirable. It found many situations in which the forces for change and the need for change were present, but no real solution or mechanism was available to produce the change. The Task Force therefore became interested in new models for the participation of young people of all classes in our society's functioning. The models of participation involved voluntary and unpaid work, remunerated work, programs in collaboration with adult segments of the society as well as those controlled by the youth themselves. By developing roles for participation, constructive change can be encouraged in directions that may replace some of the sheer protest, which reflects real sources of discontent but, typically, lacks a program for reconnecting the lives of young people with the many currents of society. The final part of the report, therefore, represents an effort to analyze and describe some of the processes mentioned above. The Task Force has been helped in this task by a contract with the National Commission on Resources for Youth, Inc. This organization has searched the country for current and viable participation models that appear to be salutary and constructive. Out of this process came the basis for specific recommendations, some of them legislative, some of them not.

The Task Force holds no brief that constructive action along the lines suggested by these considerations can eliminate mental illness or the need for clinical services for children and youth. It does hold, however, that radical change and major investments are needed if American society is to provide its young people with the opportunity for mentally healthy lives. A mentally healthy life, in the view of this Task Force, is one which has meaning and purpose and opportunity; and lives which are unrooted and thwarted are not mentally healthy in our sense, even if those so afflicted do not have diagnosable symptoms.

Summary and Recommendations

SUMMARY

We believe that every American child has the right to a mentally healthy life of well-being and effectiveness. If we are to fulfill this right, we must face squarely the social crises of our times and commit ourselves to radical social change.

At present, far too many of our children lead unrooted and thwarted lives. Caught up in a technological era marked by increasing urbanization, family mobility and stress, lack of community, preoccupation with material concerns, and fluctuating values, our young are hampered in finding a meaningful, satisfying, and productive role in life.

The major crisis of our time is a crisis in human relations. In our national confusion and fear, we have lost our capacity for mutual trust, love, and responsibility. Our children's lives are marked by a lack of bonds between individuals of different ages, generations, and social groups. Fragmentation of experience between family, work, school, and neighborhoods is accompanied by discontinuities in the steps toward responsible adulthood and by ill-coordinated specialization on the part of youth-serving institutions and agencies. Many of our young develop a feeling that they cannot control their own destiny.

Thousands of our children and youth continue to be herded into large, depersonalized institutions where custodial care, rather than remediation, is still the order of the day. Thousands of infants born this year will not survive birth, or will die before their first birthday. Thousands of others will be born with birth defects. Such risks are particularly high among our poor. The greater proportion of these tragedies could be avoided if proper nutrition, prenatal, and postnatal care were guaranteed both mothers and infants.

Evidence suggests that many surviving infants may suffer physical damage and, in turn, become "high-risk" mothers, unless society takes measures to eliminate the severe malnutrition that inexcusably still occurs among the very poor in the United States. This, however, is only one example of the many disadvantages which today's children will face, one of the many ways in which the cycle of intergenerational poverty tends to be perpetuated.

Given the increasing technological basis of our society, the present gap between the poor and the affluent will no doubt widen unless society takes steps to insure an economic floor for every American family, adequate wages and employment opportunities, and equal but high-quality services in all our institutions. Particular programs, however, may be of little value if they do not, as Dr. Robert Leon[1] notes, "go hand in hand with the development of human resources which include mental and physical well-being and all that contributes to this." It is important, Dr. Leon concludes, that we look at the "biopsychosocial" organism, not only because this can lead to an integration of present isolated programs but because we need to be more conscious of the fact that:

. . . When we consider the mental health of any socially disadvantaged group we cannot assume certain 'givens' which we take for granted when we talk about mental health for the predominant middle class—where we assume important physical, social, and cultural variables to be present. The middle class has access to and generally utilizes adequate health care and diet. Minimally adequate housing and education are usually present, and the middle-class American, for the most part, has the necessary skills to enable him to cope with the complexities of our modern society. This is not so for many . . . socially disadvantaged groups.

The process of program development must involve the client population throughout in determining their own fate. Until our young people learn that their efforts in their own behalf can be decisive and important, they will continue to succumb to the debilitating effects of apathy and defeatism. These feelings, in different guises, affect youth in all strata of our society. The increasing number of alienated youth among our middle class no longer allows us to assume that such attitudes are limited to our poor and ethnic minorities. The protest activities and the search for active involvement among other of our youth are a further reminder that attainment of the American Dream of success is not an end unto itself, that youth yearn for participation in and communication with the adult society.

1. Robert L. Leon. "Some implications for a preventive program for American Indians," *Amer. J. Psychiat.*, 125:2, August 1968.

The current lack of good mutual communications and trust between youth and the representatives of the adult society is reflected in the tendency to rely on coercive power, which has predictable consequences but which, in the long run, can only aggravate and intensify the very problems that lead to its use. Further, there is a temptation to propose and to rely on simplistic, single-factor solutions that are sure to fail with consequent disillusion and cynicism for all concerned. Our commitment to our young must include the building of mutual, reciprocal relationships between the young and the total adult world—relationships that encourage and build upon the initiative of the young and include an openness on the part of adults to communication and learning from the young, thus promoting an atmosphere of mutual respect.

We believe that meaningful participation is essential to the mental health of all our nation's children. Changes that eliminate alienation, disconnection, fragmentation, stereotypy, hostility, and apathy are as vital to the needs of our more affluent children and youth as to our more disadvantaged; as applicable to the student activist as to the black radical; as drastically required by the apathetic poverty child as by the "hippie" and other alienated middle-class youth.

Social changes on a major scale are required if all our children and youth are to enjoy full opportunity to live productive and rewarding lives to their full capacity—to enjoy optimal mental health. This, of course, does not obviate the need for more and better mental health services and facilities and for new models tailored to the needs of a pluralistic society.

In considering the broad mental health needs of our entire child population, Task Force VI has proposed a number of recommendations which are designed to narrow the present gap between the poor and the more affluent and to eliminate the present fragmentation and disconnection which characterizes both our service institutions and our interpersonal relations. These recommendations are briefly summarized below. In relation to each of these proposals, we wish to emphasize the need for mandatory built-in mechanisms of feedback and evaluation to insure that change occurs in constructive ways.

RECOMMENDATIONS

I. *A Design for Youth Involvement and Participation:*

Our proposed model would: 1) involve youth in the decisions and planning of learning programs designed for youth; and 2) utilize youth as key resources in the adult community. Financed by both private and public funds, youth of two age sectors (13–17 and 18–20) would serve in councils and programs at the local, State, and National levels. At the local level, youth would be involved both in attempts to influence adult-initiated community functions and in youth initiated activities. Youth from local councils would also serve at both the State and National levels, along with other selected youth and would be provided professional adult consultation. At the State level, youth would be involved in: 1) a continuing survey of innovative practices in local community participation programs; 2) providing consultation to youth who wish to establish a council or improve an already existing program; and 3) contact and collaboration with colleges and universities to stimulate and maintain the participation of "away-from-home" youth. At the National level, youth involvement would revolve around: 1) maintaining communication between the State programs and an active liaison with Federal programs relevant to youth; 2) reviewing of funding proposals and recruiting of applied research, documentation projects, evaluation programs, and innovations in new areas of youth participation and training; 3) the development of a directory of consultants to serve as a nationwide referral network; and 4) collaboration with the mass media to effect public recognition and awards to outstanding youth groups.

II. *Education of the Young for Participation and Growth into Adult Roles:*

On-going education of the young for active involvement and creative participation might be accomplished in the following ways: 1) inclusion in the curriculum from the first grade on of materials dealing with human relations; 2) development of the role of cross-age educational helper (i.e., teaching of the younger by older students) as a continuous part of each student's learning experience from the third grade on; 3) collaboration with youth in the planning and management of the learning environment, e.g., continued leadership training and weekly "leadership clinics" in which leadership problems are analyzed, leadership skills are practiced, etc.; Task Forces composed of students and faculty committees to develop the goals, criteria, and tools for evaluating the educational program, thus involving youth in "thinking through" procedures; and apprenticeship for potential leaders under the direction of older students in leadership roles; 4) inclusion in the curriculum of more practical training to prepare children and youth for adult roles (e.g., citizen, productive worker, mature loving spouse, and intelligent parent); and 5) training for social problems through action research, problem solving, role playing, etc.

III. *Coordination and Integration of Community Socialization and Educational Services:*

Illustrative patterns of needed change include: 1) "regional teams" and "direct workers seminars" in which both professionals and volunteers can exchange information, discuss techniques and problems, and decide courses of action relevant to the child population served; 2) identification of key policy and program leadership in all sectors of the socialization community who can, through joint efforts, explore needs for collaboration on developmental projects, identify needs for pooling and coordinating resources, conduct leadership training, etc.; 3) collaboration of influential youth with adults so that youth can help adults understand youth's point of view and provide adults with opportunities of communicating with youth about important problems; and 4) development of new patterns of Federal and State effort which will promote, support, and give guidance to creative coordination at the local community level in the planning and delivery of services.

IV. *Inservice Training of Parents:*

Programs of training and support for parents, including both pre-service and inservice parent training, should be considered a national priority. Central and state funding should provide for research and innovation in parent education and in the development of programs of education for children. Examples of parent training would include models such as weekend "inter-generational laboratories" in which parents, teachers, and students meet in problem-solving groups to develop sensitivity and collaboration within the educational community, and "family unit laboratories" which include parent-child activities, separate age groups activities, staff demonstrations of family unit functions, male-female role relations, etc.

V. *Programs for the Pre-School Child:*

Voluntary universal nursery schools should be recognized as a "public utility" and be made available to *all* children on a half-day basis, for a full day for working mothers, and for extended periods on a round-the-clock basis to meet the needs of family crises or emergencies. These schools should be expertly staffed and programmed, both as parent-education and child education centers.

VI. *Extension of Public Education:*

Quality education should be available and continuing throughout the pre-school years. Free public education should also be extended beyond the high school years to provide equal opportunities for all youth. Publicly supported junior colleges should be designed to train youth in the various "working-class" occupations, including technological and human services jobs.

VII. *Further Experimentation in Education:*

Throughout the educational system, the curriculum should be planned to maximize the potential of each child, be relevant to the child's background and interests, and make a constructive contribution to the child's background and interests, and his identification with his cultural and ethnic background. Experimental programs that have been successful in countering school dropout rates should be delineated, utilized, and expanded. Further experimentation along the lines of the "community-centered school" should also be encouraged. In addition, there is a need for expansion of adult retraining and educational programs. Research efforts should be designed to carefully delineate the type of training which will be most relevant to the working-class child and to the kind of employment that will most likely be available and of interest to him as an adult: however, efforts also should be made to find ways of increasing the interest of working-class children and youth in "formal" education, per se, and of educating the educators themselves in the importance of training children oriented toward blue-collar work to achieve a sense of competence in, and importance of, the occupational world around which the working-class way of life revolves.

VIII. *Public Education in Population Problems:*

The impending crises wrought by over-population can only be solved by an enlightened public. We recommend a continuous national educational program aimed primarily at the teens and twenties of all social and economic groups. The content of this program would be the need to limit reproduction.

IX. *The Self-Renewal Model—Guidelines for the Development and Maintenance of Programs:*

One of the greatest needs for education at all age levels is an emphasis on training for self-initiated learning and competent change-ability or self-renewal. This effort can be effective only if procedures spread this competence to the total population through extensive and high-quality programs, and only if such training is begun at an early age. The implementation of a self-renewal model requires: 1) long-range planning (one possible design is to utilize successful procedures of large corporations); 2) mechanisms of research development and training (examples might include combining research and training, the retrieval of significant knowledge relevant to a particular program, etc.); 3) dissemination and utilization mechanisms (e.g., panels to review and evaluate new techniques, regular "sharing of practices" institutes where innovative teachers share their ideas with colleagues, etc.); and 4) evaluative review (e.g., involving staff in a program of continuous evaluation and revision of on-going efforts devised to serve children).

X. *A Guaranteed Income Maintenance for the American Family:*

A number of such programs have been devised. We suggest that different areas of the United States effect alternate assistance models in order to determine which are most feasible, effective, and devoid of stigma.

XI. *The Training of Professional Child and Youth Workers:*

Such training should center on creative adaptability, an orientation toward continued professional learning, training in inter-disciplinary teamwork (including leadership and training of paraprofessionals and volunteers), and in sensitivity to interpersonal relations on the job. Such training should include undergraduate apprenticeship opportunities that provide involvement and contact with the "real community" (including youth-serving agencies) and a means of integrating such field experience with class work. Use should also be made of training materials (e.g., video and audio tapes, record players with study guides, etc.) to allow professionals to work at home, to provide materials for self-initiated groups of colleagues, or a leadership guide for a leader of inservice training programs to use as part of a training session.

XII. *The Recruiting and Training of Volunteers and Paraprofessionals:*

Illustrations for future designs include: 1) a Community volunteer bureau which will: employ a variety of survey techniques to identify the skills, interests, and availability of community manpower; collaborate with community agencies and programs to help connect them with needed manpower; and take initiative in helping agencies coordinate their training programs to make more effective use of professional trainers from various agencies; 2) leadership teams which will employ both indigenous and outside workers to help overcome some of the present problems in recruitment and service in deprived areas; 3) built-in hierarchical steps from volunteer to paraprofessional status, both for youth and adults; and 4) the development of professional, paraprofessional, and volunteer teams.

XIII. *Alternatives to Institutional Care:*

This Task Force supports the trend away from commitment to large custodial-care-type institutions. We support the use of alternative modes of care (e.g., community-based facilities, group homes, foster care, etc.)

where such arrangements provide adequate facilities, expert staffing, and other provisions essential to good child care. In the area of delinquency, for example, community-based programs that encourage youth participation and train in social competence need to be expanded. Similarly, successful job training programs for delinquents ought to be increased. Greater efforts are also needed to provide high-quality care to the mentally retarded. In addition to increasing the traditional psychiatric and psychological services, experimental programs which have successfully trained the retarded in self-initiated behavior, and those which have increased cognitive and social skills, should be greatly expanded so as to decrease the number of totally dependent residents in institutions.

In addition, preventive programs need to be established to counter the malnutrition, lack of prenatal and postnatal care, unstimulating home environments, and other factors correlated with mental retardation. Programs should focus on increased prenatal care, increased care and sensory stimulation for premature infants, and enriched programs to provide the type of stimulation necessary to counter familial retardation. Supervision of screening and placement, as well as provision of legal recourse, are also required to counter the tendency to relegate the poor and non-English-speaking disturbed children to state hospitals for the mentally defective. A wide range of community remedial mental health services are needed for the mentally and emotionally disturbed so they can be kept near or with their families. Increased funding is needed for services and for the training of greater numbers of professional and paraprofessional mental health workers.

XIV. *A Comprehensive Multi-Service Center Model:*

Future program designs for community mental health centers should be greatly broadened along the lines of the multi-service center concept, to include welfare and social services, well-parent/child clinics, family planning, general health care, V.D. clinics, treatment centers for drug addiction, etc., in addition to mental health facilities.

Such a model would consist of a number of multi-service centers, each serving defined populations and each under unified direction. These centers would operate as the central unit in a system of satellite neighborhood stations backed up by specialty services at the community level. One essential component would be the involvement of the people served at every stage of organization, administration, and delivery of service. To achieve actual working integration of services, the following minimal requirements would have to be met:

a. There must be a single director of all health and welfare services for each neighborhood service area.

b. He must have executive authority over the deployment of all manpower, money, and materials.

c. It is essential that restrictions on the use of categorical monies be removed at Federal, regional, state, and local levels through modifications of their enabling statutes and agency regulations so as to permit local service agencies to develop: (1) common professional standards; (2) common standards for physical facilities; and (3) common definitions of populations served.

The Poor in the Affluent Society

INTRODUCTION

Poverty and Mental Health

This Task Force contends that mental health is dependent upon many factors. Among the most important of these are good physical health; a stable family life; a wholesome environment; a well-functioning society; and community and societal values and attitudes that enhance individual self-esteem, intellectual and emotional development, and equal opportunity to experience all that is required for optimal mental health.

Poverty is one of the greatest barriers to optimal mental health. Because the effects of poverty on the physical and mental health of children are so far-reaching, Task Force VI thought it imperative to point not only to these effects but to some of their causes. Thus, we have documented the extent of some of the environmental and social deficiencies in our country which are most detrimental to children. We have concentrated particularly on the lack of proper food, housing, education, and physical and mental health care because these are such crucial determinants of child development. Added to these are various discriminatory attitudes toward the poor which lower self-esteem and perpetuate poverty, dependency, hostility, and poor mental health.

None of these deficiencies should be singled out as the primary target for change. Change in the direction of promoting sound mental health requires a concerted effort, one which will simultaneously attack the many

This chapter and the next, Children of the American Dream, were prepared by Barbara J. Sowder, M.A., of the Joint Commission on the Mental Health of Children.

17

adverse conditions of impoverishment and deprivation. Such a program will be costly. Not to undertake this effort will be even more costly, not only in economic terms but in terms of our most important resource—our children and youth.

Poverty, U.S.A.

As a nation, we represent only 6 percent of the world's population; yet we own almost 50 percent of the world's wealth (Golenpaul, 1967). The attainment of a high level of income and industrialization in the United States has resulted, however, in a new type of poverty. Here the ancient struggle against famine has been won. Nevertheless, we find large segments of our population malnourished and living in relative deprivation, becoming ever more aware of the inequality which they must endure in a land of affluence. Because of the changing nature of poverty, income level as a single indicator has become an inadequate measure of such inequality. Rather, there are other dimensions in the life situations of the poor such as educational and social mobility, basic services, status and self-respect, which must be considered as a part of the measurement of poverty (Miller et al., 1967).

Such a multidimensional view of poverty is of particular relevance to those who must plan and implement mental health services for the poor. The creation of adequate services rests, in part, upon our knowledge and understanding of the varying life styles, values, and attitudes which prevail among our poor populations and, in part, upon society's willingness to provide the necessary financial base and manpower to make adequate services a reality.

We recognize, of course, that the present overwhelming need for services reflects many of the problems created by harsh environmental conditions. These conditions perpetuate the cycle of intergenerational poverty and the consequential high incidences of delinquency, crime, and mental illness, as well as the drug addiction so often supported by panhandling, hustling, prostitution, and other such activities. A reduction of such ills must aim at eradicating poverty itself. The seeds of such social change have already been sown. The willingness of the American people to carry on such change will be a reflection of our society's concern for its children, their future, and the world that they, both rich and poor, will inherit and help to shape.

Who Are the Poor?

The line which separates the poor from the nonpoor, or the poor from the very poor, is not clear-cut. Estimates vary according to the criteria of measurement and range from 30 to 50 million persons. The following government figures should be viewed as a conservative estimate, based on bare minimum subsistence needs:

In 1966, 29.7 million persons were living in poverty, as defined by the Social Security index.[1] This number represented one in seven of the noninstitutionalized population.[2]

Of those families[3] counted as poor, one in three were nonwhite whereas only one in ten were white.

One-half of those living in poor families were children. Those under 18 totaled 12.5 million. Another 6.6 million children were living in families whose incomes were barely above the poverty line.

Thus the figures show that in 1966 *one-fourth of our nation's children were living in poverty or near poverty.* Further, *the nonwhite child has almost four times the chance of being raised in economic deprivation as the white child* (Orshansky, 1968).

Changes in the Poverty Profile

Due to higher earnings and increased job opportunities, the number of poor has decreased since 1959 when 39.8 million were considered poor by the Social Security index. The decline in number, however, obscures such important facts as:

The number of near poor decreased only from 15.8 million to 15.2 million between 1959 and 1966.

The one and one-half million poor families headed by a female in 1966 represented only a slight decline from the 1959 figure. Further, the number of poor in these families actually *increased* by one-tenth. These "fatherless" homes included four and one-half million children in 1966.

The proportion of nonwhites[4] among the poor rose from 28 percent in 1959 to more than 32 percent in 1966 (Orshansky, 1968).

Income Levels and Unemployment Among Minority Groups

While the median wage and salary income received by nonwhite workers increased 10 percent between 1965 and 1966, the disparity between white and nonwhite families in this area is still large. For example, Negro families, as of March 1966, had an income only slightly more than

1. The implied level afforded an income of about $65 weekly for a nonfarm family of four (more for larger ones, less for smaller ones).
2. Another 5 million persons would have been added to this figure if the count had included the 2 million in institutions and the aged and parent-child groups who were living with more fortunate relatives.
3. That is, households with two or more persons.
4. Ninety-two percent of the nonwhite population are Negroes (*Health Care and the Negro Population,* 1966).

half that of white families. This held true whether or not the Negro families were headed by a male or by a female (U.S. Bureau of the Census, 1967). Another example is the American Indian. Fifty percent of Indian families have an income of less than $2,000 a year, and about 75 percent of *all* Indian families have incomes of less than $3,000 a year (Striner, 1968). Although not entirely a nonwhite population, the plight of domestic migratory workers is reflected in the fact that the average income for this group was $1,307 in 1966 (Bennett, 1967).

Unemployment accounts for much of the poverty among minority groups. For example:

Nearly one-half of the Indian working-age population is chronically unemployed (Striner, 1968).

In 1967, the unemployment rate for Negroes was double that for whites (*Report of the National Advisory Commission on Civil Disorders,* 1968).

According to a sample survey in the Bronx in 1966, Puerto Rican youth in the 14–19 age group had an unemployment rate of 24 percent while those 20–24 years of age had a rate of 19 percent. Comparable rates for Negroes in the Bronx during this same period were 10 and 16, respectively (*Manpower Report of the President,* 1968).

The Geography of Poverty

In 1966, about one-fourth of the white poor and two-fifths of the non-white poor lived in central cities. Many rural areas—especially those dependent upon farming and mining—also have high rates of poverty. The southern United States, however, continues to have the lowest income levels.

Almost one-half of all nonwhites live in the southern United States. The economic plight of this region is reflected in the fact that only one-fourth of southern whites and almost none of the nonwhites had an income of $10,000 or more in 1966. Further, this region contained almost 50 percent of the nation's poor—two-thirds nonwhite and one-seventh white. Among these southern poor, over one-third of the nonwhite men and 7 percent of the white men had been fully employed during the year (Orshansky, 1968). Corresponding rates for the poor but fully employed elsewhere in the country were 10 and 4 percent, respectively (Council of Economic Advisors, *Economic Report of the President,* 1967).

The Need for Better Jobs

As the data indicate, it is not more jobs that are needed for many of the poor but better ones. In general, the poverty-prone jobs are those that require unskilled but often hard physical labor. There is little doubt that this situation breeds a sense of frustration and defeatism which affects large numbers of children. In 1966, 4.5 million impoverished children were in a home where the male worked constantly and nearly one million more were in a family where the woman held a job all year. Three-fifths of the men had no more than three children to support. Of the approximately 1.5 million poor families headed by a fully employed male under 65, seven out of ten were white and presumably not subjected to discriminatory hiring practices. Five out of six of all male heads under 65 had worked some time during 1966. The majority of those who did not were disabled (Orshansky, 1968).

The Failure of Antipoverty Measures

Clearly, our welfare measures and antipoverty programs have not met the need. All are linked to a means test of one kind or another which results in a loss of self-respect to those served. It must be emphasized that most of the poor do not receive assistance from public programs but, where they do, it seldom eliminates the cycle of poverty. In 1965 five out of six households receiving assistance were still counted among the poor (Orshansky, 1968). The *Report of the National Advisory Commission on Civil Disorders* (1968) points out that, overall, only a fraction of the ghetto poor were touched by the five key federal programs (manpower, housing, education, welfare, and community action) in the three major cities which the Commission studied. For example, recent "antipoverty" programs reached only 2 percent of Detroit's poorly housed and one-third of the jobless in New Haven. Many programs do not provide jobs for the unemployed or else train for jobs which do not exist.

Further, we have yet to make the financial commitment required to solve the problem of poverty. The cost for such an undertaking has been estimated at $25 billion. To the average person, this seems like a staggering amount; yet, it represents only 4 percent of our $800 billion gross national product. In long-range terms, such an investment would be sound economics, since tax funds would be increased through greater human productivity and through decreases in the diversion of monies for various welfare measures. More important, of course, would be the human benefits—the greater health and happiness of our citizens.

The Right of the Poor to Greater Benefits

The right of the poor to receive a greater share of our national affluence can be argued on a number of grounds. The humanitarian appeal needs no defense. Likewise, the argument that poverty is far too costly to our nation financially appeals to many as sound economics. Tax figures provide yet another kind of argument in favor of the poor.

For example, it is estimated that a larger proportion of the total anti-poverty tax burden is borne by those earning less than $4,000 than by any other income group. Figuring on the basis that about half of the public antipoverty tax is social insurance and that those earning less than $4,000 pay 23.1 percent of that while they pay 12.1 percent of all other taxes, this group's share totals $8.6 billion, or approximately 18 percent of the total, as calculated by 1960 income figures (Ornati, 1966). A more recent article states that the poor (the bottom 20 percent of families) receive only 5 percent of the national income, yet they pay an average of 30 percent of direct taxes of all kinds. In contrast, 90 percent of American million-aires pay no income taxes at all, according to an estimate by economist Milton Friedman (Bagdikian, 1968). The familiar accusation that the poor fail to carry their share of the tax burden thus seems grounded in myth. With greater justification it might well be asked whether the poor receive their fair share of tax benefits.

The Need for an Ecological Approach

While statistics provide numerical indices of poverty, they reveal little about the life of the poor. The proliferation of studies in recent years has barely begun to shed light on the complex factors that affect the physical and mental health of the poor. They have, however, indicated that an ecological approach is the most feasible method available to mental health workers. Children of poverty cannot be understood except in relation to the environment that surrounds them (Minuchin and Haley, 1967). This Task Force, therefore, has addressed itself to those multidimensional aspects of poverty which it believes bear on the mental health of the poor and suggest that a holistic approach be adopted to solve such multivariate problems. We begin our analysis by looking at the life conditions in our urban and rural slums and then move on to more specific forms of deprivation. However, we do not limit ourselves to "diagnosing" the problems of poverty but recommend what we believe are constructive directions for change.

We have not directed our efforts to any single audience, but to all the American people. If we seem to emphasize the deficiencies in government programs for the poor, we do so believing that collective commitment to change can, will, and must be expressed through those who determine policy and the direction of programs. "No man is an island," as John Donne stated so poetically. The poor, like each of us, live in and are affected by the total complex of our society. To be effective, any commitment to eradicate poverty must begin at the "grass roots" and permeate our total society. It must be expressed not only through economic support for needed programs but through daily individual interpersonal relationships which truly reflect the democratic and humane principles upon which America was founded.

CONDITIONS OF LIFE IN THE DEPTHS OF POVERTY

Urban Areas

Herbert Gans has stated that the two uppermost problems in cities today are *"poverty"* and *"segregation"* (1966, italics in the original). Poverty is particularly prevalent in our central cities which now contain about 10 million persons counted as poor (Orshansky, 1968). Residential segregation is an even greater problem for large proportions of Negroes and other minority groups,[5] since it affects both the poor and nonpoor. Unless changes occur, the ghetto will be home for many of tomorrow's children. *At present, the twelve largest central cities contain one-third of the total Negro population*, and it is estimated that, by 1985, approximately 20.8 million Negroes will be living in central cities (*Report of the National Advisory Commission on Civil Disorders*, 1968).

The great migration of rural Negroes during this century has resulted in an influx of large numbers of poorly educated, unskilled, and semiskilled workers into the larger cities. Often displaced by mechanization, many Negroes looked to the city for a better way of life. Most, however, were met with the harsh realities of discrimination, lack of adequate housing, and little or no employment for workers without skills. The result for many has been confinement to the most depressed areas of our cities, a reality which has bred much bitterness and frustration.

As a consequence of this migration, almost all Negro population growth is occurring within metropolitan areas, whereas most white population growth is occurring within suburban areas.[6] This situation has fostered a sense of polarization and separatism between peoples of different social classes and ethnic backgrounds. Children experience interpersonal relationships mostly with people similar to themselves and often learn either to fear or deride those different from themselves.

Nearly a fifth of our central city residents live in deprived ghetto neighborhoods where recorded unemployment runs as high as 10 to 15

5. This includes a quarter of a million American Indians (U.S. Senate . . . *Federal Role in Urban Affairs*, 1966); 12.1 million of the 14.8 million urban Negroes (*Report of the National Advisory Commission on Civil Disorders*, 1968); most of the 859,247 urban Puerto Ricans (U.S. Bureau of the Census . . . *Puerto Ricans in the U.S.*, 1960); and the unknown number of other Spanish-speaking persons, Orientals, etc.

6. From 1950 to 1960, the percentage of Negro metropolitan growth was 98 percent, and the percentage of white suburban growth was 78 percent (*Report of the National Advisory Commission on Civil Disorders*, 1968).

percent for adult men and 40 to 50 percent for teenagers. A survey of one slum area revealed a "subemployment" rate of 33 percent—a figure 8.8 times greater than the national overall rate (*The American Federationist*, 1967). Urban Indians and Puerto Ricans sometimes experience greater impoverishment than Negroes. For example, in 1964 slightly over half of New York City's poor were Puerto Ricans who, as a group, represented less than 10 percent of the population[7] (Fitzpatrick *et al.*, 1968).

Many of the urban poor are fully employed. A 1966 Labor Department survey of slums found that a fifth of those working full time earned less than $60 a week. Forty percent of all families surveyed had incomes under $3,000 a year. The plight of the poor urban dweller becomes more obvious when these figures are contrasted with the fact that the urban family of four, at that time, required about $7,000 a year to maintain a modest standard of living. Eliminating amenities reduced this figure to $5,000. According to government reports, a fifth of those living within city limits earned less than this amount. Within ghetto areas the estimates loomed to 60 to 70 percent.

The result of such poverty is badly overcrowded housing, inadequate diet, poor medical care, and few books and other essentials for one-fifth of our urban dwellers and almost three-fourths of those living in ghetto areas (*The American Federationist*, 1967).

Studies carried out in several large cities indicate that the very poor urban dweller may find little security or pleasure in his life, especially in public housing projects or other congested dwelling units.[8] A sense of fear and distrust is common, as are outbursts of violence. Many contacts are conflict laden. In this environment children have little chance to learn interpersonal skills or to develop a sense of trust in others (Chilman, 1966).

The physical environment also makes child-rearing difficult. Poor sanitation and garbage controls breed rats and vermin and increase the risk of disease. Of an estimated 14,000 rat bites in 1965, most were in ghetto areas (*Report of the National Advisory Commission on Civil Disorders*, 1968). Inadequate fire and police protection add to the hazards of slum life and lead many ghetto residents to feel that whites and white neighborhoods are given priority in these services. Likewise, recreational facilities in homes and slum communities are often lacking or are insufficient in number, and poor families cannot provide the means for transportation to

7. These data appeared in a proposal submitted to the Office of Economic Opportunity.

8. The conclusions may well represent some middle-class bias. Further research is needed, not only of the poor, but also of the middle class, who—while they live in better circumstances—may experience some similar psychological problems; e.g., the sense of alienation commonly expressed by urban dwellers. The conditions of poverty, as Chilman (1966) points out, call for adaptive behaviors different from those required by the middle class.

facilities outside their areas (Miller *et al.*, 1967). Thus, at an early age the streets are used for recreational activities, and "street life" becomes one of the major environmental influences on the slum child. Often insulated from the larger world, many children become fearful of venturing beyond their own familiar world. Their lives become totally centered around a few blocks of the inner city.

Within the ghetto, male unemployment results in family breakups and generates a system of ruthless and exploitative male-female relationships. The plight of the Negro family is indirectly portrayed in Clark's (1965) presentation of the facts of life in the Harlem ghetto—the facts and figures of the overcrowdedness, danger, disease, unemployment, crime, and drug addiction.[9] His vivid description of the feelings of despair, escapism, defeat, and agony of the slum dwellers conveys the ever persistent pathology which has become a common way of life. Symptoms of maladjustment to urban living have been similarly portrayed among the American Indians (Ablon *et al.*, 1967), and among the Puerto Ricans (Minuchin *et al.*, 1967; Sexton, 1965).

The real, yet unofficial, apartheid of the urban slums fosters an acute sense of alienation and isolation. Ralph Ellison (1966:11), appearing before the Senate Subcommittee on Executive Reorganization, summed up the Negro child's feeling of alienation. His description may well represent, with some variations, the sense of alienation felt by other urban minority-group children:

These are American children, and Americans are taught to be restless. Our myths teach us this, our cartoons . . . the television cameras. He gets it from every avenue of life . . .

So you see little Negro Batmen flying around Harlem just as you see little white Batmen flying around Sutton Place. It is in the blood. But while the white child who is taken with these fantasies has many opportunities for working them into real life situations, too often the Negro child is unable to do so. This leads the Negro child who identifies with the heroes and outlaws of fantasy to feel frustrated and to feel that society has designated him to be the outlaw, for he is treated as one. Thus his sense of being outside the law is

9. We do not know the extent to which drug addiction is a public health problem among the poor. The *Task Force Report: Narcotics and Drug Abuse* of the President's Commission on Law Enforcement and Administration of Justice (1967) states the average heroin addict is likely to be male, poorly educated and unskilled, and a member of a disadvantaged ethnic minority group. Data on Negroes indicate that narcotics addiction is heavily concentrated in low-income Negro neighborhoods, particularly in New York City. Just over 50 percent of the 59,720 addicts known to the U.S. Bureau of Narcotics at the end of 1966 were Negro and lived in New York State, mostly in Harlem and other Negro neighborhoods (*Report of the National Advisory Commission on Civil Disorders*, 1968). However, there is some indication that within the past three years, the percentage of Negro drug addicts has leveled off and is actually declining at a time when the number of addicts generally is rising at an increasing rate (Zinberg, 1968).

not simply a matter of fantasy, it is a reality based on the incontrovertible fact of race. This makes for frustration and resentment. And it makes for something else; it makes for a very cynical and sometimes sharp perspective on the difference between our stated ideals and the way in which we actually live. The Negro slum child knows the difference between a dishonest policeman and an honest one because he can go around and see the numbers men paying off policemen . . .

Now that so much money has been thrown into neighborhoods, supposedly, the papers tell us so, the slum child feels very cynically that it is being drained off, somehow, in graft. He doesn't know. He doesn't have the information. I don't even have it. *All he knows is that this promised alleviation of his condition isn't taking place.* (emphasis added)

Rural Areas

Contrary to American folklore, rural living is generally more conducive to poverty and poor health than to well-being. Life for many rural children means isolation from the main currents of American culture, low-quality education, and few, if any, physical and mental health services. With the decline in employment opportunities, more and more rural youth are forced into urban life, for which they are often ill-prepared.

Currently, it is estimated that 40 percent of the nation's poor reside in rural areas which contain less than a third of our population (Bennett, 1967). Farming, in particular, is a poverty-prone occupation. Although the agricultural population has declined, almost 11 million still live on farms (U.S. Bureau of the Census . . . Farm Population, 1968). One out of four of these persons ranks among the counted poor (Orshansky, 1968). Although a substantial proportion of nonwhites are poor farmers, 85 percent of all poor farm families are white. Currently, farm poverty represents largely the aged, the poorly educated and the unskilled, and the rural population of the South (Ornati, 1966).

The low wage scale of hired farmers—particularly migrants—tends to lower the average farm income. For example, in 1966, 2.8 million people worked on farms for cash wages, most of which were below the poverty line (Bennett, 1967). However, at the heart of agricultural poverty is "the increasing differential, insufficiently recognized, between the return from capital investment and that from hand labor" (Ornati, 1966).

Life for migrant children is particularly difficult. In 1966, one-fifth of all migrant family heads traveled, accompanied by 140,000 children under age 14. An estimated 50,000 migrant children travel when they would normally be in schools, and large numbers do not attend school at the beginning and end of school semesters. Although Congressional legislation in 1967 banned minors from some of the hazardous occupations in agriculture, the Fair Labor Standards Act does not grant migrant children the same protection as children in the general population. Doubtless, many migrant children will continue to work in the fields rather than attend school. They, like so many other relatively uneducated farm children have, at present, only a slim chance of being upwardly mobile adults.

A number of efforts are now under way to counter the plight of agricultural workers. Unionization is one such effort, but only the United Farm Workers Organizing Committee, AFL–CIO, in California has been strong enough to make any substantial gains. Nationwide, some UFWOC activities have met with organized resistance, including arrests, judicial repression, and violence. Efforts by poor farmers to organize cooperatives have also met with public opposition and are beset by additional problems, such as lack of funds for hiring trained management, and the lack of training programs for co-op members and boards. Despite these barriers, cooperatives have proven beneficial and remain one of the most promising of self-help efforts (Bennett, 1967).

Government programs are insufficient in view of the many problems faced by the rural poor. While these programs have benefited some, funds for agencies which can help the poor to help themselves, such as the Farmer's Home Administration, are simply not designed to offer much aid to the poor. The Citizen's Board of Inquiry into Hunger and Malnutrition in the United States contends that in 1967 less than 5 percent of federal farm payments went to the nearly 43 percent of farmers who are classified as small family farmers with gross incomes below the poverty line. On the other hand, almost 55 percent of such payments were made to large producers with gross incomes over $20,000 (*Hunger, U.S.A.*, 1968). In addition, discriminatory policies still exist in agricultural programs, such as the Federal Extension Service (Bennett, 1967).

The paradox of extreme poverty in American agriculture has been noted by Higbee (1963): "It is ironic that within that very segment of the population which suffers most from the overproduction of food, there are farmers and farmhands who suffer from malnutrition because they cannot afford to eat properly." More than 300 poverty-stricken counties, many of them southern, have yet to apply for federal food assistance programs such as food stamps or free commodities[10] (*Hunger, U.S.A.*, 1968).

There are, of course, other rural areas characterized by poverty, such as Indian reservations and the severely depressed areas of Appalachia. Although the majority of Indians tend to cling to the rural scene, areas

10. On June 3, 1968, the federal government announced that it would operate food-donation programs in 42 counties that refused to handle the program. This move is part of the Agriculture Department's drive to get federal food relief programs operating in 1,000 of the lowest-income counties in the nation (*New York Times*, June 3, 1968).

such as Appalachia are undergoing large-scale out-migration, particularly of youths and young adults. The desire of rural youth to move to the city stems from the discrepancy between what they have and the signs of affluence they see in the larger society. However, many are not prepared to compete in the urban environment. They find themselves limited by urban hiring practices, such as the stress on seniority. Rural youth, especially those from disadvantaged groups, are also likely to fall short of the schooling required for many jobs in the city (Burchinal, 1965). This situation reflects both the low-quality education in many rural areas and the high dropout rates. For example, in 1960 over 2.3 million rural youth left school before graduating, and almost 200,000 of these did not complete the fifth grade (Bennett, 1967).

From present indications, the decline of employment opportunities in rural areas will continue. Without the introduction of new industries, more and more rural youth will be forced to seek jobs in the cities, and their problems, increasingly, will have to be met as a compounded aspect of our urban conditions. Currently, rural areas receive less than one-third of the total funds for federal programs, even though the National Advisory Commission on rural poverty maintains that the 40 percent of the nation's poor in rural areas require more than 40 percent of the funds because of the higher cost of serving people in low-population density areas. There are a few federal programs which are primarily directed toward the rural disadvantaged.[11] Although the total funding for these programs may be inadequate to the need, these efforts do offer promise. Other antipoverty programs are still too limited in funding for rural areas. For example, only 20 percent of those in training under the Labor Department's manpower and development projects are rural residents, despite policies which have increased the number of "disadvantaged" participants from one-third to two-thirds. Administrators of the projects explain that rural areas lack the necessary equipment, teachers, and jobs for trainees.

---

11. A breakdown for various programs in rural areas and the amount of funding is as follows (Source: Bennett, 1967).

Neighborhood Youth Corps	$113 million	or	34 percent
Job Corps	$ 84 million	or	40 percent
VISTA	$ 13 million	or	52 percent
Operation Mainstream	$ 23 million	or	100 percent
Title V Work Experience	$ 30 million	or	30 percent
Title II Community Action Program	$207 million	or	27 percent
Title III funds ($33 million for migrant and $24 million for rural loans)	$ 65 million		percent not given

The OEO Head Start program also shows an inequity in rural/urban grants. Of the 680,000 youngsters enrolled in the summer of 1965, only 169,000 lived in rural areas. OEO's job training programs have trained 243,000, but only 49,000 were from rural areas (Schorr, B., 1968). Other inequities can be noted in the above footnote.

One promising new program has recently been added by the Senate—a $50 million effort to improve the "lot of the rural poor, so they won't have to move to the cities" (*Wall Street Journal*, October 26, 1967).

DAMAGE RESULTING FROM DEPRIVATION DUE TO POVERTY

Malnutrition

The effects of malnutrition on human development are not completely understood. However, the fact that peoples of developed nations are taller and heavier than those of underdeveloped nations points to the relationship between physical growth and nutrition. This stunting effect of malnutrition on growth was further confirmed among German children who were malnourished because of wartime conditions (Acheson *et al.*, 1962) and among British and U.S. children of low socioeconomic status (Acheson and Fowler, 1964; Hundley *et al.*, 1955). Less conclusive, but more startling, are findings from Serbia (Cabak and Najdanvic, 1965) and Mexico, both of which link serious malnourishment in childhood with subsequent subnormal mental development. The Mexican study suggests that protein deprivation between the ages of six months and a year and one-half results in permanent and irreversible brain damage in some infants (Cravioto and Robes, 1965). Such findings are further supported by studies in animal behavior and brain chemistry.

Complex environmental factors in industrialized countries such as the United States make it difficult to isolate the role of nutrition in development. From official statistics, one would conclude that malnutrition is not a serious problem in this country. For example, in 1965 only slightly over 3,000 deaths were listed as being in some way connected with hunger or malnutrition (*Vital Statistics of the United States*, 1965). However, one study contends that these figures mask a lack of documentation that is related to a host of complex professional and bureaucratic practices[12] (*Hunger, U.S.A.*, 1968). There is some support for this contention. For example, Jones and Schendel (1966) suggest that the extensive forms of malnutrition which they found in poor Negro infants in South Carolina

12. Such practices include insufficient training of physicians in identifying malnutrition, failure of hospitals and public agencies to require and/or compile statistical data on malnutrition, etc.

may account for the fact that the death rate for Negro babies in that state is twice that of the national rate. Further, a high correlation exists between poverty and malnutrition and poverty and high postneonatal mortality rates.[13] In virtually every state of our nation, the infant death rate in the poorest county dramatically exceeds the infant death rate for the wealthiest county. This phenomenon is explained on the basis that malnutrition lowers a child's resistance and increases his susceptibility to disease and parasitic infections (*Hunger, U.S.A.*, 1968).

Hearings before the United States Senate in 1967 revealed that hunger, malnutrition, and slow starvation are extremely prevalent in Mississippi, Alabama, Kentucky, West Virginia, the Southwest, in northern and southern Negro ghettos, and among natives in Alaska (U.S. Senate . . . *Hunger and Malnutrition in America*, 1967). Later investigations by the Citizens' Board of Inquiry into Hunger and Malnutrition in the United States found concrete evidence of chronic hunger and malnutrition in every part of the country. This group estimates that the number affected is at least 10 million (*Hunger, U.S.A.*, 1968).

Migrant workers suffer from malnutrition proportionally more than any other group (Delgado *et al.*, 1961; Johnston, 1963; Siegel, 1966). This is especially true for Negro migrants (Mayer, 1965). Malnutrition is partly attributable to low income and partly to lack of education and improper kitchen equipment and storage facilities (Siegel, 1966). Malnutrition is also prevalent among Indians, and may well be related to the high postneonatal mortality rate among this population. A conference on Indian health concluded that iron supplements administered to Indian infants during the first year of life would greatly diminish the high incidence of respiratory diseases (O'Connell, 1967).

From records and other evidence available in large cities, there is little doubt that Negro slums represent the greatest concentration of "anemias, growth failure, dermatitis of doubtful origin, accidents of pregnancy and other signs associated with malnutrition" (Mayer, 1965).

Seemingly the most prevalent—or at least most recognized—manifestation of malnutrition in the United States are the nutritional anemias. Although the extent of protein anemia remains undetermined, iron deficiency anemia is known to be common among poor infants and children. The recorded incidence of iron deficiency anemia among youngsters in impoverished communities ranges from 30 to 70 percent (*Hunger, U.S.A.*, 1968). This deficiency is commonly associated with late weaning, bottle rather than breast feeding, and excessive milk intake, all of which are common practices among lower socioeconomic groups (Schulman, 1962; Haughton, 1963; Filer and Martinez, 1964; Werkman *et al.*, 1964a). In

13. Postneonatal mortality rates state the incidence of deaths among infants aged one month to one year.

some cases these practices also reflect the apathy of the impoverished mother and her psychological unavailability to the child. The child, in turn, responds by seeking gratification from the bottle, rather than demanding a relationship from his mother. He may remain infantile and self-centered and fail to reach out into the environment for satisfaction and challenges. Follow-up studies suggest that these children continue such behavior past the second year of life and that they have more illness and behavior problems than their "control" counterparts. Coupled with barriers stemming from lower socioeconomic status, such children are likely to be headed for school difficulty, delinquency, and other problems (Werkman *et al.*, 1964b).

It is possible that the low educational attainment and poor sociability noted in many poor children may be linked to malnutrition. Cravioto, Delicardie, and Birch (1966) suggest three possible indirect effects which malnourishment, or suboptimal health care, may have upon the learning process:

(1) Loss of learning time, due to the lessened responsiveness of the child to his environment.

(2) Interferences with learning during critical developmental periods.

(3) Changes brought about in motivation and/or personality. For example, lessened responsiveness to the environment at an early age may generate apathetic behavior which in turn functions to reduce the adult's responsiveness to the child. This may result in a cumulative pattern of reduced adult-child interaction with subsequent consequences for stimulation, for learning, for maturation, and for interpersonal relations. The end result may be significant backwardness in performance on later more complex learning tasks.

The effect of hunger on children was vividly portrayed in a testimony before a Senate subcommittee in 1967 by six doctors who made a first-hand investigation of malnutrition and starvation in the Mississippi Delta region. One portion of their report reads as follows:

We saw children whose nutritional and medical condition we can only describe as shocking—even to a group of physicians whose work involves daily confrontation with disease and suffering. In child after child we saw evidence of vitamin and mineral deficiences; serious untreated skin infections and ulcerations; eye and ear diseases; also unattended bone diseases; the prevalence of bacterial and parasitic diseases as well as severe anemia with resulting loss of energy and ability to lead a normally active life; diseases of the heart and lung —requiring surgery—which have gone undiagnosed and untreated; epileptic and other neurological disorders; severe kidney ailments that in other children would warrant immediate hospitalization; and finally, in boys and girls in every county we visited, obvious evidence of severe malnutrition, with injury to the body's tissues—its muscles, bones, and skin, as well as an associated psychological state of fatigue, listlessness, and exhaustion.

We saw children afflicted with chronic diarrhea, chronic sores, chronic leg and arm (untreated) injuries and deformities. We saw homes without running water and live with germ-bearing mosquitoes and flies everywhere around. We saw homes with children who are lucky to eat one meal a day—and that one inadequate so far as vitamins, minerals, or protein is concerned. We saw children who do not get to drink milk, don't get to eat fruit, green vegetables, or meat. They live on starches—grits, bread, Kool Aid. Their parents may be declared ineligible for commodities, ineligible for the food stamp program, even though they literally have nothing. We saw children fed communally— that is, by neighbors who give scraps of food to children whose own parents have nothing to give them.

. . . We do not want to quibble over words, but "malnutrition" is not quite what we found; the boys and girls we saw were hungry—weak, in pain, sick, their lives are being shortened; they are, in fact, visibly and predictably losing their health, their energy, and their spirits. They are suffering from hunger and disease and directly or indirectly they are dying from them—which is exactly what "starvation" means (U.S. Senate . . . Hunger and Malnutrition in America, 1967:46, 47).

Another testimony related the incident of five small children in Appalachia who tore apart and devoured a chicken before it could be cooked. It was the first meat they had had in three months (ibid). Reports from Iowa tell of people whose hunger leads them to salvage food from garbage dumps (Arnold, 1967).

Dr. Robert Coles spoke before the Senate subcommittee about the psychiatric aspect—what it means for a child and his or her parents to be chronically sick and hungry. To the mind of a four- or five-year-old child, the pain becomes, perhaps, more than a concrete physical factor of life. Such harsh realities bring to the child's mind "a reflection of his worth and a judgment upon him and his family by the outside world. They ask themselves what they have done to be kept from the food they want or what they have done to deserve the pain they feel."

Speaking from his clinical experience, Dr. Coles stated that in both the North and South, one can see how persistently sickness and hunger in children can live on in adults. These people come to doubt any offer, to mistrust any favorable turn of events. They have learned to be "tired, fearful, anxious, and suspicious." They experience a kind of starvation "in which the body is slowly consuming itself." This bitter experience, in Dr. Cole's opinion, breeds potential recruits for riots in cities (U.S. Senate . . . Hunger and Malnutrition in America, 1967:52, 53).

The eradication of malnutrition is a most urgent need if we are to fulfill the right that each American child should have to enjoy the benefits that affluence has bestowed upon our nation. While the prevalence of malnutrition reported before the Subcommittee on Manpower, Employment, and Poverty is not—as Dr. Senn pointed out—comparable to the famine and starvation in India and other countries, the slow and chronic starvation of many American children is inexcusable, since *we have the technological means to guarantee every citizen an adequate diet.*

Yet our food programs[14] do not provide a diet that meets the minimum standards of intake of protein, vitamins, and minerals. Further, they reach only 18 percent of the poor. For example, 4 million children—two-thirds of all impoverished school-age children—either paid for their lunch or went without in 1967. The commodity distribution and food stamp programs do not exist in more than a third of our poorest counties. Where they exist, they reach only an average of 12 percent of the poor in any county. Many persons are ruled ineligible for various reasons, even though their income may be below the poverty line.

The commodity distribution program provides only a limited diet because it is geared to the commercial market. The amount given is not enough for a month's supply.[15] Often the poor cannot find any means of transporting commodities from the distant distribution depots.

Similar problems exist in the food stamp program, even though it was designed to correct the deficiencies of the commodity program. The price of stamps proves prohibitive to many. Further, the stamps must be paid for in cash and the minimum amount be purchased, or no purchase can be made. These are requirements that many of the poor cannot meet. Inequities also exist in the ratio of exchange for families of different sizes and incomes. Local merchants often impose additional hardships by raising food prices on food distribution days. Even more discouraging are the nutritional studies which indicate that those participating in food stamp programs are only slightly better off nutritionally than nonparticipants. This situation might be improved if greater efforts were made to educate the poor in how to plan nutritional meals on a low budget.

The Citizens' Board of Inquiry into Hunger and Malnutrition in the United States claims that the failure of these programs is not due to inadequate money or staff but to the mode of administration and the policy adopted by the Agriculture Department. They further state that no attempt is being made to use full statutory power to fulfill the purpose of these programs. For example, in 1967, $200 million appropriated for feeding

14. The array of food assistance programs includes Commodity Distribution Program, Food Stamp Program, National School Lunch Program, and School Milk and Child Nutrition Program.
15. Some time in the summer of 1968, surplus food packages were increased from 14 to 36 pounds, per recipient. The additional commodities offered 22 to 23 different foods, rather than the present 16. Emphasis was placed on the needs of infants, young children, and pregnant women. However, the retail price of this increase in food is only $11.75 monthly, per recipient (White, 1968).

the hungry was returned to the Treasury Department (*Hunger, U.S.A.,* 1968).

Recently, the Department of Agriculture has instituted a few measures to rectify existing conditions. So far, however, such efforts are limited—despite the attention that the mass media has given to this problem. Up to this time, for millions of our children, there is often no food, no milk, no meat—only hunger

Housing

In the United States today, there are nearly 6 million occupied sub-standard dwellings[16] (*Report of the National Advisory Commission on Civil Disorders,* 1968). Eighty-eight percent of substandard housing is occupied by people with incomes less than $6,000 a year (Schorr, A., 1966a) and those earning under $2,000 are more than twice as likely to occupy such dwellings as persons in the general population, according to 1960 census figures (*U.S. Census of Housing,* 1960).

The percent of occupied housing not meeting specified federal criteria is presented in Table 1. As noted, the disparity between the white and nonwhite figures is striking. About 3 in 10 nonwhite households still live in substandard housing, as compared to less than 1 in 10 among whites.

Table 1.—PERCENT OF OCCUPIED HOUSING NOT
MEETING SPECIFIED CRITERIA,
BY LOCATION, 1966

	NONWHITE	WHITE
UNITED STATES	29	8
Large cities*	16	5
Suburbs	29	4
Smaller cities, towns, and rural	64	14

SOURCE: U.S. Department of Commerce, Bureau of the
Census (Preliminary data for 1966).
* Of 50,000 population or more in metropolitan areas.

Although the poor put a higher percentage of their income into hous-ing, they are less able to maintain or enhance any housing investment. Loans and public help are generally unavailable; thus they are likely to do without adequate food, medical care, and clothing in order to afford hous-ing (Schorr, A., 1965). Nor do the poor benefit substantially from federal housing expenditures. For various reasons, they are seldom eligible for

16. By U.S. Bureau of Census standards, housing is classified as substandard when (1) sound but lacking full plumbing; (2) deteriorating and lacking full plumbing; or (3) dilapidated.

public housing. While the subsidy system supposedly evens out the differences between the poor and nonpoor, statistics reveal that the nonpoor benefit most from federal housing activities (Miller *et al.*, 1967). As Harrington (1968) states:

In thirty-one years this society has built eight hundred thousand housing units for the poor, and in thirty-four years it has financed over ten million units of housing for the middle class and the rich . . . the effect of the housing program has unintentionally . . . been to widen the gap between the two and increase the agony of poverty in the United States.

While suburbia is being built with federal credit, and the urban renewal program concentrates on constructing commercial and luxury facilities, the number of nonwhites living in substandard housing in central cities increases. Even though many poverty families are displaced by urban renewal, planning for their relocation is neglected and there has been little replacement of low rental housing. Most families who are moved from condemned or substandard housing move into other substandard dwellings (Schorr, A., 1966a). Such frequent moves have a deleterious effect on childrens' school adjustment, peer-group relations, sense of personal identity and general trust in the environment.

Urban problems are compounded by reduced tax bases resulting from the migration of industry and upper-income families to the suburbs. Industrial relocation has increased the problem of the already inadequate mass transportation facilities for low-income city dwellers (*The American Federationist*, 1967). Thus, many of the urban poor become more and more trapped within the depressed areas of our cities.

The association of poor housing with other factors has been studied in several cities. In one city, an area dominated by poor housing had double the number of ambulance runs and fire calls, four times the number of visiting nurse calls, and fourteen times the number of people on welfare as compared to a middle-income area in the same city. In another city, the poor housing area produced 36 percent of the city's juvenile delinquents and 76 percent of tuberculosis cases, although it represented less than 25 percent of the city's total population (Lee, 1967:202).

For some groups, housing is particularly hazardous to well-being. For example, home for the migrant child may be a tent, a duck coop, or an automobile. The houses of many southern families and Indian families are without potable water, sanitary toilet facilities, refrigeration, or central heating (Bennett, 1967; O'Connell, 1967). Thus, children are exposed to bitter cold, danger of fire in winter, and insect-borne disease.

Poor housing conditions are highly correlated with pulmonary diseases, especially among nonwhites (Ornati, 1966). Such environments are also conducive to many accidents caused by faulty electrical installations, poor lighting, falling plaster, and the like. Lead poisoning is still a serious threat to children in impoverished areas because measures have not been taken to remove lead paint from old housing (Ingalls *et al.*, 1961; Griggs *et al.*, 1964; Jacobziner, 1966). The rats and vermin which thrive because of improper sanitation control not only spread disease but create fears related to physical harm. Such fears often plague children in nightmares and probably produce long-lasting personality disturbances.

In addition to physical hazards in slum dwellings, overcrowding results in interrupted and insufficient sleep. This not only increases the child's vulnerability to infectious disease but diminishes his attention span for learning. Crowded conditions also result in overstimulation, since there is no insulation from either the sexual or argumentative actions of adults and older siblings. As Solomon (1968) notes, the relatively calm state of mind ordinarily observed in latency-age children is often replaced by a perpetual excitement with sex or violence among impoverished children. This hinders the process of education and school adjustment and contributes to the impression that these children are "unreachable." Prolonged babyish behavior, resulting in poor social adjustment, also has been correlated with lack of privacy and overcrowded homes (Grootenboer, 1962).

The physical environment of the slum child has been aptly described in a report by the President's Commission on Law Enforcement and Administration of Justice:

What the inner-city child calls home is often a set of rooms shared by a shifting group of relatives and acquaintances—furniture shabby and sparse, many children in one bed, plumbing failing, plaster falling, roaches in the corners and sometimes rats, hallways dark or dimly lighted, stairways littered, air dank and foul. Disrepair discourages neatness. Insufficient heating, multiple use of bathrooms and kitchens, crowded sleeping arrangements spread and multiply respiratory infections and communicable diseases. Rickety, shadowy stairways and bad electrical connections take their accidental toll. Rat bites are not infrequent and sometimes, especially for infants, fatal. Care of one's own and respect for other's possessions can hardly be inculcated in such surroundings. More important, home has little holding power for the child . . . it is not a place to bring his friends. . . . The loss of parental control and diminishing adult supervision that occur so early in the slum child's life must thus be laid at least partly at the door of his home.

The physical environment of the neighborhood is no better. In the alley are broken bottles and snoring winos . . . yards, if there are any, are littered and dirty . . .

In addition to actual dangerousness, lack of recreational facilities has been shown to be linked to negative attitudes toward the community and those attitudes in turn to repeated acts of delinquency. . . .

Crowding has a harmful effect on study habits, attitudes toward sex, parent's ability to meet needs of individual children; clearly, crowding intensifies fatigue and irritability that contribute to erratic or irrational discipline. . . .

Fighting and drunkenness are everyday matters. Drug addiction and prostitution are familiar. The occupying-army aspects of predominantly white store ownership and police patrol in predominantly Negro neighborhoods have been many times remarked; the actual extent of the alienation thereby enforced and symbolized is only now being generally conceded (*The Challenge of Crime in a Free Society,* 1967:61–63).

Despite the hazards involved in living in substandard housing, only 23 percent of the health departments of cities with populations over 100,000 have engaged in programs of housing hygiene through enforcement of the code of the Housing Act of 1947. For example, in New York City approximately 2.5 million residents live in 583,000 one- and two-family units described as "forgotten slums." There are neither city regulations or ordinances nor state regulations or statutes that establish legal minimum conditions for occupancy (Mood, 1965).

Better housing was shown to improve psychological and physical well-being in one study involving low-income Negro families living in public housing. Morbidity was found to be statistically better for this group in persons under 35 years of age, especially for those under 20, when compared to a control group living in slum housing. Childbearing data also showed fewer complaints of illness, a lower incidence of premature births, and fewer deaths. Women reported more positive attitudes concerning their surroundings and indicated, particularly, their pleasure in the added privacy and in the safer play environment for their children. Neighborhood pride and participation was also higher, and the women showed improvement in self-concepts and psychological well-being after moving into the new facilities (Wilner *et al.*, 1962).

Nevertheless, the literature contains many complaints against public housing by low-income groups. Rents, for example, may be higher in public housing than in substandard dwellings, and many prefer to stay in familiar neighborhoods (Duhl, 1963). Public units are often too small to accommodate large families. Further, regulations may exclude extended families and thus exclude potential caretakers for the children of mothers who work.

Housing reform policies have had many adverse psychological effects, some of which stem from the "charity" aspects of the programs (Duhl, 1963). There is also the "visibility" of subsidy housing. The most conspicuous example, as Harrington (1968) notes, is on Chicago's South Side—a "big high-rise segregated barracks . . . a big jail for poor people where poor people can see only poor people."

Thus, most planning efforts merely lower self-esteem and perpetuate practices of discrimination that result in feelings of alienation and isolation. Future planning, therefore, must provide more than adequate housing units for the poor. Such units must be fitted to the needs of the poor—both economically and psychologically. The recent trend of mixing low-income and middle-income housing is a step in this direction. Efforts should be made to optimize a sense of community, one in which the poor can actively participate. Facilities should be readily available to accommodate the varied needs of the poor, including recreational and educational opportunities which encourage participation across class, sex, and age lines, and the Universal Nursery School proposed by this Task Force.

Incidence of Physical Illness

The level of the nation's overall health is related to a number of factors, e.g., its economic progress, its level of education, its public health policy, and its housing.

The differentials in the health of our poor and nonpoor reflect these factors. The poor, as noted, are more prone to certain diseases related to inadequate nutrition, sanitation, and housing. They also suffer more from accidents characteristic of hazardous occupations and unsafe home environments. Lower rates of immunization appear to explain the greater impact upon poor children of such diseases as poliomyelitis, diphtheria,[17] whooping cough, etc. (Ornati, 1966).

Overall mortality differentials for whites and nonwhites show that nonwhites have higher rates of many diseases.[18] Poor children everywhere show higher disease rates. In urban areas, child hospitalization rates are highest among impoverished populations (Cornely, 1962). However, many disorders go undetected. For example,

Jacobziner *et al.* (1963) examined 22,900 apparently well infants and preschool children in 78 New York City child health centers and found defects to be significantly higher among poor nonwhites and Puerto Ricans. Studies of Head Start children also point to the high incidence of undetected and untreated disorders among poor youngsters.

Causality, as Arnati points out, operates not only through factors linked to inadequate income—including the ability to buy better health care—but also through such factors as the failure of the poor to identify minor symptoms, a limited knowledge of hygiene, and less frequent use of free medical facilities.

These factors, however, are operative both before and after birth for the poor child. They are highly related to the physical status of our new-

17. Diphtheria is more prevalent among the southern poor. It attacks mostly children under 15. The rate for nonwhites is six times higher than for whites. Fatality rates are lower among immunized groups, even where only one or two immunizations have been given (*Diphtheria in the United States* . . . , 1966).

18. Nonwhite rates are higher for all forms of tuberculosis; influenza and pneumonia; diseases of the heart and other hypertensive diseases; vascular lesions affecting the central nervous system; and malignant neoplasms (Chase, 1965). Also more prevalent among the poor are arthritis, syphilis, and diseases of the female genital organs (Ornati, 1966).

born. Currently, many women come to childbearing after a childhood marked by neglect of their health and nutrition. They receive little or no prenatal care. One result is an increase in the number of birth defects. Such handicapping conditions often produce great emotional stress in children so afflicted, and for their families as well. Such stress is compounded among poor families because they lack the financial means to provide the needed services for their handicapped child.

Infant mortality rates are also higher among the poor. For example, rates among migrant workers and among many ghetto populations are more than double the national overall rate (Siegel, 1966: *Summary of Vital Statistics*, 1960). The rate for American Indian babies exceeds the national figure by 70 percent, and among those that survive the first month of life nearly a third die before their first birthday, largely from *preventable* diseases (U.S. Senate . . . *Federal Role in Urban Affairs*, 1966). The death rate for rural children and youth, ages 5 to 24, is still twice that of their metropolitan counterparts (Burchinal, 1965).

Death, in fact, is much more common among the poor at all ages. Maternal mortality rates, for example, are four times higher among nonwhites than among whites (Anderson and Lesser, 1966). We do not as yet understand all the mental health implications for children who experience death of family members and neighbors many times in their lives. Nor do we yet know how the loss of a child affects parents and their interactions with surviving children. However, pervasive thoughts or experiences relating to death probably have many adverse effects, ranging from fear of death to a desensitization of the meaning of life and death.

The higher maternal and infant deaths among the poor are correlated with a number of factors. Some of these factors, in turn, may not result in death but may account for the high incidence of physical and mental disorders among the poor. Anderson (1958) suggests that the current infant mortality rate is not entirely a function of the economic status of the family or of the mother's educational level. Rather, it may reflect the presence of psychological problems and the mother's lack of ability and training in "mothercraft."

However, the high infant and maternal mortality rates seem to be linked to the lack of prenatal care among the poor. Data show that only four out of ten poor mothers have prenatal care in contrast to seven out of ten among the nonpoor. Nonwhites, proportionately, receive less prenatal care than whites (Ornati, 1966). It has been demonstrated in various studies that these rates do not reflect innate biological weaknesses but that higher-income whites and nonwhites have the same prematurity and infant mortality rates (Anderson, 1958).

The lack of prenatal care is also related to the incidence of premature birth. For example, studies in New York and Chicago show that the prematurity rate is from two to three times higher among low-income groups, as compared to higher-income groups. In a study by Knoblock and Pasamanick (1960), the prematurity rates for the white upper-economic group, the white lower-economic group, and the nonwhite groups were 5.0, 7.6, and 11.4 percent of all births, respectively. Further, this study demonstrated an association between socioeconomic status, the presence of complications of pregnancy, and the subsequent development of neuropsychiatric disorders in children. Investigations of control populations, consisting of children not known to have neuropsychiatric disability, showed that the important complications of pregnancy increased as the socioeconomic status decreased, that is, there were 5 percent in the white upper-economic fifth, 10 percent in the lower-economic fifth, and 15 percent in the nonwhite group. Other factors contributing to the high incidence of prematurity among nonwhites have been suggested by a number of studies, e.g., nutritional practices, maternal health, the mother's prior growth achievements in childhood, birth spacing, grand multiparity, and illegitimacy (Shapiro et al., 1960; Thomson, 1963; Donnelly et al., 1964; Pakter et al., 1961).

Extent of Mental Illness

The relationship that sometimes exists between physical and mental disorders is shown in the many studies which delineate the association between mental retardation and such variables as prematurity, complications of pregnancy, low socioeconomic status, as well as lower occupational levels, lower educational attainment, and broken homes (see, e.g., Wortis, 1964).

It is now believed that only about a quarter of the mentally retarded have brain damage or an organic defect. The other three-quarters have milder forms of retardation, show no obvious brain damage, and have few physical handicaps. These usually come from the poor strata of our society, typically census tracts where the median income is $3,000 per year, or less.[19] As much as 15 percent of this group lives in deprived rural areas and in urban ghettos (PCMR Message, 1968). Puerto Ricans in New York constitute about 9.1 percent of first admissions to state schools for the retarded, although their proportion of the state population is only 4 percent. No refined analysis has been made, but Fitzpatrick et al. (1968) suggest that cultural, language, and class barriers may result in a diagnosis of retardation where it, in fact, does not exist. These investigators also

19. Only 1 percent of the nonorganically mentally retarded come from high-income and well-educated groups. Exact statistics for all types of retardation among children are lacking.

question whether these cultural and social differences might not account, in part, for the reported high incidence of schizophrenia among Puerto Ricans and the fact that a large number of these children are placed in "Special Schools."

Ablon *et al.* (1967) raise this same question in regard to the low incidence of severe mental disorders reported in the studies on American Indians. These studies do point to high rates of alcoholism, neurosis, and social incapacity. Further, childrens' chances for successful social adjustment appear to be lowered through apathy, poor learning, and general withdrawal. Mental breakdowns, however, are reported only infrequently, although they are known to increase with expanded detribalization and acculturation. Since these changes are generally accompanied by a greater degree of poverty, causality may be partly attributable to economic deprivation. However, the accompanying social disintegration also produces cultural conflict and undermines the Indian child's sense of cultural identity. He becomes caught between two worlds, not quite belonging to either.

It is also quite possible, as the authors point out, that the reported low incidence of mental illness among Indian children is simply a function of our lack of knowledge of these people. They note that we once viewed the Negroes as simple and happy people who seldom developed mental health problems. We now know that these stereotypes resulted from our ignorance. We may be similarly mistaken about Indians, since persons involved in epidemiological studies estimate that 20 percent of the Indian population is in need of some type of psychiatric care.

Differing cultural patterns compound the difficulties of determining the incidence of mental illness. The problem is made more complex by the extensive poverty among oppressed minority groups.

A number of factors hinder any definitive statement concerning the relationship between poverty and mental illness. These include the lack of standardized psychiatric classification; difficulties involved in making comparable different income segments of the population (since it is imperative that standards of the patient's own social class be used, Bean *et al.*, 1964); the different expectations, conceptualizations, and tolerance levels concerning mental illness among different class segments (which may allow some members to go undiagnosed, tolerated within the home, etc.); and lack of other standardized criteria which hinder drawing generalizations from various investigations.

While some studies suggest a link between poverty and increased risk of severe mental illness, these are seriously questioned on the basis of validity, methodology, etc. (see, e.g., Dohrenwend and Dohrenwend, 1965; Gruenberg, 1968). Such studies point to the high number of poor persons who are admitted to state and private hospitals (Faris and Dunham,

1939; Schroder, 1942; Hollingshead and Redlich, 1958; Pollack, 1966), and thus to the relationship between inadequate services and low SES. However, we do not yet have definitive knowledge that poverty *produces* behavior disorders. Reliable incidence studies of different behavior disorders are lacking, and correlation between different types of socioeconomic deprivation and varying types of behavior disorders has not yet been established (Redlich, 1967).

Figures on the incidence and prevalence of mental illness among poor children are simply unavailable.[20] However, analysis of Head Start children revealed that 10 percent of these youngsters were crippled in their emotional development by the age of 4. For the child population, in general, one source estimates that 4 million children under 14 are in need of professional help because of emotional difficulties. Between 500,000 and 1 million of these are thought to require immediate professional care (National Committee Against Mental Illness, Inc., 1966). A review of various surveys conducted through school systems indicates that between 2 and 3 percent of school children are in need of some kind of professional care. An additional 7 to 12 percent are thought to need help for emotional problems (Rosen *et al.*, 1968). Kohlberg (1968) has reviewed many of these studies dealing with school surveys. He notes that the label "positive adjustment" is less likely to be given lower SES children. But, as he points out, these surveys usually depend on teacher and peer ratings or on intelligence quotients rather than on clinical assessments. The possible cultural biases in both methods need no elaboration.

Some workers feel that sampling and population problems have led to invalid generalizations about the mental health of the poor. Specifically, they call attention to the variability of life styles among low-income groups and suggest that global references to "the poor," "the disadvantaged," "the culturally deprived," and so forth, are but designations of what is now recognized to be a number of subgroupings and subcultures. Much more research is needed before the characteristics of these various groups can be stated with certainty. For the present, a much more meaningful and operationally feasible method is that of distinguishing the "stable" from the disorganized among the poor (Minuchin *et al.*, 1967; Lewis, 1961; Miller, 1964).

Evidence suggests that the stable and the disorganized families of the poor differ in patterns of family organization, child-rearing practices, and in their ability to tolerate poverty. The disorganized group exhibit the general characteristics of the poor; e.g., the "separate" lives led by wives and husbands in their daily existence, the almost exclusive entrance into peer-group relationships among the children, the action-seeking of adoles-

---

20. This holds for the entire child population.

cents for experiences outside the home, the rejection of nonmaterial middle-class values, etc. In addition to these characteristics, the more "stable" among the poor exhibit certain strengths which enable them to withstand the adverse effects of poverty (Gans, 1962; Kohn, 1963). For example, Pavenstedt (1965) found that very young upper-lower-income children experienced a good deal of order and stability in their environment. Although their homes were not intellectually stimulating, later testing in school revealed no great language or behavior problems. Among very low-income families, however, activities in the home were impulse-determined, and consistency was totally absent. Parents often failed to discriminate between children or failed to distinguish between the child's role and their own. Communication by words was almost nonexistent. Behavioral problems among these children were noted upon entrance to kindergarten or grammar school. Self-perception was low, and language achievement was seldom attained. They became "immature little drifters" who, without anyone to relate to, failed to learn communication and came to grips with only certain circumscribed areas of their existence.

Malone (1963) described many behaviors of children from disorganized slum families which predispose them to later chronic acting out and impulse disorders. Such children exhibited low frustration tolerance, impulsivity and unreliable controls, dominant motor discharge, poor sense of identity, marked use of imitation, little constructive play or use of fantasy, language retardation, and a tendency to concrete thought. Malone (1966) stresses the impact of the "real dangers" present in the lives of these children. Such dangers put pressures on the child to grow up fast, but the resulting early independence and premature coping and defensive ability do not lead to full independence in later life: "Genuine mastery and flexible adaptability are forfeited."

Drawing from studies of the disorganized poor, Beiser (1965) has delineated certain personality traits, level of skills, and the state of psychological well-being which seem to characterize these populations. Among personality traits listed are the lack of future orientation, inability to defer gratification, apathy, and suspiciousness. Skills needed to master today's technological culture fail to develop. Such skills include those related to such basic personality functions as perception, cognition, and the use of language. "Social skills," which include a broad repertoire of abilities, are also important, although the study of these has been largely neglected. Evidence suggests, however, that the disorganized poor tend to see others in "block form"; that is, they lack discriminatory abilities to assess motivations of others accurately or to recognize affect both in others and in themselves. Their psychological well-being is complicated by a number of symptoms—peptic ulcer, eczema, and other psychophysiological reactions; palpitations, apprehensiveness and depression, sleeplessness, the hallmarks of psychoneurosis; and conditions usually labeled sociopathic (e.g., alcoholism). Some workers postulate a predominance of hysterical-type features in the personality with a tendency to aggressive impulsive behavior (Reissman *et al.*, 1964) and an early blunting of affective responses to the tragedies of a harsh environment (Malone, 1966).

Deutsch (1963) suggests that disadvantaged children are subjected to "stimulus deprivation" in the home and that this accounts, in part, for their later difficulties in school. However, Minuchin *et al.* (1967) note that, in some areas of the environment, sensory stimulation may be more intense for slum children than for the more protected middle-class child. Certainly the slum child's perception is not faulty when he roams the street —which makes difficult any explanation as to why such children do poorly on tests of figure-ground spatial relations. Lowered performance on many types of tests, however, may be attributable to the fact that impoverished children develop somewhat different language, verbal, cognitive, and attentive skills than do nonpoor children and thus are handicapped by tests which are largely based on middle-class norms. Although these different skills are often useful and functional to the disadvantaged child in his own habitat, they are often nonfunctional or even dysfunctional in other settings. It seems, in fact, that the poor child, throughout his life, is subjected to disadvantages which have a cumulative effect and leave him ill-prepared to compete in our predominantly middle-class society.

Such children, as Smith (1968) points out, belong to "a submerged minority . . . trained in *in*competence that leaves them unable to benefit from most 'opportunities' that are opened to them." A sense of competence, as Smith notes, is an essential component of the motivation required to master one's environment, and both motivation and competence are intricately bound to one's attitudes toward the *self*.

While the child's sense of self is partially molded by his family, family socialization patterns and interactions alone may not determine the child's total view of himself or his total competence—or lack of competence— in mastering his environment. A person's location in the social system may play an equally strategic role. At the crux of competence are "hope" and "self-respect." Opportunity provided by the social system corresponds to hope; respect by others provides the social ground for respect of self; and power, "the kingpin of our society," evokes respect and guarantees the means to opportunity. Restricted opportunity not only blights hope but bars one from the acquisition of the knowledge and skills required for effectiveness. Lewin (1948), as Smith notes, demonstrated that contempt and withheld respect may lead to "self-hatred" and to debilitating defensive maneuvers. The lack of power entails an overall vulnerability and creates dependency.

Both familial and societal factors interact and impinge, extrinsically and intrinsically, upon the child's formation of the *self*, that is, "the entity around which a person's enduring orientations to the environing world are organized." Erikson (1959), as Smith points out, delineated many of the elements which we currently believe essential to a healthy self concept: trust and confidence, initiative and industry, autonomy, and, particularly, hope. On the other side of the coin, Smith notes, "are self-doubt, passivity, dependence, fatalism, and despair. No one will question which of these lists goes with the Haves, which with the Have Nots!"

This theory of incompetence which springs from powerlessness and hopelessness is particularly relevant to nonwhite children, especially those in urban ghettos. Racial discrimination denies the nonwhite child the social ground required for respect of self. Social inequities have limited the nonwhite's opportunities and consequently his motivation and achievements. Power and a voice in his own fate have traditionally been denied the nonwhite.

Low income, as Chilman (1966), Lewis (1967a), Jeffers (1967), and others have shown, is clearly related to family conflict and instability. This relationship is particularly marked among nonwhites. In 1966, 29 percent of nonwhite children were not living with both parents, as compared to 9 percent of white children (U.S. Department of Labor, *Social and Economic Conditions of Negroes in the United States*, 1967), a fact that bears a relationship to the "man in the house" welfare regulation. Negro children from disorganized families are likely to live in mother-centered households, which may contribute to a confused masculine identity and a subsequent drive toward exaggerated masculinity. Self-hatred and lowered self-esteem are often evinced at a young age. Many such children come to view the world as hostile, believing success is tied to prostitution, pimps, sports celebrities, etc., rather than to "middle-class respectability" (Pettigrew, 1964).

Even when socioeconomic factors are controlled, profile analyses of Negro and white children indicate that they do not live in comparable environments. Keller (1963) found the most striking variation to be in self-evaluations. In her study, 80 percent of Negro children showed unfavorable self-other comparisons in contrast to only 30 percent of the white children.

Henry (1965) found that Negro families whom he studied in St. Louis lacked "the essential strength of hope." "What happens," he asks, "to a person who has no expectations or hopes for himself?" His behavior, Henry explains, is disorganized, without background or direction. "What is left of him is the irreducible ash—*the survival self*—the flight from death. The survival self must concentrate on those experiences which give it continual and vivid reassurance that it is alive—heightened perhaps and smoothed by drugs or alcohol . . . sociologists of the middle-class background contemptuously refer to this state as 'hedonism' . . . it is not—'it is flight from death' " (italics in the original). Life without any real hope of upward mobility is vividly portrayed by Liebow (1966) in his account of Negro men in Washington, D.C.

Many of the character styles of the poor child are necessary for adaptation to his own environment and would be considered symptoms of maladjustment in the middle-class child (Schneiderman, 1965). The incompetence that goes with powerlessness and hopelessness, especially in the ghetto child, gives rise to much deviant behavior which can be interpreted as an escape from self and the world. However, much of this behavior— deviant by middle-class norms—is directed toward alternative modes of competence which become normative within the subculture when legitimate channels for attainment of goals remain closed (Smith, 1968). It follows then, that symptoms produced by the impoverished child may not have the same significance as those produced by the middle-class child (Wilking and Paoli, 1966). Professional workers often fail to recognize this distinction.

While this Task Force acknowledges the cultural relativity of much lower-class behavior, one fact cannot be ignored: *The poor child, in general, is denied optimal mental health because he is denied an environment which fosters the competence required to adapt and function within the superordinate society.*

Rehabilitation programs, to be effective, must find ways of building upon and redirecting the competence which many slum children channel in socially deviant directions (Smith, 1968). Such programs, as well as effective treatment for the disturbed poor child, must be developed from the knowledge of the varying life styles of the poor. Much more research is needed to complete our knowledge of how poverty and social disorganization produce harmful effects and of how different adaptive and cognitive styles affect ego development. However, the mental health problems of the poor cannot be solved solely by professional mental health workers. The alleviation of these problems requires changes in the social, economic, political, legal, educational, and medical institutions of our society. To accomplish these objectives, the poor must be given equal opportunities to participate in the affluent society. Under existing conditions, the distrust, sense of alienation, and the hardships produced by poverty can only lead to an increase in the incidence of mental illness in the United States because the poor no longer believe that poverty is inevitable and irreversible.

Optimal mental health cannot be bred into a people who are denied the basic necessities of life and the sense of personal dignity so highly prized in our culture. Meaningful rehabilitation of the mentally ill cannot be accomplished by a system of "charities," to be given or withheld by arbitrary selection means. So long as the American Medical Association blocks the institution of adequate policies on the controversial issues involving equal care for the poor, large-scale rehabilitative issues will be unsuccessful (Polier, 1966).

LACK OF SERVICES FOR THE POOR

Increased facilities and manpower are needed to meet the physical and mental health needs of the American population in general. The need is particularly acute for those in low-income groups who cannot afford the cost of private care and who, for many reasons, may fail to use those facilities which are available to them. For many of the poor, however, facilities and treatment are nonexistent. For example, although there are just 12 percent of the nation's physicians and 18 percent of the nurses practicing in rural areas, they must serve 30 percent of the nation's population. The inaccessibility of medical care means an additional expense in travel and working time for rural people, many of whom cannot afford medical fees at all. Many migrant children go untreated because mobility prevents them from meeting established requirements for medical benefits. Three-fifths of the counties identified as migrant home base or work areas have not yet been touched by the Migrant Health Act services (Bennett, 1967). Facilities and services for nonurban Indian groups have increased in recent years; however, they are still poorly developed (Ablon *et al.*, 1967). One promising innovation in meeting the health needs of our rural, migrant, and Indian reservation population is the traveling clinic (Straus, 1965).

In urban areas, one out of every four or five babies is born to a family dependent on hospital outpatient clinics for its *total* medical care. Facilities for prenatal care are either nonexistent or are not used (Cornely, 1962), sometimes because eligibility is based on income and admits only the most destitute. Data from several large cities have indicated that between one-fifth and one-half of the women delivered in municipal hospitals have had no prenatal care, or else have received care too late for it to be effective. The majority of these women were from socially and economically deprived populations ("A look at problems in prenatal service programs," 1966; Anderson and Lesser, 1966). Currently, among migrant workers, an estimated 16,000 mothers will not have prenatal care (Bennett, 1967). In many isolated rural areas, the poor are still dependent upon midwives, and both the mother and infant go without subsequent medical care.

The 1965 amendments to the Social Security Act required the states to make maternal and child health services available to all children by 1975. As a result, 54 special projects, both in rural areas and large cities, are in operation and by the end of June 1967 had registered 237,000 women (new pregnancies) for medical, clinical, family planning, and other health services. Patients are currently being admitted to the program at a rate of 9,000 each month. The programs that have been in operation for over two years show what appears to be a reversal of the trend toward increasing infant mortality. For example, in Chicago in 1965 the infant mortality rate in a population from low-income census tracts served by this program was 34.5 of the 14,380 infants born, as compared to the rate of 57.4 of 9,044 births in a similar income population not served by this program. These projects have brought quality care to high-risk maternity and prematurely born groups by bringing maternity clinics into the neighborhoods where the patients live (U.S. Department of Health, Education, and Welfare, *Programs for the Handicapped,* 1968). Expansion of such programs is recommended.

During childhood, the children of the poor may not receive any health care. In 1963[21] only 7.5 percent of the children under 17 whose family's income was less than $2,000 visited a pediatrician, as compared to 33 percent of those in the $10,000 and above income level (U.S. Bureau of Census, *Vital and Health Statistics,* 1966). Data from a National Health Survey show that poor children are hospitalized less often but remain in the hospital longer (Coll, 1965). Negro children receive about half as much attention from doctors as white children. Among poor Negroes, only one out of ten children is likely to see a pediatrician as often as once yearly (*Health Care and the Negro Population,* 1966).

Most of the 600,000 children between the ages of 3 and 5 who attended Project Head Start Developmental Centers in 1965 had never been to a physician or dentist and had not received immunizations. Of the 16–21-year-old youths who enrolled in the Job Corps programs, the majority had never been to a physician, and many came from homes where at least one parent had a physical and/or mental handicap (U.S. House of Representatives, *Subcommittee on the War on Poverty Program,* 1965).

The poor tend to bear ill health stoically or to rely on patent medicines or home remedies. They lose more work per year and pay more proportionally for treatment. The majority have no hospital or surgical insurance. Sixty percent earning under $2,000 are uninsured as compared to only 19 percent earning over $7,000 (Eichorn and Ludwig, 1966). The increased cost of medical care has hit the poor hardest[22] and their situation is worsened by the fact that they need care most. By late 1950, 44 percent of families earning less than $5,000 were reported as having serious problems because of medical expenses (U.S. Bureau of the Census, 1964).

21. July 1963–June 1964.
22. For example, the increase in cost of medical care between 1953 and 1958—in mean gross charges per family for personal health services—was only 16 percent in the family income class of $7,500 and over as compared to 49 percent in the $2,000–$3,499 class (Ornati, 1966).

Although designed to provide care for the poor, Medicare and Medicaid are proving far too costly to state and local governments. Many plan to cut their health care budgets drastically ("Don't get sick," 1968).

Income and availability of services, however, are not the only factors involved in the utilization of services by the poor. Education is more highly correlated with frequency of visits to the physician than is income[23] (Ornati, 1966). Poor education often hinders the identification of symptoms, and lack of experience with professionals leads many to hesitate in seeking early treatment. Many feel stigmatized and out of place in professional surroundings (Miller *et al.,* 1967). The stigma is particularly felt where care involves charity. This feeling is often fostered by professionals, many of whom, as Breslow notes, feel that those who receive public care are "clinical material":

The latter expression and the tone in which it is usually uttered, betrays an attitude toward people which is destructive of the mutual respect which is necessary for good medical care. The long wait in uncomfortable surroundings, after a difficult trip, to receive care which is too brief, from a hurried doctor who is frustrated with the knowledge that he can only make a fragmented contribution and whose attitude says 'clinical material'—these aspects of care to those most in need have left deep scars. Is it remarkable that people do not like such experience and tend to avoid it? Compounding the difficulty, many health professionals have projected the responsibility for resistance to this kind of treatment onto the people themselves by calling them *apathetic* or part of the *hard core* (Breslow, 1967:1095, italics in the original).

In addition to this depersonalization, many service structures are too rigid to be able to serve the poor, e.g., clinic hours are not fitted to those who work; facilities may be difficult to reach—particularly in rural areas; and services are often so fragmented that the poor lack the means and perhaps the tenacity to follow up on referrals to different agencies (Hoff, 1966). In addition, discriminatory practices still exist in some areas (U.S. Senate . . . *Hunger and Malnutrition in America,* 1967).

The inadequacies of services for the physical care of the poor exist also in the mental health field. The need for additional facilities and manpower are, in fact, even more acute, and treatment methods in need of more radical revision. An overview of the psychiatric services to children in the United States, undertaken by the Biometry Branch of NIMH, reveals that recent increases in facilities and professional man-hours have not kept pace with the increase in demands for services. Estimates of expected manpower resources show that if the present patterns continue one cannot provide even the current level of service by 1972 (Rosen *et al.,* 1968).

23. Except for those in income classes under $2,000 who, regardless of age or education, have significantly less frequent physician's visits (*Public Health Bulletin,* 1960).

In addition to the manpower problem, the traditional mental health strategy is criticized on other grounds. For example, Gladwin (1967) notes:

There is a growing doubt that clinical diagnoses as currently made provide an adequate basis for predicting overall social and occupational effectiveness, except in cases of marked symptomatology. The requirement of the clinical model that people come into the clinic and present themselves for help around an articulated problem means that help is given only to those best able to help themselves. Those people who most need help are most likely to remain beyond the view of the clinician and thus to go untreated.

This has been shown in a number of studies which indicate that poor children do not receive the same treatment in public hospitals and clinics as their more affluent counterparts. Furman et al. (1965) found that the public clinic[24]—in contrast to the voluntary clinic—is overloaded, has a relatively limited control over intake, and offers a curtailed service to the very poor and to its referring agencies (which are mainly the courts and schools). Middle-class children, deemed to be "good treatment cases," receive most of the treatment, whereas poor children receive mostly diagnostic and testing services. Hunt (1962), comparing the treatment received in a child guidance clinic, concludes that the poor child falls into a group for which psychotherapy is not generally considered the treatment of choice. Poor children are generally referred elsewhere.

Studies of class status, as related to various aspects of treatment, reveal that custodial care and organic therapies increase as the socioeconomic status of the patient decreases (Hollingshead and Redlick, 1958; Redlick et al., 1953). Acceptance for psychotherapy—as well as discounts in fees for therapy—increase as the socioeconomic status of the patient increases (Hollingshead and Redlick, 1958; Schaffer and Myers, 1954; Brill and Storrow, 1960). The higher the socioeconomic status of the client, the greater the likelihood that the therapist will decide on analytic rather than supportive therapy (Winder and Hersko, 1955) and, given similar symptomologies but different socioeconomic statuses, lower-class persons are likely to be diagnosed as more disturbed, to be given a poorer prognosis, and to be more frequently diagnosed as being psychotic or as having a

24. However, treatment in clinics appears to depend also upon such factors as the patient's age, diagnosis, sex, and the referral source. Of the 339,000 children under care in clinics in 1966, two-thirds were adolescents. Of these, more of the 18- to 19-year-olds received treatment than those age 14 to 15. Almost half of the adolescents with psychotic, neurotic, and personality disorders have received treatment, but only one-third of those with brain syndromes and only 14 percent of those mentally deficient received this service. Irrespective of age or diagnosis, more boys than girls were treated. Also, children referred by mental hospitals were more frequently treated than those referred by other agencies (Rosen et al., 1968).

character disorder than are middle-class persons.[25] The termination of services initiated by therapists increases sharply as social class declines (Schneiderman, 1965), as well as terminations by the client (Schaffer and Myers, 1954; Baum *et al*.,1966). The patient's chances of being listed as "socially improved" decreases the lower the social class of the patient (Cole *et al*., 1962) and follow-up, in general, is provided only to the more affluent (Myers *et al*., 1965). There is also evidence of ethnocentric biases among professionals which results in less-intense and less-prolonged treatment. Problems in treatment are compounded when low SES is added to ethnicity (Yamamoto *et al*., 1967). Langner *et al*. found that Negro and Puerto Rican children in Manhattan are less likely to see a psychiatrist than are white children, irrespective of SES (Unpublished MS, 1967). Segregated mental institutions, staffed with unempathic personnel, create additional problems for Negroes (Coles, 1966). State-supported mental health clinics are reluctant to accept Indian referrals (Ablon *et al*., 1967).[26] Treatment is further hindered because professionals lack training in the language and culture of different ethnic groups (see, e.g., Fitzpatrick *et al*., 1968).

Evidence indicates that the poor seek psychiatric help only after they are unable to function because of psychotic symptoms. Most commonly, they are committed to a state mental hospital (Hollingshead and Redlich, 1958; Myers *et al*., 1965; *Action for Mental Health*, 1961). The proportion of poor children in state mental hospitals is undetermined, but probably quite high. Data from Maryland show a much higher percentage of poor children, as compared to affluent children, in state hospitals (Pollack, 1966).[27]

Children under 15 are the only age group which show an increase in first admission rates to mental hospitals (Rosen *et al*., 1968). The greater proportion of children confined to these institutions are adolescents, for whom separate facilities are seldom available. A recent survey of state hospitals shows that approximately 13 percent provide separate units for children. An additional 26 percent provide services to children but no separate units (Star and Ruby, 1965).

25. This bias was consistent despite variations in the psychologists' origins, experience, theoretical position, etc. (Haase, 1964).

26. Many of the studies mentioned above relate to adult populations. How extensively all of these factors can be applied to the population of poor children remains to be determined. There is some evidence that the relationship between class and maintenance of contact in intake, diagnostic evaluation, and psychotherapeutic treatment is not as universally true for the children as for the adults in the lower socioeconomic strata (Hunt, 1962; Tuckman and Lavell, 1959; Baker and Wagner, 1966).

27. This trend was not noted for children classed just above the poverty line (i.e., $3,000–$4,999). This group relied very heavily on outpatient facilities. A small percentage of the very poor were shown to be in private mental hospitals.

Further, the situation in mental hospitals today is reminiscent of that which Greenblatt described in 1957, in which there were about twenty untrained "watchdog" attendants to every nurse and doctor (Greenblatt et al., 1957). According to a recent NIMH survey, 21 state hospitals are without any psychiatrists, and 91 state institutions have only one to four psychiatrists ("Survey of Mental Health Establishments—Staffing of Patterns and Survey Methodology, October 1965"). Figures for 1965 show the ratio of physicians working full time in public mental hospitals is one for each 102 patients. Only 35 percent of these physicians are psychiatrists; another 20 percent are physicians doing their training in psychiatry. The ratio of all types of mental health professionals[28] is 1 to 19 (Joint Information Service of the American Psychiatric Association and the National Association for Mental Health, 1968).

Despite our current belief in total milieu therapy, and our knowledge of the fact that "institutional neurosis" results from placement in large institutions which can deliver little more than custodial care, the greater proportion of our institutionalized mentally ill children continue to be housed in large institutions. This holds true also for most of the retarded, the physically handicapped, and the delinquent. Noninstitutionalized care and care in smaller institutions remain largely the prerogative of the more affluent.

Facilities for the mentally defective are shockingly inadequate. In 1960 the 78,333 mentally retarded youngsters under 20 represented almost one-half of the total child resident population in the United States (U.S. Department of Health, Education, and Welfare, 1965). This represented an increase of almost 60 percent since 1950. Although nonwhites are probably underrepresented in these institutions, the increase in nonwhite children was three times that for white children (i.e., 160 and 52 percent, respectively). Combined with homes for dependent children, facilities for the mentally handicapped housed only 37 percent of the nonwhite institutionalized population in 1960, as compared to 60 percent of the institutionalized white population[29] (U.S. Bureau of Census . . . Inmates of Institutions, 1963).

While all countries show a decline in the use and construction of the "big closed mental deficiency colony" and a greater use of community resources (e.g., training to help the mentally defective reenter normal community life) (Soddy and Ahrenfeldt, 1967), such efforts are still on a small scale in the United States. Little progress has been made in this country in the area of institutional care (Dybwad, 1960). Of the 720

28. Nineteen percent of these professionals are physicians. Others include: psychologists and psychometrists (5 percent), social workers (12 percent), registered nurses (44 percent), and various ancillary therapists (21 percent).
29. Correctional institutions housed 40 percent of the nonwhite population.

institutions for the mentally retarded operating in 1960, 11 percent accommodated fewer than 50 persons and served only 5 percent of the retardate population. Forty-seven institutions reported between 1,000 and 1,999 residents and 17 reported 2,000 or more. Thus, 9 percent of the institutions, the majority operated by state agencies, housed 65 percent of the institutionalized retardates[30] (U.S. Department of Health, Education, and Welfare, 1965).

While treatment of the retardate population depends upon the extent of retardation, and upon its etiology, i.e., whether it is organic or non-organic (since remediation is more successful with the latter), the effects of custodial care in a large institution only increase the symptomatology and the chances that institutionalization will become an enduring way of life. The low IQ reported for a greater proportion of retardates[31] may be, in part, a function of institutionalization, since studies have shown the occurrence of decreasing IQ subsequent to confinement (Zigler, 1966).

The large number of retardates from the poverty population are the most likely candidates for placement in large, custodial-care-type institutions. An effort is currently being made by Division of Mental Retardation, Rehabilitation Services Administration, through the Hospital Improvement Program, to serve some 35,000 retardates in 88 institutions and 100 projects by the year 1969. The program offers many advantages, the prime one being an emphasis upon methods designed to decrease the number of totally dependent residents in institutions.[32] Some experimental programs have offered promise. For example, those diagnosed as familial retardates are shown to be capable of having their behavior patterns modified (Kirk, 1958; Zigler, 1966); the severely retarded have proved to be capable of self-initiated behavior and speech development (McKinney and Keele, 1963); self-confidence has been improved through participation in community activities (Dayton, 1963), and prerehabilitation training for employment has proved feasible with young adults (Young Adult Training Institute and Workshop, 1966). Better institutional practices have been found to increase the cognitive and social capacities of retardates (Richardson, 1964). Clinics that provide comprehensive evaluation and give counsel to parents are also a promising development (see Dybwad, 1960). However, even the Hospital Improvement Program reaches only approximately a third of the institutionalized retardates.

Greater efforts are needed to provide high-quality care to the mentally

30. The number of institutions reported here excludes those hospitals which provide psychiatric care to retardates but includes homes which combine treatment of the physically handicapped with treatment of the mentally retarded.

31. Eighty percent of the present retardates have an IQ under 50 (Tarjan, 1965).

32. Data obtained by personal communication with personnel in the Division of Mental Retardation, Rehabilitation Services Administration, May 1968.

retarded. There is a need for additional psychiatric facilities, especially in view of the fact that the incidence of major behavioral disorders is higher for institutionalized retardates than for the general population (Heber, 1964). Preventive programs need to be established to counter those variables noted between poverty and retardation. Programs should focus on increased prenatal care, increased care and sensory stimulation for premature infants, and enriched programs for preschool children which will provide the type of stimulation necessary to counter familial retardation. Supervision of screening and placement, as well as provision of legal recourse by the poor, is also required to counter the tendency to relegate the poor and non-English-speaking disturbed children to state hospitals for the mentally defective—a categorizing that is likely to result in permanent placement.

Institutional practices in the field of delinquency are equally outmoded. A number of studies indicate that delinquency rates are higher among certain lower SES groups, especially those in socially disorganized areas (Conger *et al.*, 1966) and among groups such as Indians who are undergoing cultural conflict (Ablon *et al.*, 1967). The question of whether or not delinquency should be equated with emotional disturbance in all cultural subgroups is still being debated. However, even if such behavior is "normal" among certain subgroups, the consequences of ensuing legal measures are not likely—by most correctional means—to produce emotionally healthy results. For youth 15 and over, placement is generally in jails, workhouses, reformatories, or prisons (U.S. Department of Health, Education, and Welfare, 1965). Testimonies before the Senate Subcommittee on Employment, Manpower, and Poverty in 1967 revealed that some 100,000 children were incarcerated in adult prisons in 1965. Of the 833,507 juveniles taken into custody, only 2.9 percent were referred to a welfare agency. One-third of the juvenile courts in the nation have no caseworker or probation officer available to them, and 83 percent have no regular access to any psychiatric or psychological assistance for the treatment of offenders. In 1965 most training schools were still operating custodial programs—at an annual cost of $144,600,000. Despite the lack of success with institutional programs, state and local governments—without federal grants—plan a 42 percent increase in training school capacity by 1975. Little financial support is planned for community-based programs, even though these have been proved successful (U.S. Senate . . . *Juvenile Delinquency Prevention and Control Act*, 1967).

Surveys of state and local agencies reveal that training schools are used for various purposes other than those for which they were intended, e.g., as maternity facilities, detention homes, care places for the mentally retarded and/or children with severe psychiatric problems, etc. Placement in foster care and group homes—although seemingly successful probation alternatives—are limited ("Correction in the United States," 1967).

Figures for all types of correctional institutions showed a sharp increase in nonwhite populations between 1950 and 1960—76 percent in training schools and 92 percent in other types of correctional facilities (U.S. Department of Health, Education, and Welfare, 1965). Of all institutionalized children in 1960, 18 percent of white children, as compared to 40 percent of nonwhites, were in correctional facilities, a fact which suggests that there may be vast inequities in the handling of behavior problems from children of different social and racial backgrounds (Rosen *et al.*, 1968). Although public training schools with populations less than 150 showed the lowest returnee rate, 44 percent of the public training schools in 1963 had populations over 150. The recidivism rate increased as the child population of the institution increased (U.S. Department of Health, Education, and Welfare, 1964).

The rising delinquency rate—particularly among the poor, and especially among the ghetto population—makes imperative a preventative approach. The inability of most correctional institutions to truly rehabilitate delinquents calls for a greater effort to utilize means which have proved—experimentally and practically—to be effective. Group homes, foster care, and other noninstitutionalized community-based programs which encourage youth participation are one such example, particularly programs that include training in social competence. Job training programs also offer potential. However, any such programs must be more than crash efforts which offer hope to disadvantaged youth only to breed further discouragement because funds, manpower, etc., are either insufficient or are withdrawn by power agencies. We must, as Leonard Cottrell, Jr., stated before a Senate subcommittee, deal directly with the cultural, social, and economic processes which give rise to delinquency. For these purposes, the conventional individual casework and psychotherapeutic approaches are inadequate (U.S. Senate . . . *Juvenile Delinquency and Control Act, 1967*). In fact, psychiatric intervention appears ineffective with habitual delinquents. In a review of the data on delinquency, as related to psychiatric treatment through court-connected child guidance clinics, Rodman and Grams (1967) conclude that efficacious treatment is dependent upon effective diagnosis, upon the placement operation, and upon the treatment programs for each *type* of delinquent (italics in the original).

Rural children are another group that need special attention. Of the 2,007 outpatient clinics open on April 30, 1965, only 234 were in rural areas.[33] During this same year, rural clinics served 25,000 children—only 8 percent of the total clinic cases served in the United States. Only slightly over half of these were open full time—as compared to almost three-

33. A rural place was defined in this study as one located in a county in which 50 percent or more of the population lived in towns of less than 2,500 persons and where the county was not included in a standard metropolitan statistical area (Rosen *et al.*, 1968).

quarters of those in urban areas. In addition the rural clinics were pro-vided only 5 percent of the professional man-hours available to all clinics. Rural clinic services tended to be brief, often consisting of only psychologi-cal testing. This reflects the lack of these services in schools and other community agencies (Rosen *et al.*, 1968). Considering that one-third of the nation's child population under 18 resides in rural areas, that the incidence of poverty is high in such areas, and that the psychiatric out-patient unit is often the only available mental health facility for rural youth (especially those who cannot afford transportation to urban areas), it is apparent that many of these youth go untreated.

Referrals for the poor child are usually made by the court or schools, both of which may reflect the ethnic and social class bias of middle-class professionals. Such referrals, for children who are emotionally disturbed, may be deferred longer, the lower the social class of the child (McDermott *et al.*, 1965). For the very poor, no referral may ever be made, despite the fact that the child's emotional disturbance is recognized (Kozol, 1967). School mental health facilities are, in general, inadequate, especially in small school districts. As a result, early identification of children needing treatment is insufficient.

We do not have in the United States, as Gorman (1968) points out, any comprehensive, coordinated method of providing services to fit the total needs of the child. We might, as Gorman argues, emulate the Soviet Union's child care arrangements. Such care begins on an intensive, meticu-lous basis, with the pregnant mother. After the child is delivered, notifica-tion is made to a children's polyclinic which provides most of the medical and psychiatric services for children in kindergarten and school. The 70,000 pediatricians in the USSR are trained to detect emotional problems in children and have an intimate knowledge of the child, his family, and his homelife. Any emotional disturbance is reported to the child psychiatrist of the polyclinic staff. Pediatric care—as well as educational facilities—are provided in the nurseries. Specialized nurseries, sanatoria, and Residential Forest Schools are available to handle psychiatric disorders in children—always with the goal of rehabilitation. The neuropsychiatric dispensary psychiatrist who works at the polyclinic is expected to follow the emo-tionally disturbed child, regardless of his living unit, from the onset of disturbance until the age of 15.

In the United States, on the other hand, there is a fragmentation of services, a lack of manpower, and a welter of agencies with stringent intake procedures. No one has been delegated the responsibility for the child. No organized system of follow-up exists, and complete life history data are usually nonexistent. Our 15,000 pediatricians generally have no psychiatric training, although they are a promising source of manpower for purposes of early prevention and intervention.

Our present child mental health care network is inadequate for the needs of all our children. The poor, however, receive the least care although they may, as many feel, be the group most in need of mental health services.

The present inadequate care of the mental health of the poor revolves around a host of complex problems, some of which stem from the attitudes of the poor themselves. For example, the lower class are more likely to attribute their mental health problems to physical causes and to believe that such problems should be physically treated (Hollingshead and Redlich, 1958). Whereas the middle class regard mental illness as being amenable to treatment, lower-class persons hold negative attitudes which equate mental illness with severe forms of disorder, e.g., "craziness" or "insanity." Often they regard such conditions as hopeless (Riessman and Scribner, 1965). When they do not receive the expected medical-psychiatric interview from the therapist—whom they expect to play an active but permissive role—they may drop out of treatment (Overall and Aronson, 1963). Often the poor are unaware of facilities that are available to them —further evidence of their isolation and alienation from the mainstream culture. Many of these attitudes are caused by or reinforced by the attitudes of the professionals, by monetary barriers to treatment, etc.

Gladwin (1967) notes that one of the most promising strategies that have been proposed to surmount some of the difficulties mentioned above is the development of programs built around the goal of social competency. For the poor—except for cases of extreme symptomatology—this would entail the teaching of those middle-class skills and perceptions that are essential to the opening up of avenues of choice and opportunity. For emotionally disturbed children, programming could be designed along the lines of Project Re-ED. To effectively implement a social competence model, however, clinical practice and training must include knowledge about social systems in a form that is meaningful and useful to practitioners.

There are indications that many of the poor are tired of having things done *to* them and *for* them. They are tired of experts who teach them what to do but who do not listen to what the poor themselves want done. They are disenchanted with unequal schools and inadequate medical care. Normand *et al.* (1963) note that the poor are also becoming more sophisticated about mental illness.

Two new approaches seem promising in improving mental health services for the poor. One involves the inclusion of lower socioeconomic groups in the planning and implementation of mental health programs. The use of paraprofessionals and indigenous workers appears to be another way.

Studies have shown that indigenous personnel are able to break through some of the barriers between the poor and the professionals. Because these workers understand the language and the problems of the poor, and of the particular neighborhood with which they are familiar, they can serve as an effective communicative link between their people and the professionals. They prove to be excellent referral agents and are able to aid the poor through the labyrinth of our present fragmented and bureaucratic service agencies. They are successful in reaching people who are often inaccessible to the professionals, particularly when they go directly into the homes. The compatibility of language and culture often allows the nonprofessional mental health aide to establish rapport easily with persons in need of help.

As community agents, the nonprofessional workers act as a catalyst in creating interdependence and self-help efforts. Their use in a multiservice center was found to improve the quality of services and to be conducive to the development of community competence and autonomy (Peck and Kaplan, 1967).

DEFEATISM

There are many indications that the poor develop a sense of defeatism and hopelessness concerning their chances for upward mobility in our competitive society. The dynamics of such attitudes spring from a host of complex factors related to our cultural and socioeconomic system and to the manner in which these factors impinge, psychologically and materially, upon the lives of the poor.

Defeatism, in fact, may be reflected in the attitudes of the very young, as Kozol (1967) so vividly portrays in his account of Negro children in the Boston public schools. Crowded housing, poor health, inadequate educational opportunities, the need for added income, attitudes of the more affluent, and value systems within poverty populations—all tend to lessen the child's motivation to compete within the educational system, thus greatly lessening his chances to escape the cycle of poverty.

By adolescence, the poverty youth's sense of hopelessness may well have made him just another statistic. The school dropout rate, which increases as the parent's income decreases, is consistently higher where poverty is most concentrated—among urban slum, rural, and nonwhite populations. In 1964, about 64 percent of all school dropouts came from families with incomes under $5,000, and only 10 percent from families with incomes over $7,500 (U.S. Bureau of the Census . . . *School Enrollments, October 1964*, February 8, 1966). For some groups the dropout rates are unusually high. In the metropolitan North and West, Negro students are three times as likely as white students to drop out of school by the age of 16 or 17. Further, in these areas 20 percent of the eligible Negro population is not enrolled in school, in contrast to 6 percent of the eligible white population (Coleman *et al.*, 1966). Father Bryde states that the national Indian dropout rate from the eighth grade to the twelfth grade is 60 percent (in Ablon *et al.*, 1967).

The factors related to the high dropout rate among poverty populations are numerous and complex, stemming both from the child's home environment and the inadequacies within our educational system. The child of poverty is likely to begin school with a number of disadvantages. Typically, his parents are school dropouts who married young and have more than the average number of children (Orshansky, 1965). Ill-education and financial problems lessen the young parents' chance of providing a home environment which fosters the type of intellectual stimulation and language development required to compete within the educational system. "Disadvantaged" children are likely to be placed within crowded, understaffed, and dilapidated schools in which there are not only an insufficient number of textbooks and materials[34] but a type of curriculum which has little relevance to their lives or may, in the case of the nonwhite children, contain curricular material which is actually detrimental to the building of a healthy self-respect.

Thus, the roots for dropping out are often nourished in both the home and school. The child, handicapped by language differences, lack of books and of study space, and often by the indifference of teachers, may fail to learn to read in the early grades. Thus, his chances for dropping out are greatly increased.[35] The cumulative effect of being behind in the early years is well recognized. The poor child who may be only one year behind his more affluent counterpart in the first or second grade may be four years or more behind at the high school level. For example, it is estimated that 85 percent of the eighth grade students in Harlem are "functional illiterates," i.e., their reading level is not above that of the fifth grade (Larner, 1966). The prevalence of inferior intellectual functioning among various minority-group children, particularly the Negro and the American Indian, has been consistently reported[36] (e.g., Peterson, 1923; Schuey, 1958; Cole-

34. Educational expenditures are often less in central cities. The Syracuse University study of school expenditures by Campbell *et al.*, shows that in thirty-five of the largest metropolitan areas in 1962, expenditures in the inner cities—where there were many low-income families—were $145 per pupil less than in their contiguous and more affluent suburbs (summarized in the *Carnegie Quarterly*, 1966).

35. Three times as many poor readers as good readers drop out of school and 80 percent of good readers, in contrast to 45 percent of poor readers, graduate (Plenty, 1956).

36. Eighth grade pupils in Central Harlem in recent years had a mean IQ of 87.7 as compared to an average of 100.1 for New York City (Moynihan, 1965). A normative study of 1,800 Negro elementary school children in five southern states yielded a mean IQ of 80.7 (Kennedy, 1963). According to the most recent classification system accepted by the American Association of Mental Deficiency and used by the U.S. Public Health Service, the average child in the latter study was "borderline retarded" (Heber, 1961). A high percentage of Indian children are edu-

man *et al.*, 1966). How much this can be attributed to health factors, home environment, and sometimes language difficulties, and how much to the inferior education and testing methods to which the poverty child, and particularly the nonwhite child, is subjected has yet to be determined.

Poor school attendance, often aggravated by lack of proper clothing, improper diet, and insufficient care of illness or accidents, furthers educational retardation among the poor (Liddle and Rockwell, 1963). One mother explained why she had kept her children home from school: "There was no food in the house, and I didn't want them to have to go to school hungry and then come home hungry too. I felt that if I kept them with me, at least when they cried and asked for a piece of bread, I would be with them to put my arms around them" (Jackson, 1966). Mobility hinders attendance among migrant groups (Bennett, 1967). Among Indian children, native values may oppose those of the white middle-class educational system. The conflict engendered lowers the Indian child's motivation, and permissive parental attitudes provide no counter to absenteeism (Ablon *et al.*, 1967).

The cumulative aspects of educational retardation breed a sense of defeatism in both the student and the teacher. While many inadequacies within our educational system could be solved by greater financial expenditures and curriculum revisions, such measures will prove inadequate as long as educators lack empathy and understanding of children of the poor, especially children from varying ethnic groups. The tendency to deal with the poverty child in depersonalized terms—by calling them, for example, "animals" or "niggers" (Kozol, 1967)—undermines the child's image of his self and his belief in his own competence; hence, the circular pattern of the educational dropout and the ensuing consequences.

The reasons for dropping out given by the school may vary from that given by the student and/or his parents. The school records in Connecticut showed "16 years old" and "work" as the most frequent reason for dropping out of school, whereas students and parents placed considerably more weight on indifferent or discouraged student attitudes toward school. Financial reasons were given approximately the same weight by both parents and students; however, fewer Negroes than whites reported that their motivation was lack of money, even though incomes for Negroes were lower (*Comparative Study of Negro and White Dropouts in Selected Connecticut High Schools*, 1959).

Perhaps a major determinant of the high dropout rate among Negroes

---

cationally retarded when scores on standardized achievement tests are compared to whites (Ablon *et al.*, 1967). A study of public schools by the U.S. Office of Education ranks Indians the lowest of all the ethnic groups in educational achievement (Coleman *et al.*, 1966).

stems from the fact that education may not be the same avenue toward upward mobility that it is for the white individual in our society. Despite increases in the median educational attainment levels of low-income whites and nonwhites, the difference between the percentage of whites and non-whites with high school diplomas or college educations has remained stable over the past decade. Children of families at the bottom of the occupational hierarchy still have much less chance of moving into upper-level jobs. The chances of the white manual worker's son moving into an upper-level job is slightly more than double that of the Negro manual laborer's son. More disturbing is the finding that among Negro sons of white-collar fathers, 72.4 percent went into manual occupations, whereas only 23.4 percent of their white counterparts did so (Miller *et al.*, 1967). No doubt the reasons for this downward mobility are complex, including discriminatory employment, unequal pay, etc. But perhaps the failure of our society to eradicate these discriminatory practices reflects even more the failure of our educational system.

When compared to high school graduates, youths who drop out of school are shown to have much more difficulty in finding employment, lesser chances of progressing to skilled or semiskilled employment, to have higher rates of unemployment after their first job, and to be far more likely to earn wages below the poverty level (David *et al.*, 1961). The relationship between educational level and income is dramatically shown in the 1967 statistics. Family heads over 25 who had less than eight years of schooling had a median income of $4,142, and those with less than four years of high school had a median income of $7,187; whereas the median income level of high school graduates was $8,338, and that for college graduates was $11,870. What the median figure alone does not portray is the fact that from 48 to 75 percent (depending upon the educational level) of those with less than a high school education were earning less than the national $7,579 median income of all family heads. Only 35 percent of high school and about 17 percent of college graduates fell below the annual median wage. The lower the educational level, the greater the proportion of those below the poverty line (U.S. Bureau of the Census . . . "Income in 1966 of Families and Persons in the United States," 1967). In part, this situation is due to the fact that a large proportion of the ill-educated poor do not work full time.[37]

The disastrous consequences of low education upon the choice or lack of choice in the working role perpetuate the sense of defeatism among the poor and affect their attitude toward work. The lower-class youth are as often fired for poor work attitudes as for poor work performance (Brager,

37. In 1966 one out of six of the male heads of poor families had been out of work and actively seeking a job sometime during the year—an unemployment rate almost three times that for heads of nonpoor families (Orshansky, 1968).

1964). Such persons may work but fail to work up to capacity. Friend and Haggard (1948) found that those fired for poor work attitudes (i.e., those who were low in work adjustment and achievement) disliked run-of-the-mill competition, were indifferent to improvements in physical working conditions, promotion-on-merit atmosphere, a sense of group belongingness, and to congenial fellow workers. There was a tendency for such workers to defeat themselves and to spoil their job chances by excessive drinking, quarreling, and absenteeism. They seemed to "marry the wrong person" and to have large families which they had difficulty in supporting. Correlational analysis linked these tendencies to self-sabotage to certain attitudes toward the family, e.g., parental rejection, antagonism toward the father, resentment or dependence or domination by families. They appeared to reenact in the working situation the pattern they resented in their early life, and frequently expressed an attitude of being shortchanged at home and on the job.

For the urban slum youth, the lure of the streets may become a fixed pattern—one that will prevent him from developing punctual habits and other attitudes necessary to succeed in employment.[38] In a recent article Stewart Alsop speculates that there may be a point at which the Negro adolescent becomes psychologically unemployable. He quotes Julius Hobson, a Negro activist and former head of CORE for the Washington, D.C., area, as saying:

There's a psychological thing there. . . . A man who's lived on his wits, sleeping till ten in the morning, on the hustle in the streets or the poolrooms—he figures a guy working eight hours a day for eighty bucks a week just isn't smart. If you just get a guy like that a job and turn him loose, you're wasting your time —he won't last a week. After thirty, maybe twenty-five, a man living on his wits reaches a point where he just won't hold a regular job. You've got to catch them young. (Alsop, 1968)

A number of studies indicate that even the fully employed and "stable" poor view employment in survival terms. Work is not expected to be a source of personal satisfaction. The reasons for this orientation are highly complex; however, some are obviously tied to the fact that available jobs have little status in our society. They are merely time-serving occupations which fail to engender pride in being trained or utilized to fulfill one's capacity.

A sense of defeat may be perpetuated by other factors which interact with the poor and the world of work. For the Negro and other minority

38. A Conference on the Effective Utilization by Industry of the Hardcore Unemployed emphasized the importance of training in good work habits as a necessary part of job training. (Sponsored by the Division of Personnel Psychology of the New York State Psychological Association, May 2, 1968.)

groups, union membership may be denied because of discriminatory practices or regulations. Some unions require a high school diploma for apprenticeship, thus barring many school dropouts. For many, the possession of a police arrest record prevents their being considered for any except marginal employment.[39] Once the ghetto youth has been arrested for any type of offense, however minor, it virtually assures him a future place on the roles of the hardcore unemployed.[40]

Rapid technological advances have brought about important changes in the relationship between work and education. As Ornati (1966) notes, employment today depends increasingly upon certain skills, for example, the ability to pass aptitude tests, fill out questionnaires, use correct words, etc. Formal education is being linked more and more to jobs that previously were not so restricted.

Technological changes have "displaced" many groups whose previous employment was not dependent upon formal education but on the ability to work within a constricted area of employment, for example, coal miners, meat-packers, automobile workers, and farmhands. Large numbers of these workers are now unemployed. The general upgrading in hiring practices eliminates many from competing in the labor market. The displaced miner who, a few years ago earned $27 a day, typifies the fate of many displaced workers and the effect technological changes have had upon their children.

For many men in Appalachia today, the only means of survival is to be classified as disabled under one of the welfare programs. Among people who have traditionally linked pride and independence with the ability of the male to provide for his family, dependence upon welfare has given rise to a high incidence of psychosomatic and neurotic symptoms and to a weakening of strong kinship ties. Male employment is scarce, and many jobs are seasonal, often paying less than welfare. Industrial work, when available, tends to employ the female rather than the male, thus fostering the sense of defeatism which has been noted in many Appalachian men—an attitude which they pass on to their sons. Some men who are unsuccessful in seeking employment leave their families so their children can be fed by becoming eligible for a Public Assistance grant. Retraining programs have not been highly successful, especially for older workers. Like many other programs, these have offered limited opportunities, most of which involve employment outside the area. For many ex-miners and other poor Appalachians, their life situation has bred not only a dependence upon welfare but a rationalization of its

39. The recent enlightened trend in this area is to consider convictions rather than arrests.
40. Both government and private programs designed for the hardcore unemployed are beginning to select trainees who possess police arrest records.

merits. A recent article on poverty in Appalachia cites these people's attitudes as being antithetical to work. Work is viewed as subordinate to life, and survival through other means—such as welfare—a more desirable alternative (Weller, 1965). With so little belief in the future, many children drop out of school and many are faced with mental health problems (Public Health Service, 1964).

Some attempts have been made to uplift the lives of children in areas where technological changes have brought about greater poverty. One such program is the Child Development Group of Mississippi. This program was begun with sufficient federal financing, manpower, etc.—seemingly, in all ways, planned to accomplish its intended purpose—only to meet with public and political opposition. Almost all those who have examined CDGM's program view it as the most daring attempt yet made to tackle the problem of rural Negro education. However, CDGM accomplished much more than preschooling. Once alienated and apathetic Negro sharecroppers and town dwellers were brought into effective organization which they themselves helped to administer. Despite its success, funds were delayed for the program for several months because of the opposition of a Mississippi delegation ("How do you fight it," 1966). Although CDGM is still operating, refunding is currently being negotiated and the future status is unknown. CDGM may well become another of the all too familiar examples of disconnection and fragmentation in the lives of the poor—another glimpse of what life might be if it were not for the barriers separating the poor from the affluent.

The mental health implications of the failure of CDGM may well be the same as that which Parker and Kleiner (1966) postulate for the civil rights movement in general. In essence, Parker and Kleiner hypothesized that the civil rights movement raises the Negro's aspiration level. The authors felt that if there is not a concomitant increase of expansion of opportunities for the American Negro, mental illness may consequently increase. Whether or not this prediction is correct remains unproved; however, there is little doubt that the situation of the American Negro today has led to an increase in protest and violence. The Negro today, as Duhl (1963:293) notes, is "coming out of limbo. He has had to locate himself between the white society's rejection of him and his rejection of himself." In greater and greater numbers, Negroes are beginning "to take on the new demands of *somebodiness*" (italics in the original). A new awareness has bred a new type of malcontent. "Now we have television," said one angry man interviewed in Watts, "and we can see the difference between the way the whites live and the way we live" (U.S. Senate . . . *Federal Role in Urban Affairs*, 1966:2603).

Despite the new awareness among the poor and ethnic minorities, feelings of defeatism still pervade. Recent trends in many of the programs aimed at poverty groups tend to perpetuate frustration and a sense of hopelessness because hope is offered and then withheld. The poor, as a group, remain alienated from the workings of the larger society. They are not active in citizen activities. In fact, the less the financial stability of the family, the less the participation in activities of the broader community and in voluntary associations (Caplovitz, 1963).

The poor remain largely outside the political structure of our society. Studies have shown that even voting decreases as incomes decrease[41] (Scammon, 1967; Caplovitz, 1963). There are a number of factors which account for the lower voting rates among the poor, for example, *de facto* resistances to Negro voting, residence requirements, English-language literacy, loss of voting rights because of imprisonment, high cost of voting in some areas through restrictive laws requiring a greater investment of time or money to register and vote, etc. The poor are also less likely to possess the intellectual resources (e.g., rules of participation, reading and writing skills, etc.), the material resources that can be used to increase political effectiveness, and the social resources (e.g., affiliation with organizations, work groups, etc., that can provide support for political actions) which are known to favor effective political participation (Milbrath, 1965). A number of studies have shown that the poor do not feel that they can adequately influence governmental activity through the voting process. Negroes, regardless of class, are less likely than whites to attempt to influence local and national governments. A study by Almond and Verba (1963) found that Negroes are ready to participate in terms of interest and organization but do not yet believe that they can actively effect change.

This same disparity between interest and participation has been noted by some educators in relation to participation in Parent-Teacher Association meetings in ghetto schools. Low participation is mostly due to the fact that the agenda has little if any relevance to their everyday lives. Educators indicate that ghetto parents will attend if they can see the relationship of the meeting to their world, e.g., the protest initiated by CORE and staged by the parents to protest Kozol's dismissal from a Boston school (Kozol, 1967).

While radical revisions are needed at many levels of our society to uplift the lives of the poor, both white and nonwhite, our educational system remains the most viable method of increasing the poor child's chances of helping himself. By broadening our educational system to include large-scale adult education and retraining programs, the life conditions of many poverty children will be improved. Both become in-

41. Figures by Miller *et al.* (1967) show that the voting rate for income groups $10,000 and over is 84.9 percent. The rate drops to 62.7 percent in the $3,000–$4,999 group; 57.6 percent in the $2,000–$2,999 income group; and to 49.6 percent in families below $2,000.

creasingly important as the link between education and upward mobility becomes more and more entrenched in our socioeconomic system.

Besides adequate education for the child and large-scale education and retraining programs for the adult, both of which are aimed at raising the level of competence required to compete within the superordinate society, an additional avenue for effecting change is the organization of the poor to win political, economic, and social goals. Although previously it has been almost impossible to organize the poor in their own defense, there are growing signs of unity.[42] The organized protests of welfare mothers, the co-ops of poor farmers, and self-help community programs such as that of Saul Alinsky should be encouraged. Only full and active participation in American society can overcome the sense of alienation which the poor have endured—physically through isolation, and psychologically through the attitudes of affluent Americans. Full participation, particularly for the nonwhite poor, requires a change in the policies and viewpoint of the more affluent citizens who determine not only the power structure of institutions, but also, to some extent, the self images which the poor and different ethnic groups have of themselves within the American context. Most efforts to benefit the poor have been piecemeal and fragmented. The poor have had no real voice in policies dealing with their own fate, and many times can benefit by such policies only at the expense of their self-integrity.

Until the poverty child can be shown that his own efforts on his own behalf can be decisive and important, he will continue to succumb to the debilitating effects of apathy and defeatism. This phenomenon is eloquently summed up by Robert Coles (1967:18, 19) and by a ghetto mother whom he quotes:

One thing is certain, though: ghetto childhood tends to be short and swift. The fast moving, animated children I see everyday soon enough grow old rather than grow up, and begin to show every sign of resignation described by writer after writer. At twelve or thirteen these children feel that schools lead nowhere, that there will be jobs for only a few, that ahead of them is the prospect of an increasingly futile and bitter struggle to hold on to what ever health, possessions, and shelter they have.

'They is alive, and you bet they is, and then they goes off and quits,' said one mother, summing it up for me. 'I can tell it by their walk, and how they look. They slow down and get so tired in their face, real tired. And they get all full of hate; and they look cross at you, as if I cheated them when I brought

42. The Southern Conference Educational Fund (SCEF, 1968) lists several projects in which for the first time powerless whites are united with blacks for a common goal. An example is The Grow Project (Grass Roots Organizing Work) in New Orleans, which aids in establishing coalitions between whites and blacks for such items as a union drive at a factory, a co-op effort, or for a political campaign.

them into the world. I have seven, and two of them have gone that way, and to be honest, I expect my every child to have it happen—like it did to me. I just gave up when I was about fourteen or so. And what brings us back to life is having the kids, and keeping them with us for a while, away from the outside and everything bad. . . .'

DEPENDENCY PERPETUATED

Affluent Americans show little understanding of the problems of poverty. The attitudes of the majority, as Ferman *et al.* (1965:xv) have stated, are a "mosaic":

. . . The poor are viewed with some compassion but are also frequently seen as immoral, unmotivated, and childlike in their behavior. There is still a public lack of appreciation of the dehabilitating effects of poverty and the stresses that result from a lack of adequate resources. Hostility and racial prejudice may be directed toward some of the poor. In some cases, these attitudes permeate the leadership elites of communities, making the task of poverty reduction more difficult. In truth, history has widened the social distance between the poor and the affluent since life in suburbia makes it possible for the affluent to carry on day-to-day activities with little intimate awareness of the poor or their problems in the crowded urban ghettos.

Although our more humanitarian impulses have given rise to a host of welfare agencies and programs, our ambivalence toward the poor is reflected in the very policies of these welfare measures. The plight of the poor is attributed to their own lack of initiative. Thus we tend to ignore the weaknesses in our socioeconomic system which have created a welfare system that perpetuates dependency—the very condition which it was intended to destroy.

Nor have we attempted to lift out of poverty many who are truly unable to keep themselves. A government analysis released in April 1967 indicated that less than 1 percent of the 7.3 million Americans on public welfare could be self-reliant if employment were available. Besides the aged, blind, and severely handicapped, over 50 percent of this number were dependent children (Bennett, 1967). Nowhere is America's ambivalence toward the poor more apparent than in the welfare measures which are supposedly designed to aid its children. As of January 1968 over 4 million were in Aid to Dependent Families programs.[43] Nationwide, the average monthly payment was approximately $40 per recipient—a sum far below the poverty line. Payments varied from state to state,

43. Formerly Aid to Dependent Children program. The data above also include families in the AFDC, unemployed-parent segment of the program effective in 21 states.

ranging from $8.40 in Mississippi[44] to $61.70 in New York (Department of Health, Education, and Welfare . . . "Advance Release of Statistics . . . ," 1967). It is evident that such sums can do little to interrupt the *cycle* of poverty.

AFDC caseloads continue to increase each year, despite decreases in unemployment rates and the fact that social insurance now covers many who were formerly eligible for AFDC. The increase is especially notable in urban and nonwhite cases, and in the proportion of families needing assistance because of desertion, divorce, separation, and unmarried parenthood. These changes represent, in part, important changes in American society, such as greater residential mobility, expanding urbanization, rising living costs, and increased family disorganization (Burgess and Price, 1963). Although AFDC was intended to aid poor children, there is a good deal of public opposition to the program on the grounds that it tends to serve lazy, promiscuous, and undeserving persons.

Recipients and advocates of the program express dissatisfaction over the gaps in coverage and low level of payment, as well as statutory requirements and administrative practices. A main point of contention is the fact that in most states benefits are available only when a parent is absent from home. Many unemployed fathers choose to leave their families rather than see them go hungry. Thus, the system encourages family disorganization and perpetuates dependency on welfare. The program also appears to discourage incentive to seek employment through regulations requiring deductions of certain proportions of outside incomes earned by adult recipients. Complaints are also leveled at welfare workers, particularly where casework and investigative duties are combined. Recipients feel their privacy is violated by investigations seeking to determine compliance to regulations, especially those dealing with the "man-in-the-house" rule. Further, residency requirements in many states limit the number of persons eligible. The general tendency is to require a year's residency before being eligible for payments. This plan was designed to reduce in-migration but has failed to do so (*Report of the National Advisory Commission on Civil Disorders*, 1968).

A recent Congressional amendment (81 Stat. 821, 894) to the Social Security Act (42, U.S.C., sec. 601 *et seq.*, 1964), effective January 2, 1968, may lead to a further tightening of eligibility requirements or else to a reduction in per capita payments if states and cities cannot meet the increased costs which are likely to accrue from this legislation. Under

44. All of the southern states are included among the 21 states that forfeit approximately $106 million a year in federal payments to dependent children because they will not pay enough to raise the combined state and federal minimum to $32 a month. Federal payments are related to state per capita income and account for the largest share of benefits in all southern states.

these amendments, the percentage of children who can be covered by federal AFDC grants is to remain at the percentage covered in each state in January of 1968 (ibid). Supreme Court Justice Black, recognizing the importance of the Congressional amendment, vacated a stay of judgment[45] he had granted on November 27, 1967, in the *Smith* v. *King* case[46] in which a three-judge court held that Alabama's "substitute fathers"[47] rule was a violation of the equal protection clause of the Fourteenth Amendment. In granting this stay, Justice Black delayed reinstatement of children who had been declared ineligible under the "substitute father" regulation. Thus, months of hardship were added to the lives of children who, although in need, were being punished for the behavior of their mothers. As Judge Justine Polier (1968) points out, this legal enactment recognized the legality of a common-law stepfather when legality was denied to the common-law marriage relationship. Judge Black's temporary order did not condemn the state's "substitute father" regulation. The basis for vacating the initial order was framed only in terms of the implications which would ensue if the group (representing from 15,000 to 20,000 persons) were to be added to the welfare rolls subsequent to the time limit set by the Congressional amendment, after which no federal funds will be given states for additional persons added to the welfare rolls.

The Supreme Court, in hearing the pending appeal, ruled unanimously on June 17, 1968, that a state cannot deny welfare benefits to children of a mother who "cohabits" in or outside her home with any single or able-bodied married man. By implication, the Court also ruled against similar regulations in 18 other states and the District of Columbia where, according to a Civil Liberties Union estimate, 500,000 have been denied federal aid because of the "substitute father" rules (Semple, 1968).[48]

A national survey conducted for the Public Welfare Association in 1960 by Burgess and Price (1963) was instigated to better understand some of the controversial areas which have surrounded the Aid to Dependent Children program. The study focused on the family unit, seeking to discover more about the lives of ADC recipients, both white and non-

45. *King* v. *Smith*, No. 949, 36, U.S.L.W. 3294.
46. *Smith* v. *King*, Cov. No. 2495–N (M.D. Ala., Nov. 8, 1967).
47. "Substitute father" regulations, in force in several states, provide that public assistance will be denied an AFDC family if a man is cohabitating or visiting for the purposes of having sexual relations with the children's natural or adoptive mother (unless the mother can prove that the father is physically or mentally incapacitated or is no longer cohabitating with her). The regulation assumes that the man has taken on the role of father to the children, despite the fact that he may not be their father (*Welfare Law Bulletin*, January, 1968).
48. *The New York Times* reported on June 26, 1968 that the Department of Health, Education, and Welfare announced its intention of notifying the states that deprived families are to be informed within 90 days that they may be eligible now for benefits previously denied. There is no provision for making the benefits retroactive.

white, urban and rural. The more encouraging findings of this study were the low rates of child neglect or abuse (9 percent) and the fact that in only 4 percent of the cases was the grant reported as not being used primarily for the benefit of the child. These and other findings suggest that most ADC mothers were attempting to provide the kind of family life essential for the development of the child. Other encouraging findings of this study centered around the children—one-half were participating in at least one youth organization, such as Y-Teens, Scouts, 4-H, etc., and almost one-fifth were active in two or more such organizations. Even more encouraging was the finding that delinquency and criminal rates among these children appeared to be far below the national average, and few indications of antisocial behavior were noted.[49]

Many of the findings of this study, however, were discouraging, pointing to the inadequacy of the present system. Poverty rates were high. The general environment in which ADC children lived was characterized by poor housing, overcrowding, poor diet, few basic amenities, and inadequate medical care. Many belonged to multiproblem families who were in need of considerable service from other community and welfare agencies. Education was also a problem. Less than one-fourth of the children 18 years and over had completed high school and only a few had gone on to higher education or vocational training. A striking relationship was noted between an adequate education of the parent and consequently an improved social environment and better occupational, educational, and social adjustment for the child. This points to the importance of emphasizing methods of keeping the child in school and of providing better educational vocational training. The picture portrayed by this study was not optimistic in terms of potential for independence. For some, ADC had provided a bridge enabling them to readjust to a productive life. For many others, self-reliance seemed possible only through positive programs of rehabilitation and prevention. America's dependency challenge, the authors conclude, calls for more adequate financial assistance and a more meaningful coordination of services in terms of health, education, vocational training, testing and guidance, and community projects.

The growing discontent with welfare policies has led to some revisions in legislation. Residence requirements have been ruled unconstitutional in a number of lower courts. Alabama's restriction removing persons from welfare because of the birth of an illegitimate child has been successfully challenged.[50] Other aspects under legal attack are discriminatory policies against Negroes and the restrictive legislation and administrative actions

49. This was a nationwide survey which, on this variable, did not delineate the difference between white, nonwhite, rural, and urban populations.

50. Alabama conceded to the Supreme Court that its regulations barring welfare to needy children because of a mother's illicit sexual behavior "have virtually done nothing to change behavior" in that state (MacKenzie, 1968).

which keep poor people from public assistance to which they are entitled (Bennett, 1967). The poor themselves are beginning to unite and to seek means to implement their rights.

Revision of the AFDC and other welfare measures is particularly relevant to the Negro and other minority groups. A study in 1964 revealed that 56 percent of the nation's nonwhite children receive AFDC at some time during their childhood, whereas only 8 percent of the white children are so assisted (Moynihan, 1965). Another Department of Labor survey in 1966 revealed that 30 percent of the population of both East Harlem and Watts, and 40 percent of the Bedford-Stuyvesant children and 25 percent of the adults received welfare (*The American Federationist*, 1967).

Our welfare measures have not tended to foster stable, intact families. While a broken home is not necessarily associated with mental illness (Langner and Michael, 1963) and a stable one-parent home may be better for the child than an unstable, two-parent home (Herzog and Sudia, 1967; Lewis, 1967b), the absence of a male figure does appear to have strong effects on children. Evidence indicates that children who have no adult model with whom to identify have difficulty in deferring gratification and this seems to be associated with poor social responsibility, lessened orientation toward achievement, and a greater likelihood of delinquency (Mischel, 1961). Also female-headed households are poorer than those headed by men. This is especially true in Negro households, since working Negro women average only two-thirds the annual income of white women (U.S. Bureau of the Census, 1965).

Ironically, our welfare measures provide least to the child within the context of his own family and more to the child the further he is moved away from a familial environment. For example, the AFDC child receives over $60 a month in New York. The same sum is paid to a legally responsible relative for care of the child. For foster home care with strangers this amount is doubled, for varying types of institutional support this amount is tripled, and care for the emotionally disturbed varies from $500 to $1,200 a month. We suggest that systematic cost analysis be made in order that the tax dollar may be more efficiently utilized in the care of children.

While institutional care, foster homes, group homes, etc., may be necessary alternative modes of care for some children and may, in some cases, provide a comparatively better environment than would the home, there are many children for whom such alternatives would be unnecessary if their families were provided the means for their care and/or if proper community treatment facilities were available. The present system of alternative modes of care does not guarantee quality care. The alternatives are costly to the nation in terms of expenditures and often costly to the child in terms of psychological stability.

There is a growing recognition that the United States lags behind other nations in failing to provide an economic floor for the American family.[51] To date, 62 nations, including all the countries of Europe, have adopted family allowance programs. Under the highly successful Canadian system, payments are made on behalf of all children,[52] irrespective of the economic status of their parents. Cost is borne by the federal government. Studies have shown that the payments have benefited children, and the number of cases of misuse of payments by parents has been infinitesimal (Vadakin, 1967).

A number of assistance programs have been devised in the United States, for example, public assistance, in-kind programs (e.g., medicare, food stamps, rent subsidies), social security, negative income tax, guaranteed income or universal (or partial) demogrant (i.e., payment without income test to the whole population, or limited only by age) (Schorr, A., 1966b). Some of these programs, of course, have been in effect for some time, although most have come in for severe criticism because of their limited coverage. Others currently are being proposed as a solution to income maintenance or support.

However, most experts agree that a system of income maintenance cannot completely obliterate the concomitants of poverty. Many services will have to be provided. Among the most important of these is realistic training for work and job opportunities. This will require revisions in high school vocational education and in various programs designed for dropouts, the unskilled, the handicapped, and other special groups. Some current programs are worthy of note and provide a basis upon which to expand training efforts.

Among the exemplary training programs were those carried out by the National Institute of Labor Education (NILE). NILE, under a grant from the Department of Labor, has successfully trained members of minority groups who, because of poverty, limited education, or race, have not benefited proportionately from training opportunities. It has also encouraged and instigated organized labor's use of its facilities and abilities to establish preapprenticeship, institutional, and on-the-job training programs for youths who formerly did not qualify because of stipulations for apprenticeship in the various labor organizations. Not all unions or company representatives complied with the program. Prejudice against school dropouts and minority groups was implicitly expressed. The suc-

51. The Advisory Council on Public Welfare (1966) states there are many advantages to the states in such a national floor—for states with low standards, it would act as a lever in upgrading the economic level of the whole population; and where standards are higher it would remove the argument for residence restrictions based on the assumption that assistance serves as an incentive to migration.

52. There is one exception to this universal payment—that is, the stipulation that the child must be in regular school attendance. The regulation was designed to counter the school dropout rate. Vocational training fulfills this requirement if the course of instruction provides sound preparation for entering the labor market.

cesses of the program, however, are proof of the practicality of training disadvantaged youth for skilled and semiskilled occupations as a means of solving the serious shortages of such workers, on the one hand, and severe unemployment among young people, on the other (*Final Report . . . on OMAT Project . . .* , 1965).

Another promising development is the increasing recruitment of human service workers from among the ranks of the poor. In 1967 there were approximately 50,000 of these new "nonprofessionals." About 50 percent of these positions were produced for "indigenous" personnel by the Office of Economic Opportunity. Another 25,000 or more part-time preschool aides have been employed through Operation Head Start. Title I of the Education and Secondary School Act provides for the future employment of some 40,000 teacher aides. Thousands of others will probably be employed as home health aides through the Medicare program (Riessman, 1967). Job definitions for nonprofessional workers have been developed independently by a number of programs, such as Lincoln Hospital Mental Health Service and Mobilization for Youth. In addition to the positions listed above, jobs include community action aides, housing service aides, homemakers, and parent education aides (Reiff and Riessman, 1964).

A number of cities and universities around the country are implementing nonprofessional or paraprofessional programs designed to permit hierarchical steps from the entry position up to the professional status. This requires a redefinition and reorganization of job structures so that training, upgrading, and added education can be built into the program. One such plan is being developed in the Newark school system. The plan proposes that individuals with less than a high school education go through training steps while working full time, beginning with an entry salary of around $4,000 per year and becoming professional teachers in five to six years (Riessman, 1967).

Programs like those just described provide opportunities for people to contribute in meaningful ways to our society. Such employment has increased both the economic security and the self-esteem of many who were formerly dependent upon public resources. Although there has been some professional opposition to the use of paraprofessionals, the main objections seem to center around the amount and quality of training the worker has received. Recent research on the effectiveness of using paraprofessionals indicates that these workers evidence high morale and considerable involvement in their work, and that they are beginning to be accepted by professionals (Riessman, 1967). As we pointed out in the previous section on mental health services, indigenous personnel can solve many service problems which remain unmet under traditional methods.

Under existing conditions, overwhelming and impossible tasks are assigned to the public service sector. Experts in the mental health manpower field have long recognized that traditional training methods cannot produce the ratio of professional manpower needed to meet the increasing demand for service. Our services are presently terribly overburdened. Further, many are hampered by attitudes and regulations that are degrading to the poor. As a result, our professional services have become highly depersonalized. The inability to meet the needs not only destroys the self-esteem of those being served but also the self-esteem of those providing services.

This direct depersonalization is most apparent in our slum schools where, as noted, educators may actually refer to children as "animals," and in our hospitals and clinics where the poor are viewed as "clinical material." It is also reflected in the treatment received in our welfare agencies as well as in our welfare legislation. It is found in our courts where the poor are shuffled through in an almost "assembly line" process.

Much of this depersonalization treatment comes from a lack of understanding and is promoted by concepts such as the "culture of poverty." However useful on a theoretical basis, such concepts easily fall into misuse. Professionals and the lay public alike accept the "traits" described under such categorization at face value, applying them as if the poor were a homogeneous group rather than heterogeneous subcultures with varying value systems. Many assume that the "traits" of dependency, defeatism, and hostility included in the "culture of poverty" concept are a *chosen* way of life rather than the direct consequences of adapting to a life of poverty. Such assumptions are used to justify lesser service and differential treatment on the basis that the poor neither deserve, expect, nor want better services and treatment. Planning based on such assumptions also overlooks the strengths which exist in some poor neighborhoods, particularly the interdependence existing through kinship and community ties. In many ways, the efforts of poor people to assist one another resemble the traditions of frontier days. Much can be done to strengthen this interdependence and the efforts toward self-help through strong leadership provided by indigenous workers.

In summary, there are many advantages in training the poor for human service jobs. The poor stand to gain in employment, self-direction, and increased as well as more humane services. Service agencies benefit through increased manpower, which means more efficient and personalized services. Society, overall, benefits through the productive use of its natural resources and the alleviation of suffering.

HOSTILITY AND SOCIALLY DEVIANT BEHAVIOR

Child abuse, child neglect, delinquency, crime, vandalism, and general social deviancy are reportedly far more prevalent among lower socioeconomic groups. Historically, crime statistics have shown that youth between the ages of 15 and 24 are the most crime-prone group. Currently, this trend is increasing, the highest rates being in inner-city slums, especially in those which have become racial ghettos.

Statistics, of course, do not portray the true incidence of crime. Some of the recent growth rate in youth crimes is attributable to the increase in our youth population and to better police reporting of crimes. In addition, the lower rates among suburban middle-class youth are partly a function of the differential treatment accorded the more affluent—a fact which reflects the existing inequities in our law enforcement and legal institutions. Yet, despite the unreported delinquency in suburbia, there appear to be factors in the social environment which lead to more frequent crimes in the lower socioeconomic areas of our cities. Increased urbanization, the abundance of material goods which provide motives for stealing[53] (our fastest growing crime), the paucity of employment opportunities for youth, the gap between American ideals and American achievements, and the weakening of traditional institutions—especially parental authority —are among the changing social conditions which seem linked to the recent increase in youth crimes.

Youth everywhere—on the campuses, in the suburbs, and in the slums—are sorely discontented. However, it is the young in the slums who are most embittered by existing social inequities. Many slum youth have not experienced stability and warmth from either their parents or society at large. This experience has led them to expect little from life, although their desires are much the same as those of their more affluent counterparts.[54] For example, the automobile has become a "status" symbol for all youth. For the more affluent, this desire may be fulfilled by parents; however, the slum youth finds this status symbol unattainable—except by illicit means. While the more affluent youth may seek relationships among his peers within suburban recreational facilities or in his own home without adult interference, the slum youth often has recourse only to the streets where his activities are subject to police interference. As Niemeyer (1968) notes, *"these young people have no way of organizing themselves for positive purposes"* (emphasis added).

In many ways, the poor child is caught between two worlds. Everyday life—especially in the urban slums—entails adaptation to a dangerous, frustrating, and threatening environment. For many poor children, hos-

53. As noted in the next chapter, shoplifting is far more prevalent among affluent youth, although they are less likely to be prosecuted for this offense than are poor youth.

54. Hyman Rodman (1966) poses what he terms "The Lower-class Value Stretch," in which he states that the lower-class person, without abandoning the general values of the society, develops an alternative set of values. The lower class stretch the values so that lesser degrees of success also become desirable; and thus in many areas they have a wider range of values than the middle class.

tility pervades the home as well as the streets. The adaptations which the poverty child must make to these conditions may be conducive to survival in his natural surroundings; however, these adaptations thwart the development of the type of competence needed to succeed in the middle-class institutions—the other world in which he must function.

Beiser (1965) hypothesizes that the very poor from disorganized communities tend to lack the developmental experiences which Eric Erickson postulates as being essential to a well-integrated personality. Their childhood experiences tend to produce mistrust rather than trust, doubt and a sense of powerlessness rather than autonomy, indecisiveness instead of initiative, a sense of failure rather than mastery, isolation instead of intimacy, and despair rather than ego integrity. Inconsistencies in disciplining practices often lead to difficulties in interpersonal relationships, especially with authority figures. When an act results in retribution in one instance and not in another, authority comes to be seen as "capricious and punitive." Thus, a spontaneous violent discharge of emotions frequently begins to characterize the life style of the child—a tendency which is augmented by the sense of frustration and powerlessness.

Although research findings are far from conclusive, evidence to date indicates that family life is the most important determinant in delinquent behavior. Reviewing the studies on delinquency, the President's Commission of Law Enforcement and the Administration of Justice concluded that an unstable home, characterized by paternal unemployment, inconsistent discipline, and, especially, rejection of the child, is associated with delinquent behavior. A summary of this Commission's findings suffices to portray the conditions which typify the lives of delinquents from the slums.

Typically, the delinquent slum youth lives in a harsh environment, a neighborhood low on the socioeconomic scale of the community. He may well be a school dropout and is probably unemployed. He is 15 or 16 years of age—younger than his counterpart of a few years ago. He is one of several children—perhaps representing several different fathers—who lives in a mother-centered household. He may belong to a broken family or one which has never had a resident male head. Or, the nominal male head may be an alcoholic, imprisoned, etc. In short, the youth has never known an adult male well enough to identify with him. The youth's life has been characterized by an early independence and an erratic kind of authority which is no longer effective by adolescence. Like his more affluent counterpart, he is rebellious. However, his environment offers few alternatives for the role of rebel.

His parent, or parents, may well express an interest in the youth and may desire to keep him out of trouble. But, having long been accustomed to making decisions for himself, the slum youth values his independence.

He seeks ego-enhancing experiences among his peers, who become more important than parents and other authorities, and in the lure of the slum community he seeks an adult model and an achievable goal. Often the example of a successful career is linked to a criminal who has gained prestige in the community. Being denied access to traditional positions of status and achievement, the slum youth may emulate this prestige model who, in turn, seeks such youths to recruit and train in the criminal enterprise (*Challenge of Crime in a Free Society*, 1967). Chein *et al.* (1964) found the most striking aspect of the life style of delinquent boys to be a lack of order and meaning in their existence. This sense of "aimlessness" is accompanied by random efforts at creating some pattern of meaning to existence.

The study by Chein and his collaborators, however, deals largely with another socially deviant response of youths in poverty environments—that of drug addiction. While LSD is a problem for a small group of upper-middle-class kids, the children of the poor are much more likely to turn to heroin.[55] These investigators found that the epidemic areas in New York City generally consisted of relatively concentrated settlements of under-privileged minority groups (Negroes and Puerto Ricans). Their lives were characterized by poverty and low socioeconomic status, low educational attainment, disrupted family life in which a disproportionate number of adult females served as family heads, and highly crowded housing. The areas were densely populated and teeming with adolescents.

While delinquency rates were also high in these areas, evidence from this study does not suggest that delinquency is a consequence of drug use—exclusive, of course, of narcotics violations. Drug use, however, tended to be associated with utilitarian violations but not with crimes of violence or other behavior disturbances. Adolescent female drug users characteristically obtain money for drugs through prostitution, which may account for the large number of rape charges in neighborhoods with many prostitutes who are legally minors.

Chein *et al.* (1964) found that drug-using gangs diminished street warfare. In areas with the highest rates of both addiction and delinquency, two different themes were found in the orientation of delinquents—one which gave emphasis to the negativistic aspects of living and one which was characterized by a sense of futility. Both themes draw in attitudes that are favorable to the use of narcotics, but the sense of futility is more dangerous. Not only is futility associated with the rejection of reasons which might serve as deterrents to addiction, but the basic mood is one that can be relieved by the psychopharmacological effects of narcotics.

55. Although a small sample of female addicts was studied, this investigation centered mainly around 2,950 males, ages 16 to 20, who were involved with drugs from 1949 to 1954 in New York City.

The one factor which Chein and his associates found to be more distinctly related to drug use than to delinquency per se was that of cohesive family living. Although many delinquents came from unstable families, almost all addict families were characterized by disturbed relationship between the parents, e.g., divorce, separation, open hostility, or lack of warmth. The mother usually became the dominant figure and the father, when present, failed to establish a warm relationship with his family. Among female users, both parents were typically distrustful or manipulative of authority figures. The few drug users from more cohesive families were more likely to make frequent efforts to break the habit, but only if they were among the nondelinquent users.

Thus, among both delinquents and addicts there appears to be a correlation between an unstable family life and subsequent development of socially deviant behavior. Legal and psychiatric efforts to correct such behavior are seldom adequate to effect rehabilitation. Wide gaps still exist between our knowledge and its implementation through law. For example, in the *Gault* case,[56] the Supreme Court upheld juvenile rights, stating that "neither the Fourteenth Amendment nor the Bill of Rights is for adults only." While specific rights were guaranteed juveniles, these applied only to adjudicatory hearings, not to the dispositional process. As Polier (1968) notes: "*Gault* may protect some children from unfair hearings and wrongful findings, but it will not provide one dollar's worth of professional mental health services or one hour of care for any troubled child." Similarly, the Supreme Court, considering the compulsive craving of the addict, held that criminal punishment for addicts constitutes cruel and unusual punishment.[57] Nevertheless, punitive approaches prevail, and proper treatment has been developed only in a few areas. Thus, the punitive atmosphere which the child experiences in the slums is continually repeated in the larger society. While proper treatment may occur in some instances, more often the sick are removed and confined from the community (and out of sight), "only to be released to return to old haunts and to behavior that originally produced the symptoms of their problems—which remain untouched, unmodified, and persistent" (ibid). In fact, legal and psychiatric decisions often reflect moralistic ideas concerning the family which may *actually be detrimental to the welfare of the child and do little to remove him from a hostile atmosphere*. For example, if psychiatric agencies refuse to commit an antisocial, or otherwise hostile adult, the court may return that adult to his family without consideration for the children in the family. The psychiatrist may put the welfare of his client above all else and recommend as "good therapy" the visitation and/or custody of children by a sick parent whom he is treating—often without considering the con-

56. *In the Matter of Gault*, 87 Sup. Ct. Rep. 428, 18 Lawyers Ed., 2d 527 (1967).
57. *Robinson* v. *California*, 370 U.S. 660 (1962).

sequences of such a decision upon either the other parent or the child. Similar examples of society's failure to act in behalf of children, or to provide proper provisions for children, could be enumerated ad infinitum. In the case of delinquents, the consequences of inaction have been aptly summarized by Polier (1968), who states that we are dealing with "yesterday's neglected children on whose behalf the community failed to act."

This failure to act is most apparent in our inner cities, many of which have now become racial ghettos from which nonwhites find little means of escape. The differences in the crime rates in disadvantaged parts of the cities as compared to other city areas is illustrated by a comparison of crime rates in five police districts in Chicago in 1965. The data, as cited by the Kerner Commission, indicated that one very low-income Negro district had 35 times as many serious crimes against persons per 100,000 residents as a high-income white district. Furthermore, low-income Negro districts had significantly higher crime rates than did low-income white areas, seemingly because of the higher degree of social disorganization in the Negro areas. Although three times as many policemen were assigned to the high crime area, crime rates for offenses against both persons and property were 4.9 times higher than in the lowest crime area.

The facts indicate that the high crime rates in racial ghettos are committed by a small minority of residents and that the principal victims are the residents themselves. Negroes, like whites, tend to commit crimes within their own groups. For nonwhites, the probability of suffering from any index crime (except larceny) is 78 percent higher than for whites. For all index crimes together, the arrest rate for Negroes is about four times higher than that for whites.

The problems associated with high crime rates generate widespread hostility toward the police. This is especially true in the ghetto, where the policeman is a symbol not only of law but of the entire system of law enforcement and criminal justice.[58] He becomes the target for all the injustices in that system—e.g., the wide disparities between the sentences given to the poor and the more affluent, the assembly-line justice in teeming courts, the antiquated correctional facilities, and other basic inequities which the system imposes on the poor. The policeman, however, has been assigned an almost impossible role. On the one hand, there are those citizens who cry for more repressive tactics to counter the growing crime rates; on the other, are groups who regard the police as agents of repression. In the ghetto, the policeman becomes more and more a symbol of

58. A federally financed study of police operations in three northern cities found that 27 percent of the policemen studied were observed or admitted to "some form of misconduct that could be classified as a felony or a misdemeanor." Examples were shaking down traffic violators, accepting payoffs to alter sworn testimony, or accepting payoffs for protection of organized criminal groups. The research group indicated that the majority of those involved in such misconduct were assigned to slum areas (Burnham, 1968).

the society from which so many Negroes are alienated. At the same time, police responsibilities in the ghetto have grown as other institutions of social control have lost their authority—the schools because many are old, inferior, and segregated; religion because it has lost meaning for many; career aspirations because they are totally lacking; and the family because its bonds are so often snapped, as the Kerner Commission remarked. The Commission adds: "It is the policeman who must fill this institutional vacuum, and is then resented for the presence this effort demands."

Negroes state that police brutality and harassment occur repeatedly in Negro neighborhoods. A survey conducted in three cities for the President's Commission on Law Enforcement and the Administration of Justice found that, while most police-citizen contacts occurred without antagonism or incident, abuses were largely against the poor; however, more than half of these poor were white. Verbal discourtesy was more common than abuses involving force. In ghettos, complaints centered around harassment of interracial couples—or what sometimes only appeared to be an interracial couple—as well as dispersal of street gatherings, the stopping of Negroes without obvious basis, and the presence of aggressive "preventive patrols." These incidents, together with contemptuous and degrading verbal abuse, are blows at the dignity of poor citizens. The breaking up of street gatherings is most often directed toward youths. Often unemployed and seeking escape from uninhabitable homes, these youths find meaning in existence among their peers on the streets. Characteristically, they are both hostile to the police and eager to demonstrate their courage and masculinity. They believe dispersal of their gatherings is intended as harassment, whereas police often consider dispersal to be a "preventive technique."

The Kerner Commission noted that hostility toward the police may be exceeded by the conviction that ghetto neighborhoods are not given adequate police protection. Ghetto citizens believe that police maintain a much less rigorous standard of enforcement in their neighborhood, tolerating such illegal activities as prostitution, drug addiction, and street violence which are not tolerated elsewhere. Another conviction is that many calls for help are much less urgently heeded in the ghetto than in white areas. According to the Kerner Commission, there is evidence to suggest that the lack of protection in ghetto neighborhoods is not necessarily a result of different police policies. Rather, it stems from lack of personnel to handle the volume of calls. Police respond according to priorities. This, however, is viewed by ghetto residents as a dual standard. Actual instances of improper conduct by some policemen, as well as unpopular police practices, foster the overall mistrust which ghetto residents have of the police.

The riots of recent years reflect the unrest and dissatisfaction of Negro ghetto residents. While all riots developed in ways related to the local community and its particular problems, the events developed similarly over a period of time out of an accumulation of grievances which are increasing in Negro ghettos. In general, grievances center around prejudice, discrimination, police practices, unemployment and underemployment, housing and other conditions—all of which are aggravated in the minds of Negroes by the inaction of municipal authorities. Unfair business practices and underrepresentation on municipal bodies are given as reasons for the destruction of property. Criticisms leveled at the antipoverty programs center mainly around insufficient participation by the poor, as well as the lack of continuity and the inadequate funding which characterize many programs. Inadequate welfare benefits and unfair welfare regulations are also mentioned but are not among the most serious complaints. In the 20 cities surveyed by the Kerner Commission, the sense of frustration was reflected in the high percentage of rioters and nonrioters who expressed the belief that the country was not worth fighting for. Many did not feel themselves to be true citizens. Others felt they were being exploited, politically and economically, by the "white power structure." This Commission found that Negroes lacked the channels of communication, influence, and appeal that have been traditionally available to other ethnic minorities within inner-city areas. The frustration of powerlessness felt by Negroes has led some to the conviction that there is no effective alternative to violence as a means of expression and redress. More generally, however, this feeling of powerlessness has led to alienation and hostility toward the institutions of law and government and the white society which controls them. This is reflected—especially among youth—in the reach toward racial consciousness and solidarity symbolized in the slogan "Black Power."

According to the Kerner Commission, the typical rioter was, in fact, a teen-ager or a young adult. He was a lifelong resident of the city in which he rioted, a high school dropout—but somewhat better educated than his Negro neighbor—and almost invariably unemployed, underemployed, or employed at menial tasks. He was proud of his race and extremely hostile to both whites and middle-class Negroes. He was informed about politics, although highly distrustful of the political system and its leaders (*Report of the National Advisory Commission on Civil Disorders,* 1968).

In many ways, the reactions of the ghetto population epitomize the disconnection and fragmentation so common to the lives of all our nation's poor. The urban environment and racial discrimination only exaggerate and highlight that which is communicated to all the poor through their own experience and through our mass media—that is, the gap between a life of affluence and a life of poverty. Being isolated and alienated, the poor have little knowledge of the social class differences within the non-poor population. The view provided by the mass media predominantly portrays the life styles of our upper classes. Thus the gap between the poor and the nonpoor is made to appear even greater, giving rise to stereotyped ideas about life outside the ghetto which apply, if at all, only to the lives of the more affluent. Being equally alienated, the more affluent also have a distorted view of the poor. The stereotype of the childlike, shiftless, and immoral and thus undeserving poor is one such view.

Neither distorted view is conducive to positive mental health nor to constructive social change. For the poor, such distortion only reinforces feelings of hostility and despair. Further, it is the poor who suffer most when the unrealistic views of the more affluent are channeled into public policy for poverty persons. The alienation of the poor from the more affluent is typical of the general fragmentation of American life. This fragmentation, highly visible in the organizational structure of our service-dispensing institutions, equally characterizes social activities and interpersonal relationships. Very early, children learn that they must play many discreet and disconnected roles. Throughout their development, they experience little mutual interaction between different age, class, and ethnic groups. School, and "the real world," in all probability, will be experienced as unrelated, disconnected activities. Many children are also touched by the high rate of residential mobility which destroys the sense of continuity in community and friendship patterns.

Such disconnection and fragmentation bear a circular and reinforcing relationship to alienation. Distrust and hostility, dehumanization and depersonalization, are the by-products which undermine rationality. The extreme factions among both white and black racists often exemplify the irrationality born of distrust, hostility, and alienation. Certainly, the psychological benefits accruing to racist actions and attitudes must be weighed against the coexisting negative factors. For many subcultures, competence entails finding means to manipulate the system in order to gain rights. Presently there is both great distrust and hostility, each having a basis in reality. The resultant active efforts are often unplanned, sporadic, and unfruitful, pointing to the need for built-in mechanisms of change within the structures of our major social institutions.

CONCLUSION AND RECOMMENDATIONS

The elimination of the gap between poverty and affluence remains one of our nation's greatest challenges. Poverty, as the Council of Economic Advisors noted (1964:57), costs the nation doubly, "once in the production lost in wasted human potential, and again in the resources diverted to coping with poverty's social by-products." Its elimination, they noted, is sound economics. The Council, however, spoke of the more humanistic aspect which has been succinctly stated by Wilbur Cohen (1964:26):

The most fundamental reason for declaring war on poverty is a moral one. This Nation and its institutions are founded on the belief that each individual should have the opportunity to develop his capacity to the fullest. Those who are born into the world of poverty are not only deprived of the material comforts of life, but are also stunted in their emotional, intellectual, and social development, and thus effectively prevented from realizing their human potentialities.

To say that poverty and inequality of opportunity (which is both a cause and an effect of poverty and deprivation) are morally wrong is only a beginning . . .

Nevertheless, it is a significant beginning—the landmark of a major social revolution. As Huxley (1965) notes, the War on Poverty focused this nation's conscience, for the first time, on those who were previously considered the "undeserving poor." It is this segment of the population whom our humane organizations have failed to serve. These are the dispossessed who have been isolated, unheard, and denied the skills required for social competence. We are only beginning to realize that the poverty of the dispossessed is a syndrome—a constellation of interacting factors which operate in a vicious circle and involve both the dispossessed and the larger society. It will not be sufficient, as Miller and Rein (1964) note, simply to provide our *"institutions of failure* with more funds—to continue doing what they have always done in the past. *It is necessary to change social institutions so that they are more effectively responsive to* the needs of the poor . . ." (italics in the original).

If we are to break the vicious cycle of poverty, we must, as Huxley (1965) states:

apply integrated multiple interventions acting in concert throughout the system. Such interventions must be based on a holistic approach; upon an appreciation of the ecology of the subsystem, if our efforts are to act synergistically rather than antagonistically.

Task Force VI has proposed various measures intended to improve the life of the poor and the quality of American life in general. These range from economic and employment measures to restructuring of our major social institutions. However, we have not made extensive and specific recommendations in many areas because there are a number of groups whose competence on particular issues and services need not be duplicated. We could cite, for example, the recommendations of the American Council of Social Workers on public assistance; the Kerner Commission on housing, employment, and other problems facing the ghetto poor; the President's Commission on Law Enforcement and the Administration of Justice on delinquency; the Citizens' Board of Inquiry into Hunger and Malnutrition in the United States on Federal Food Programs, and so on. We believe such an exercise would be somewhat futile, since the findings of such study bodies have been made public. There is a wealth of knowledge available which is worthy of study and experimentation. Therefore, we have addressed ourselves only in a general way to some of the major problems of poverty.

One of our major concerns is that of promoting the idea of the need for establishing built-in mechanisms of change within our social institutions —change which will lend itself to the utilization of current knowledge and research findings and to individual and collective involvement. We believe that all change efforts should include built-in mechanisms of feedback and evaluation to insure that change occurs in constructive ways.

The quality of human interaction and the development of competence are basic to the goal of all constructive innovation. The achievement of the kind of genuine interaction and competence which will promote positive mental health requires full-scale training programs which will foster the psychological strengths and the social and occupational skills necessary for competence. It also requires participation and mutual interaction between and among all segments of our population—regardless of age, sex, ethnic membership, or socioeconomic class.

We address ourselves more fully to the problems of change, competence, and participation in Part II of this report. The recommendations in that section apply to the poor as well as to the affluent. The proposals which follow, however, are more specifically directed toward the problems of poverty. The main exception is our recommendation for a multiservice center, which we have placed here because it is the poor who suffer most from the present system of physical and mental health services.

Recommendations

I. *Income Maintenance*:

A number of assistance programs have been devised, e.g., public assistance, in-kind programs (e.g., medicare, food stamps, rent subsidies), social security, negative income tax, guaranteed income or universal (or partial) demogrant (i.e., payment without income test to the whole population, or limited only by age) (Schorr, A., 1966b). We need to focus on those which prove most feasible, effective, and devoid of stigma. *This Task Force suggests that different areas of the United States effect alternate assistance models,* each providing careful evaluation and feedback. In the long run, some programs may prove superior to others, or the pluralistic approach to income maintenance may prove a highly desirable method.

II. *Employment Programs*:

Congress has enacted the Scheuer-Nelson Subprofessional Career Act which will appropriate approximately $70 million to employ and train unemployed and untrained persons in these human service jobs. However, some modifications are required in the traditional concept if these nonprofessionals are to be effectively employed. As Riessman (1967) points out: *"While jobs have been created, careers have not"* (italics in the original).

This Task Force suggests that all employment programs, especially those designed for the poor, be designed on a "career" model, such as the New Careers Concept.

III. *Education*:

We are rapidly approaching a time when the high school diploma will not be a sufficient credential for some level of economic independence. Yet, many poor children are not being provided the opportunities, incentives, or help they need to advance to increasingly higher levels of education. In addition to changes suggested in other portions of this report, we recommend:

1. To counter the current high dropout rate: quality education should start and continue in the preschool years; experimental programs designed to optimize the educational interests and opportunities of the poor should be encouraged; funding should include mandatory built-in assessment and evaluation; techniques which have proven successful in reducing dropout rates should be planned to maximize the potential of each child, be relevant to the child's background and interests, and make a constructive contribution to the child's identification with his cultural and ethnic background.

2. Further experimentation along the lines of the "Community-Centered School" should be encouraged. This model has been successful among the Navaho and may be the most promising solution to the educational problems of the Indians and other ethnic minorities.

3. College education should be tuition-free at least two years beyond high school, since parental income remains the greatest determinant of who will complete college.

IV. *Comprehensive Services—A Multiservice Center*:

Federal authorization for matching funds to states provided an impetus to the developing community mental health center movement, a movement intended to provide comprehensive care for *all* persons. Much of the philosophy of this movement is meritorious; however, it is not living up to expectations, nor is care provided for the poor (Albee, 1967). This Task Force suggests that future program designs[59] for community mental health

59. The model for this comprehensive health-care system was conceptualized by Matthew Huxley, a Task Force VI member. Although the multiservice center does not appear in this form in the Commission's final report, many concepts found in

centers be greatly broadened along the lines of the multiservice center concept, to include welfare and social services, well-parent/child clinics, family planning, general health care, V.D. clinics, treatment centers for drug addiction, etc., in addition to mental health facilities. Often children (and adults) in need of help fall between available services because they may not fit the agency definition for eligibility, or they show a disorder, disease, or dismay which comes under the auspices of some other agency, and their families may not know that other appropriate services exist. When referred by one agency to another, the referral system is frequently ineffective (either by poor agency design, or inefficiency), and often the distance between the agencies of referral, or the operating hours, or the method of making appointments are in themselves an actual barrier to utilization of such services. Improved coordination of planning and funding at federal, regional, state, and local levels is essential to any such plan. Currently, fragmentation of local services, plus excessive expense gaps and duplication, are ensured by the diversity of federal and state categorical or special service agencies, each having separate and differing regulations, eligibility requirements, and agency-operating requirements at the delivery point. Even when communities desire to coordinate and integrate services to children and their parents, they may find that they are prohibited from doing so because of significantly differing regulations on the part of the funding resources. Task Force VI believes that there exists a critical need for the integration of services at the point of delivery to the family and the neighborhood.

Such a model would consist of a number of multiservice centers, each serving defined populations and each under unified direction. Such centers would operate as the central unit with an associated system of satellite neighborhood stations backed up by specialty services at the community level.

To achieve actual working integration of services, the following minimal requirements would have to be met:

a. There must be a single director of all health and welfare services for each neighborhood service area.

b. He must have executive authority over the deployment of all manpower, money, and materials.

c. It is essential that restrictions on the use of categorical monies be removed.

The Task Force believes that an essential component of such a plan

---

this model, such as integration of services and client participation, provided a framework for several proposals found in the final report. Task Force VI's model was particularly useful in the Commission's formulation of an advocacy system (see *Crisis in Child Mental Health: Challenge for the 1970's,* Report of the Joint Commission on Mental Health of Children. New York: Harper & Row, 1970).

would be the involvement of the people served at every stage of organization, administration, and delivery of service. Specifically, one such mechanism could be on the policy-making board of each neighborhood center, which should be composed of both the persons served and representatives of the power structure of the community (which will usually be larger and include a number of neighborhood centers).

We believe that it is essential that the categorical restrictions on service imposed through federal, regional, state, and local agencies be eliminated through modification of their enabling statutes and agency regulations so as to permit local service agencies to develop:

Common professional standards;

Common standards for physical facilities in which services are rendered; and

Common definitions of populations served.

Both laws and regulations at federal, state, and local levels must be collated and modified to make possible such integration, which is now impossible.

V. *Alternatives to Institutional Care*:

Task Force VI supports the trend away from commitment to large custodial-care-type institutions. We recommend that there be increased funding at all governmental levels to provide alternative modes of care, such as community-based facilities, group homes, and foster care. Funding should be sufficient to provide adequate facilities, expert staffing, and other provisions essential to good child care.

For juvenile delinquents, we recommend the expansion or creation of:

1. Community-based programs that encourage youth participation and train in social competence, and

2. Job training programs.

For the mentally retarded, we recommend:

1. Increasing the traditional psychiatric and psychological services.

2. Expansion of experimental programs which have successfully trained the retarded in self-initiated behavior and those which have increased cognitive and social skills. Programs should focus on decreasing the number of totally dependent residents in institutions.

3. To decrease the number of young children who are at risk of becoming mentally retarded, we urge the expansion of preventive programs. These should focus on:

a. Expanding prenatal and nutrition programs, especially among low-income groups,

b. Increased care and sensory stimulation for premature infants, and

c. Enriched programs to provide the type of stimulation needed to counter nonorganic retardation.

For the mentally ill and emotionally disturbed, we recommend:

1. Substantial funding for a wide range of community-based services which will provide day and night services, long-term care in residential centers and hospitals, services in the home to both the child and family, information and referral services, comprehensive developmental and psychoeducational assessment, special education programs, rehabilitative services and work-training programs.[60]

2. Substantial funding for increased manpower and training of both professional and paraprofessional workers, and

3. Expansion of Re-ED-type schools and other newer models which prove to be successful.

For all children who are institutionalized, attention must be paid to the supervision of screening and placement and to the provision for legal recourse. These measures are crucially needed, at present, to counter the tendency to relegate the poor and non-English-speaking disturbed children to state hospitals for the mentally defective.

60. Services such as these are discussed in some detail in a study jointly sponsored by the National Association for Mental Health and the Joint Commission on Mental Health of Children, Inc. See "A Comprehensive Program for the Severely Mentally Ill Child and His Family," New York: The National Association for Mental Health, Inc., 1968.

Children of the American Dream

A Collective Dream

In our pluralistic society, there are many dissonant voices and aspirations, many changing values wrought by the forces of change itself, and many variations of the "American Dream." There is, however, a central and dominant theme in the American Dream, one that is firmly entrenched in our institutions, and one that bombards our senses through our mass media—the hope for prosperity and the desire for the material advantages and pleasures which abound in twentieth-century America.

As Table 2 shows, and as the previous chapter indicates, there are many who, in all probability, have not and will not achieve this dream unless sweeping social changes are effected. Obviously, income (along with such factors as size of family, geographic residence, life style, etc.) determines the degree to which the rest of our population shares in this collective dream.

Table 2.—PERCENT DISTRIBUTION OF FAMILY INCOME, 1966

	NONWHITE	WHITE
Number of Families (in millions)	4.9	44.0
Percent (rounded)	100	100
Under $5,000	56	27
$5,000 to $6,999	17	19
$7,000 to $9,999	16	25
$10,000 to $14,999	9	20
$15,000 and over	3	10

SOURCE: Adapted from figures released by the White House, November 3, 1967, and published on that same date in *The New York Times.*

Problems Wrought by Urbanization and Mobility

Beyond the hope for material advantages, however, the dream is differently conceived by various class[1] and ethnic groups. Increased population density, urbanization, and mobility have also reshaped the dream for many, with the consequence that few children grow up in the stable small town where, as Barker and Wright (1951) show, children are likely to be active participants in the adult setting.

As a consequence of increased mobility, many children are not only "rootpruned," but rootless. Extended family ties are limited, or almost nonexistent. Often the father is away for long periods. For some children, the extended family is replaced by the extended social group, and mobility results in a greater "social adaptability." Such children appear to adapt well to leaving home and to the college or work situation.

However, some studies have suggested that mobility increases psychiatric problems in children (see, e.g., Kantor, 1965). Frustration is also experienced by other family members, as indicated by the increase of alcoholism among the wives of mobile executives. The "transient" nature of the lives of some of these families does not favor putting down roots and having a sense of involvement. For many, there is an increased avoidance of involvement or a decrease in affective relationships, both within the family and within the community. Perhaps affective relationships are further hindered because the deep sorrow of leaving behind friends has been experienced too many times.

Encapsulation in Suburbia

With the increase in mobility and urbanization, more and more of America's nonpoor children experience only the limited environment of suburbia, or of a series of suburbias. Currently, many suburban neighborhoods are being constructed without stores, shops, community services, or adequate recreational facilities. In short, the suburban child is denied interaction with adults and with the adult working world. There are seldom institutions to alleviate this loss of deep, affective relationships. Some children become "social isolates," while for others contact is limited mostly to peer groups in the confines of suburbia and the school.

1. The description which follows is based, of necessity, upon an eclectic approach. A number of divergent opinions can be found in the literature in relation to the subject areas chosen and the choice of stratification variables. No assumption is made that categorization by class denotes homogeneity within any particular class structure or that interclass similarities in attitudes and behaviors have the same meaning for persons in all class segments. As Gans (1962) notes, *considerable variation exists within each class stratum* because social mobility and other processes create innumerable combinations of behavior patterns.

Suburban areas, however, are not necessarily homogeneous.[2] One neighborhood may be comprised of varying class and ethnic groups, each being rather cohesive and alienated from all others, each with its own distinctive version of the American dream. In his study of Levittown, Gans (1967) found that the majority of residents did not move to the suburbs because they are socially and occupationally mobile. Rather, the residents' motives for moving to suburbia revolve around aspirations for greater privacy, more room, and more time to be to themselves. Once in suburbia, there is no abandonment of traditional class, ethnic, and religious subcultural life styles. The working class, the lower-middle-class, and the upper-middle-class Catholics, Protestants, and Jews, all find ways to their own groups. Further, each class contributes different services to the community. Most are highly ethnocentric and unaccepting of the existing pluralism within the community.

LIFE STYLES, VALUES, AND CHILD-REARING PATTERNS AMONG THE NONPOOR

Family Structure and Attitudes Toward the Larger World

Certain differences among these nonpoor class segments are particularly relevant to the study of child life. Gans (1962) feels that the most important —or at least the most visible—difference between the classes is one of family structure. Among the working class,[3] social relationships amidst the family circle dominate the style of life and the view of the outside world. While specific characteristics of this family circle vary widely among different groups in the working-class subculture, it differs from that of other class segments by the fact that it encompasses a large number of persons—including, in some instances, nonrelated individuals.

In the middle-class subculture, life revolves around the nuclear family and the career by which the breadwinner achieves his way into the larger

2. As Gans notes, earlier studies of suburbia depicted a single synthetic "mass culture." Through loss of traditional differences, suburbanites were depicted as being left to the mercies of the physical and social environment. Thus proximity determined friendships, the media manipulated consumer and political behavior, and the expectations of neighbors determined the remainder of social life.

3. The heterogeneity in the working class has been noted in various studies (Hollingshead and Redlich, 1958; Gurin *et al.*, 1960; Bean *et al.*, 1964; Leggett, 1964). As Miller and Riessman (1961) noted, many studies fail to distinguish between the lower class and the stable working class (i.e., regular members of the nonagricultural labor force in manual and service occupations). The income, stability, and life styles of the stable working class places them among the nonpoor and yet sets them apart from the middle and upper classes. In the area of family life, workers such as Handel and Rainwater (1964) feel that the working class is splitting into two groups, the "traditional" and the "modern." The latter is beginning to approximate lower-middle-class family patterns.

society. While contact with close relatives may be maintained, they are expected to participate only in a subordinate role. Members of the nuclear family depend largely upon one another for social and emotional gratification. One important source is child-rearing. Thus, the middle class is far more child-centered than the working-class family and spends more of its leisure time together. Outside social life is spent with friends who share similar interests, rather than among relatives, as in the working class.

Although the "professional upper-middle class" is also built around the nuclear family, greater emphasis is placed upon individual development and self-expression. While importance is attached to a career, status, and income, job satisfaction is even more important—although it is not always achieved. Such satisfaction is often the focal concern for the woman also. If she is uninterested in a profession, she may develop an intense interest in motherhood, or in community activity. Child-rearing gives the woman not only an opportunity to develop her individual achievement as a mother but to instill in her child the same striving for self-development. Consequently, the professional upper-middle class is adult-directed, rather than child-centered. Participation in the larger society is also valued and often manifested through careers or activities revolving around social service.

Among the traditional working class, the outside world is viewed in its relation to the maintenance of or destruction of the family group. While it is to be used as a means of benefiting the family group, the outside world is viewed with a certain amount of detachment and hostility. Work is considered primarily as a means of obtaining an income and of maximizing pleasures within the family circle.

The "elite" or "upper" class is also a closed subculture which places emphasis upon a large family group. Among the elite, however, ancestors are accorded a high degree of importance. One's lineage is highly related to status, and pressure is put upon the child to choose his friends, marriage partner, etc., among persons of similar lineage and status (see, e.g., Hollingshead and Redlich, 1958).

The middle class, on the other hand, makes little distinction between the family and the outside world. The latter is thought of only as a larger society which supports the aims in which the nuclear family participates (Gans, 1962). However, many lower-middle-class people do feel uncomfortable with the political institutions of the larger society. Many believe that the moral framework which guides their lives, and the sort of relations which they have with friends and family, ought also to govern organizational life and society. Any other behavior is seen as "political" and "immoral" (Gans, 1967).

The working class also reflects a "person-centered" orientation, a particularism which leads the worker to think of himself as relating to people, rather than to roles and organizational structure. But, in comparison with the lower-middle class, the worker is far more "traditional" and "old fashioned." He prefers "discipline, structure, order, organization, and directive, definitive (strong) leadership," although such leadership is not viewed in opposition to "human, warm, informal, personal qualities" (Miller and Riessman, 1961).

Child-Rearing Values

The "traditional" orientation of the worker is also reflected in parental values. Duvall (1946) found that the working class (and the lower-middle class) want their children to be neat and clean, to please adults, and to obey and respect adults. Kohn (1963) also found these values to be more highly prized among the working class. Among the latter, emphasis is placed upon the overt act. The child is expected to conform to external proscriptions. Middle-class parents, on the other hand, value curiosity, happiness, consideration, and, especially, self-control and self-direction more than the working class.[4]

Obviously, as Kohn notes, the middle-class way of life is one demanding great conformity. However, relative to the working class, middle-class conditions of life do permit and demand a greater degree of independent action. Working-class occupations, on the other hand, are more subject to standardization and direct supervision. They are also more dependent upon collective action, particularly in unionized industries. Thus, occupational security requires a greater measure of conformity to external authority.

Kohn suggests that occupational conditions contribute to parental values and consequently (though perhaps unconsciously) to child-rearing practices. The level of income and the stability of income of the middle class grant them a respectability which is problematic for working-class parents. These factors allow the middle-class parents to concentrate on the child's internal dynamics and to focus more on motives and feelings, as well as training in independence.

This concern with internal dynamics is also facilitated by the higher level of education and the learned ability to deal with the ideational and the subjective. In short, "middle-class life conditions both allow and demand a greater degree of self-direction than do those of the working class" (ibid).

4. Miller and Swanson (1958) have suggested a distinction between the "new" and "old" middle class. They feel that the rise of a bureaucratic way of life of a bygone era has resulted in new child-rearing practices. Children reared in entrepreneurial homes are "encouraged to be highly rational, to exercise great self-control, to be self-reliant, and to assume an active manipulative stance toward their environment." Children reared in "welfare-bureaucratic" homes, on the other hand, are encouraged "to be accommodative, to allow their impulses some spontaneous expression, and seek direction from the organizational programs in which they participate." These differences may also be found in lower socioeconomic groups. Gans (1962) suggests a similar distinction between the "managerial" and "professional" middle class. Such distinctions, however, are not universally accepted; see, e.g., Kohn (1963:170).

Strivings for Security: The Working Class

In comparison to middle-class persons, the worker is greatly hindered by his level of education. He does not read effectively and is ill-informed in many areas. While able to make abstractions, he does so only in a "slow physical fashion." His pragmatic orientation discourages a liking for abstract ideas and he is frequently suspicious of "talk" and "new-fangled" ideas, even though he is highly suggestible. Although somewhat radical on economic issues, he is far from liberal on such matters as foreign policy and civil liberties. He is highly uninterested in politics, though interested in mechanics. He is stubborn, "materialistic, superstitious, holds an 'eye for eye' psychology," and admires strength and ruggedness (Miller and Reissman, 1961).

Like the lower-middle class, the worker experiences a striving for stability and security. However, these are probably far more central determinants in working-class life. Instability and insecurity threaten psychological life through factors both external (e.g., unemployment and layoff) and internal (e.g., family discord, intergenerational conflict, desire for excitement, etc.). "Getting by" rather than "getting ahead" may assume upmost importance (ibid). As Kohn notes, " . . . the working class has striven for, and partially achieved, an American dream distinctly different from the dream of success and achievement." While success and achievement preoccupy the middle class—whatever their status within this strata— the worker is uninterested in mobility and class status. Security, respectability, and the enjoyment of a decent standard of living are the main foci of the worker's dream. Thus, Kohn suggests: "Working-class parents want their children to conform to external authority because the parents themselves are willing to accord respect to authority, in return for security and respectability . . . conservatism in child-rearing is part of a more general conservatism and traditionalism."

Where aspirations for upward mobility exist among the working class, these are characterized by a certain amount of unrealism. There is often a false idealization of white-collar professions and an accompanying false devaluation of blue-collar work—the latter perhaps being a reflection of the meaninglessness of such employment as factory work. For example, in a nationwide survey by Gurin *et al.* (1960), only 22 percent of skilled and 27 percent of semiskilled workers—as compared to 42 percent of professionals—reported being "very satisfied" with their jobs. Whereas 80 percent of professionals mention ego satisfaction in connection with their job, such satisfaction was expressed by only 54 percent of skilled workers and 29 percent of unskilled workers. Further, manual workers feel more inadequate on the job. Gurin and his associates suggest that self judgment of one's skill and competence in a given line of work is not only based on skill and competence but on general status considerations as well. . . . Even a highly competent unskilled laborer, in judging his ability to do his work, would be affected by an underlying feeling of inadequacy springing from the generally low status of the job.

Mental Health Implications of Working-Class Status

These findings have far-reaching implications for the mental health of working-class children. Since the role of the father as the sole breadwinner is highly prized in the working-class family, feelings of inadequacy on the part of the father affect the child's conception of the father as an adult model. The same holds for the working mother, though perhaps to a lesser degree. The instability of working-class life also affects marital relationships—the prevalence of divorce, desertion, discord, etc., being higher the lower one descends on the occupational scale of the working class (Bowman, 1964). The lower status which society at large accords to the working class also affects the blue-collarite child's conception of himself and accounts, in part, for the fact that these children limit their aspirations and may secure only their most minimal goals.

In view of the many ways in which occupation affects mental health, it follows that large-scale efforts must be made to change the negative attitudes which Americans hold of the working class. Specifically, such efforts should:

1. Educate the public in the positive contributions which the working class makes to American society;

2. Promote an understanding of the life styles among the working class;

3. Promote interaction between the working-class and other class segments through such means as those proposed in the Youth Participation Model.

In addition to according a higher status to working-class occupations, ways must be found to reduce occupational instability and to enhance satisfaction in occupations common to this class segment.

Education and Occupational Mobility

Given the high percentage of working-class children who stay within this occupational level, ways must also be found to enhance educational opportunities. At present, working-class youth are not being optimally trained in competence. In part, this is due to the cultural differences between the home and the school environment.

Among the working class, education is differently conceived than among the middle class. The lower-middle class, like the working class, value vocational training. However, the former—like other persons in middle-class strata—view education in broader terms. It is thought worthwhile even when it is not used for vocational purposes. For example, the middle class— unlike the working class—feel that college will benefit girls even though they may never work. Also, the middle class expect the schools to train their youngsters to be sociable.

· The working class, however, view education only as a means of learning techniques necessary to gaining the most lucrative type of employment. They find much of the curriculum irrelevant to this orientation. Some working-class parents neither want nor expect their children to go on to college and to the middle-class jobs for which a college education is required (see, e.g., Hyman, 1953; Kohn, 1963). Where positive attitudes exist, these are accompanied by a certain unrealism. College education, in particular, is often an unattainable goal, either because of inadequate preparation or lack of funds. The rejection of middle-class culture no doubt contributes to the fact that many working-class youths are inadequately prepared for college.

Working-class adolescents, as a whole, do leave school earlier than middle-class youth. A number of workers have attributed this higher dropout rate to the working-class child's inability to defer gratification (Schneider and Lysgaard, 1953; Chinoy, 1955). Chinoy found that working-class youths may verbally profess concern with occupational success and advancement. Nevertheless, he concludes, "they are likely to be more interested in 'having a good time' or 'having fun.' They want to 'go out,' to have girl friends, to travel, to own a car or a motorcycle."

Miller, Riessman, and Seagull (1966) challenge the adequacy of the deferred gratification pattern (DGP) as an explanation for differential behaviors between middle-class children and children from lower SES groups. In relation to school dropouts, Miller et al. feel that the DGP hypothesis is an inadequate interpretation of this behavior among working-class youth because (1) the school is less enjoyable for the working class because of its middle-class structuring, teacher expectations, and utilization of class-biased IQ tests; (2) many working-class youths are compelled to withdraw because of economic necessity; and (3) "lower income youth are, at least implicitly, being contrasted with the presumably deferred gratification middle class adolescent. A question therefore has to be raised as to whether today the latter typically give up spending money, good times, girl friends, travel, or a car in order to go to school or college . . . "

At present, our knowledge of the educational experience of working-class youth is inadequate. However, a number of studies compiled by Shostak and Gomberg (1964:121–92) indicate that there is little relationship between aspiration and fulfillment for many of these youth. The hopes which working-class parents hold for their children are likewise higher than the goals their children generally achieve. This discrepancy, between aspiration levels and achievement, is often more marked among Negroes than whites.

Recommendations on Educational Needs of Working-Class Children

The middle-class structure of our educational system has generally failed to prepare the working-class youth, either for existing employment vacancies, future employment opportunities, or college education. Our vocational training has not kept pace with the changing nature of employment since the rise of automation. Likewise, little attention has been focused on training the young along the lines of projected occupational needs and skills.

Reviewing the problem of education and employment among the working-class youth, Dansereau (1964:191) concludes:

Statistics show the greater security of the educated worker and educators have argued the need for a smooth transition from school to work life. The desired transition cannot occur without access to a reasonably worthwhile job, and the preparation for that job cannot occur unless the training is available and able to hold the student's interest. Archaic legislation regarding vocational training must be updated to provide funds for the training necessary to meet the nation's needs, to serve the majority of our future workers. If we are to mollify the blow of unemployment for the blue-collar child, we must learn his capabilities and guide his aspirations and plans accordingly. *This task must start early and stay late*; home, school, church, government, and mass media, each has its part to play.

The blue-collar child has untapped talents which are vital to our remaining in a place of world leadership regarding standard of living and human dignity. We have already allowed too many to become "lost." . . . The solution can come with joint effort. . . . Successful programs will reflect imagination and ingenuity. As to financial cost, dollars not invested in training most assuredly will join others in welfare programs of catastrophic size (italics in the original).

In consideration of the educational needs of the working-class child, the following proposals are suggested by this Task Force:[5]

1. That research efforts be designed to carefully delineate the type of curriculum and training which will be most relevant to the working-class child and to the adult role which he will most likely assume. Components of this research should include:

a. Careful consideration of future employment opportunities and

5. We recognize some of the complex and unresolved social and ethical problems relating to the kind of "meritocracy" implicit in these recommendations (for further discussion see Michael Young's *Rise of Meritocracy*). Certainly such problems should be given careful consideration.

inclusion into training programs of the type of skills which will be most relevant to future technological and "human services" jobs. In implementing research findings, training should begin with the very young, and be based on the best projections of the occupational skills which will be required by the time such youth attain adulthood.

However, precautions must be taken to avoid placement in such training along "class" lines. For example, there are middle-class children whose aptitudes and interests fall into "working-class" occupations, just as there are working-class children whose interests lie in middle-class professions. Because of parental pressure, lack of funds, etc., children in both classes now experience difficulty in pursuing a career of their own choice. If status differentials are removed and our educational system becomes more sensitive to training in competence according to aptitude and interests, positive mental health benefits should accrue.

b. Teacher training designed around projected employment opportunities and the skills which will be required to fulfill jobs in the future.

2. That immediate steps be taken within the educational system to educate the educators themselves in the importance of training the working-class child and those children oriented toward blue-collar work to achieve a sense of competence in, and a sense of importance of, the occupational world around which the working-class way of life revolves.

3. That *publicly supported* junior colleges be designed to train youth in the various trades which comprise the "working class" occupational world (including both technological and human services).

4. In view of the correlation which has been noted in a number of studies between a higher level of education and positive mental health, efforts should be made at all levels in the educational system to increase the interest of working-class children and youth in "formal" education, per se.

Although the literature is inconclusive, the data suggest that the achievement of higher status and better educational and employment opportunities should do much to enhance the mental health of working-class children.

MENTAL AND EMOTIONAL DISORDERS AMONG NONPOOR CHILDREN

Working-Class Children

At present, we know very little about mental health and mental illness among working-class children and youth. Studies dealing with working-class adults suggest that the risk of severe mental disorders decreases the higher the occupational level within this class (Hollingshead and Redlich, 1958; Srole *et al.*, 1962; Kornhauser, 1964). Nevertheless, the stable working class seems to be a "high risk" population, in comparison to middle- and upper-class populations.

Although Hollingshead and Redlich (1958) found that prevalence rates among the neurotic *patient* population in New Haven were lower among the stable working class (Class IV)[6] than in any other class, they caution against assuming that neuroses are less common among this class segment. They feel the rate may be attributable to both a lesser use of psychiatric facilities and to biases on the part of therapists. As the New Haven and other studies indicate, working-class persons hold negative views concerning mental health and are reluctant to seek psychiatric help. Further, they do not value insight therapy. Rather, they tend to seek material help in the form of pills, needles, etc. Psychiatric help is often sought only when the disorder has become severe. Therapists find verbal communication difficult and are repelled by the language and values of this class. Hence, custodial care in public mental hospital and/or somatic or drug therapies are the more common treatment mode for working-class adults. In a study of one public psychiatric hospital, Harrison *et al.* (1965) found that children of both "skilled" and "unskilled" workers were less likely to receive intensive and individual psychotherapies than were children of executive or professional parents.

Prevalence of Impairment in a Representative Sample of Children

Langner and his associates, who are currently engaged in a prevalence survey of children's psychiatric impairment and disorders in Manhattan, found that 13 percent of the children thus far surveyed had "marked" or "severe" impairment.[7] Among white children, the risk of total impairment decreased the higher the parental income and educational level. The de crease was particularly marked among children whose mothers had had graduate or professional training, seemingly because these mothers showed few signs of impairment themselves and because the data revealed a high correlation between maternal impairment and impairment in the child.

6. It should be noted that working-class persons also comprise 16 percent of the Class III (lower-middle-class) population.

7. Impairment is rated along a number of dimensions using, e.g., behavior settings (e.g., in school among peers, family interactions, etc.), psychiatric interviews, psychometric scores and profiles developed on the basis of factor analysis of mothers' reports, etc. The data are analyzed in relationship to treatment, familial practices and attitudes and demographic variables such as sex, race, SES, age (6–18), etc. However, impairment is to be distinguished from "caseness" (i.e., the need for clinical consultation or direct intervention). The findings by Langner are tentative, since they are based on an interim analysis of 400 out of 1,000 children selected from a random sample of 1,000 households representative of different income groups.

Tentative figures for these 400 children show that 8 percent of the high-, 12 percent of the middle-, and 21 percent of the low-income group had "marked" impairment, or worse. However, almost no differences were found between low- and high-income Negro children (18 percent vs. 19 percent). Little difference was noted between low-income (17 percent) and high-income (15 percent) Spanish-speaking children.[8] About half as many high- as low-income whites were considered "cases" (8 percent vs. 15 percent). High-income Spanish also showed a decrease as compared to low-income Spanish. However, 33 percent of high-income Negroes and only 21 percent of low-income Negroes were so considered. In most impairment areas, the high-income Negro child was found to be particularly unfortunate. For example, among all high-income groups, only Negroes showed any "marked" school impairment. (However, no mention is made of the quality of the schools which they attended as compared to other groups.) High-income Negro mothers were also found to have the most problems, e.g., body complaints, lack of understanding of the child, general dissatisfaction, and poor self-image. In addition, marital discord was high among high-income Negroes.

Langner and his associates feel that real environmental stresses exist in high-income Negro families, leading to greater impairment rates. Such environmental factors as prejudice and job discrimination—which in turn effect family cohesion and familial relationships—also prevent high-income Spanish-speaking children from obtaining a commensurate reduction in impairment.

Several factors point to the fact that these ethnic groups do not fully share in the American Dream. For example, over 90 percent of the Negroes and Spanish-speaking peoples in this study were excluded from most material advantages. The fact that "high income" was cut at $6,500 makes this exclusion even more apparent. Further, higher income was generally dependent upon the mother's being employed. Even college education did not prove to be a guarantee of upward mobility for these Negroes, since the low-income group contained a higher proportion of college-educated fathers than did the high-income group.

Langner and his associates feel that a "multi-factorial attack" is the only feasible solution to the problems of the high-income Negro. They note: "Whether this intervention is social or psychiatric or financial (in relieving

8. Negroes and Spanish are divided only into high- and low-income groups, even though the stated income distribution was as follows: low income—$6,499 and under; middle income—$6,500 to $10,499; and high income—$10,500 and over. High income for both is cut at $6,500 (below the $7,200 estimated to be the "adequate health and decency budget"). When they are compared to whites, it is only on the basis of high and low income. Whether any Negroes or Spanish truly fell in the high-income bracket is not stated; if not, one wonders why they were not compared with middle-income whites.

the working mothers so prevalent in this subgroup) is largely irrelevant. . . ." (Langner *et al.*, Unpublished MS, 1967). This finding suggests again the need for comprehensive and high-quality community services such as the multiservice center and the Universal Nursery School.

Statistics indicating the extent of mental illness among our more affluent children are not available. The study by Langner and his associates, is, in fact, the first systematic attempt to study behavioral and emotional problems among children on a differential class basis.[9]

We do know that increased affluence and status are related to the provision of many services and safeguards which remain unknown to our poor.

Service Deficiencies

Langner and his associates state that the 13 percent of children whom they found with "marked" or "severe" impairment are "surely more than our child psychiatric facilities could ever dream of handling." However, with "need" held constant, high income children were found to be receiving a better share of treatment than children of lower-income groups who also showed "marked" impairment. High-income children were also three times more likely than low-income children to receive an unnecessary therapeutic contact. Despite these facts, less than half of the high-income children in "need" had had any contact.

The type of therapeutic contact was found to vary widely with income and ethnic background. Negro children were three to five times as likely to see a school counselor as white children, whereas few Spanish children saw a counselor. Negroes were also more likely than other children to see a social worker. Whites, irrespective of income, were more likely to see a psychiatrist. In fact, both low- and high-income whites were the *only* group receiving psychiatric therapy while still exhibiting low impairment (i.e., "Well" or "Mild"). However, a third of the high-income Spanish children showing "marked" impairment had seen a psychiatrist—indicating that this group may have positive attitudes toward such care.

Although children in higher SES groups seem to profit most from existing services, even their needs are not being met adequately. Part of the problem lies in the shortage of manpower. This situation is compounded by the fact that professional mental health workers tend to work in large urban areas and to serve mostly the more affluent. For example, of the total professional man-hours spent in direct contact with children under 15 by child and adolescent psychiatrists in the United States in 1965, 22 percent

9. No doubt this study will be subjected to the same criticisms as the earlier Midtown Manhattan study (see Gruenberg, 1968). The figures above should not be viewed as indicative of absolute levels of prevalence or incidence.

were devoted to 8 percent of our children, that is, the child population in New York State (Whiting, 1968). Undoubtedly, many of these psychiatrists are concentrated in New York City.[10] Nevertheless, these do not seem adequate to the need.

Another problem lies in the fact that the traditional mental health strategy is not suited to all socioeconomic and cultural groups, as was noted in Chapter I. Obviously, the traditional methods are not meeting the needs of the working-class children described in this chapter. As one solution, Reiff and Scribner (1964) suggest that efforts be made to foster organized labor's participation in the planning of the mental health programs. Labor could also do much to educate the blue-collar worker in mental health concepts, in the need for early treatment, and in the utilization of existing facilities.

The feasibility of this proposal lies in the great importance that working-class persons attach to labor unions. Compared to their feeling of alienation toward major social institutions, and their reluctance to join voluntary associations connected to the large society, their participation in union organizations is relatively high (see, e.g., Hausknecht, 1964). Thus, the involvement of labor organizations provides a means through which working-class people may be actively involved in mental health programs.

The present system of services places an unusual hardship upon the working class and upon the lower-middle class. Because they neither qualify for free medical services nor earn an income sufficient to meet the cost of psychiatric care, they become as Dr. Reginald Lourie[11] notes, our "psychiatric indigents." The solution requires a broad stratagem, such as the multiservice center proposed in the preceding chapter.

We believe these centers to be a more practical and workable solution for the needs of *all* our population.

SUICIDE, SOCIAL DEVIANCY, AND DRUG USE

The all too common problems of teen-age illegitimacy, venereal disease, suicide, drug use, delinquency, and widespread alienation from society are not always categorized under mental and emotional disorders. And rightfully so. These problems, however, often reflect or create deep emotional or mental stress in individual youngsters. Our inadequate statistics indicate that most of these problems are more prevalent among the poor, but are certainly not uncommon among our more affluent children and

10. One out of six of *all* psychiatrists lived in metropolitan New York City in 1967 (Joint Information Service of the American Psychiatric Association and the National Association for Mental Health, 1968).

11. Stated before a meeting of the Executive Committee of the Joint Commission on Mental Health of Children, June 21, 1968.

youth. Wherever such problems are found, they indicate that we, as a society, have failed our youngsters in many ways. Our failure to act is often tragic.

Suicide

For reasons as yet little understood, a small minority of our youth choose death rather than life. Affluence apparently provides no guarantee against suicide or suicidal tendencies,[12] since the distribution of suicide is proportionately the same in all class strata (Shneidman and Faberow, 1961). Studies do indicate that the college population is a high-risk group when compared to their nonstudent peers. Rates at Yale (Parrish, 1957), Harvard (Temby, 1961), and Berkeley (Bruyn and Seiden, 1965), were found to be 15, 14, and 23 per 100,000 respectively, whereas the nationwide expected rates for the corresponding years for the same-age nonstudent population were 7, 10, and 13 per 100,000. For several years, suicide has been the second leading cause of death among our college population. Various reports suggest that there may be an increase in the number of college students who commit suicide, although there is no evidence indicating an increase in the *rate* of college suicide (Pennington, 1968).

The reasons for college suicide are not well understood. Seiden (1966) found that Berkeley students who committed suicide were—when compared to their classmates—usually older, in their senior year, more often a language major or foreign student, and had more signs of emotional disturbance. Although above average academically, the student who committed suicide tended to feel dissatisfied with his performance. The effects of school pressure as related to suicide have not been specifically studied. However, a longitudinal study of students from Harvard and the University of Pennsylvania indicated a rate twice that of their same-age peer group 15 to 40 years after graduation (Paffenbarger and Asnes, 1966), suggesting the factor of student susceptibility rather than academic stress.

The etiology of young suicide is not well understood. Evidence suggests that the oldest child may be more at risk than other siblings. A review of the literature shows a relationship between multiple child-parent(s) separations, parental ambivalence, a broken home, and other such factors which lead to the loss of a love object or of love. This loss may predispose a child to depression, a strong need for a father figure, or an inability to tolerate further love-object loss. This last factor is particularly cited as the precipitating mechanism in adolescent suicide attempts. The adolescent tries in earnest to establish a primary relationship with a boy or girl friend to

12. Attempted suicides, especially among children and adolescents, far outnumber committed suicides. Adolescent girls, in particular, attempt suicide (Pennington, 1968).

the detriment of any relationships with same-sex friends. Thus when the romance fails, the individual has no other significant relationships to carry him or her through the crisis (Pennington, 1968).

Social isolation appears to be the single most important factor which differentiates the young who commit suicide as opposed to those who attempt suicide (Seiden, 1967). The successful youthful suicide has substantially cut himself off from adults and peers, whereas the adolescent who attempts suicide feels as though there is someone in his environment who will answer his "cry for help." It has also been suggested that there is an increase of "emotional tension" in the American adolescent population at large (see, e.g., Farnsworth, 1957) which may contribute to the increasing suicide rate. Groups experiencing cultural conflict, such as American Indians and Puerto Ricans, also show high suicide rates (Pennington, 1968).

Those who work with the young are attempting to provide alternatives for problem solving other than suicidal behavior. Suicide Prevention Centers —whose main purpose is crisis intervention—have been established to help the individual get through the period of severe suicidal tensions. Also, attempts are being made to utilize counseling and guidance services in colleges and high schools, and pupil personnel services in elementary and junior high schools. The latter, of course, are traditional services which are already inadequate and overburdened, both because they are insufficient in number, understaffed, and too often staffed by poorly trained personnel. Expansion and improvement of these services within our educational institutions remain one of the most feasible methods of providing counseling and mental health services to our child population.

Illegitimacy and Venereal Disease

Illegitimate births and venereal disease among youth are commonly associated with the lower class.[13] We know, however, that many of our methods of data collection lend themselves unwittingly to biases which favor the more affluent and that behind these methodologies and safeguards lie much hidden evidence of malaise. Problems to which great social stigma is attached are particularly difficult to uncover among higher-income groups because of the greater protective measures afforded by both parents and our social institutions.

13. In class-related studies, the poor show higher illegitimacy rates, due to such factors as the financial costs of marriage and divorce, "man in the house" welfare regulation, the greater use of contraceptives and abortion among the more affluent, etc. Sampling biases also exist. Herzog (1967) notes that voluntary agencies tend to serve higher SES groups. These groups are given better care—including casework or psychiatric treatment—while poor unwed mothers generally receive care in outpatient clinics where emphasis is placed on sociological rather than psychiatric considerations (e.g., methods of keeping the mother off relief rolls). Also, the more affluent are likely to have help in effecting concealment of the pregnancy and subsequent adoption of the child.

In those rare instances where middle-class youngsters are singled out for study, evidence indicates that illegitimate births and venereal diseases are much more prevalent among the more affluent than had been assumed (see, e.g., Vincet, 1961; Deschin, 1961). Projections are that both problems will increase in case numbers[14] because of the increase in child population and the earlier physical maturity of boys and girls. The rise in case numbers is not expected to be entirely offset by the greater availability of birth control methods and the more effective means of treating venereal diseases.

Commentators on this state of affairs agree that sexual standards are changing. However, much of the Puritan morality remains, and many parents still refuse to discuss sex with their children. Sociologists have pointed out that such parents often view sex as something unclean which should not be talked about. Their children obtain their information on sex from uninformed peers or pornographic publications and thereby develop a sense of guilt about a curiosity which is natural and healthy. Deschin (1961) found that youngsters who received information from these sources held distorted views of sex and venereal disease and seemed more promiscuous than those who received information from a responsible adult. The failure to educate our young in responsible sexual behavior and the lingering shame and guilt attached to sex are factors which will continue to victimize and penalize many of our young, both rich and poor. It is, however, a problem area the more affluent adult world chooses largely to ignore.

Juvenile Delinquency

In fact, middle-class parents tend to deny that any acts which may be classified as "delinquent" are a major problem among their children. For example, they show little surprise when the poverty child becomes a thief. Yet, the percentage of children who steal out of need is minuscule when compared to the approximately 15,000 shoplifting thefts performed each day by affluent teen-agers. Speaking of the shoplifting trend, Municipal Court Judge Leonard Wolf of Beverly Hills told reporter Davidson (1968):

14. The illegitimacy *rate* (i.e., the number of nonwedlock births per 1,000 live births) among teen-agers has increased less than the rate among any other age group over the past 20 years and has remained relatively constant since 1957. The increase in number is related to the increase in population growth and must be distinguished from rate (Herzog, 1967).

Young people in the age group 15–24 were responsible for 53.9 percent of the total infectious venereal disease in the United States in calendar year 1965: 47.2 percent of the infectious syphilis and 54.3 percent of the gonorrhea. Among boys and girls 15–19 years of age, the incidence of infectious syphilis continues to increase at a faster rate than for all other age groups. At least one out of every 250 teen-age boys and girls in fiscal year 1966 was infected with gonorrhea. It is estimated that the number of all venereal disease cases which actually occur is approximately four times the number reported (American Social Health Association, 1967).

It's gotten worse than juvenile crime in the Negro ghetto, which parents of these well-to-do kids frequently are the first to denounce. It's a major league, hushed-up American scandal.

Evidence indicates that the typical teen-age shoplifter is the 16-year-old girl[15] whose father is a business or professional man earning $15,000 a year or more. She is given more than enough money to buy what she needs. Her clumsy methods invite arrest, but department stores—fearful of losing business—often do not prosecute. They either ignore the acts or notify parents.

Parents, upon being notified by the stores or by the police, respond to their child's behavior with shocked denial and with a certain fear of what friends will say. Often, they are overprotective and seek to shield the youth from any ensuing consequences. Typically, these youths do not see their actions as wrong nor are they aware that stealing for kicks might result in a permanent criminal record. Richard McLaughlin, chief security officer for the May Company department stores on the West Coast, told reporter Davidson (1968):

Children learn by example. They see their mothers eating grapes in a super-market without paying for them, or slipping sticks of butter into an oleo carton before going to the checkout counter, and they develop the philosophy that it's all right to steal from a big rich organization because nobody will miss it. Then they hear Daddy at home bragging about cheating his company on his expense account and the Government on his income-tax return. They're taught from childhood that anything's OK, just as long as you don't get caught.

Other reasons advanced for the shoplifting trend among affluent teen-agers are pressures by their peers to conform, and rebellion against established rules and parents who are too busy to take an interest in them. These same reasons are among the many which have been advanced to explain affluent youths' growing use of drugs such as LSD and marijuana.

Drug Use

There are no exact figures on the number of youth who use drugs. Surveys on several college campuses indicate that about 20 percent of students have used marijuana at least once and between 2 and 10 percent have tried LSD at least once. Students interviewed believe the number of drug users to be higher (Lukas, 1968). Keniston (1967) estimates the prevalence of drug use and abuse on college campuses at 5 percent of the total student population. Kifner (1968) reports that drug usage among high school students is becoming extremely widespread. This population is prone to try a "weird and dangerous variety" of drugs without sophistication or discrimination, as a means of rebelling or escaping boredom.

15. Girls outnumber boys in this crime about 20 to 1.

Since it remains to be proved that marijuana has any harmful physical effects,[16] much more concern is shown for the use of the amphetamines[17] and LSD. At least one million persons are believed to have tried LSD, and some experts feel that tens of thousands of persons are active users (Lukas, 1968). However, usage of this drug has decreased since the discovery that it *may* produce severe psychotic reactions, chromosome breaks, and serious birth defects, although there is no evidence that usage of other hallucinogens as "mind-expanding" agents has decreased. Some decrease may result, however, from the ideological shift among some college youth toward achieving "openness" without "trip"-inducing drugs.

Experts are quick to point to the increasing orientation toward pharmacological agents among the middle-class adult society. In addition to aspirin and legally prescribed barbiturates, a currently increasing minority of successful middle-class adults are using marijuana and hallucinogenic drugs, according to a national survey conducted by *The New York Times*. Many said they used the drugs to escape boredom. Others were either searching for sexual freedom or a "passageway to their own subconscious." Most of the drug users felt alienated from the mainstream of American life, but few were involved in any social causes. While adult usage of marijuana, the amphetamines, and the barbiturates cuts across social class lines, drug abuse is more frequently found in the middle class. However, it is among our young that drug usage is increasing most rapidly, suggesting that the next generation may be even more dependent upon drugs than this one (Arnold, 1968).

YOUTH CULTURES AMONG THE NONPOOR

Drug-using Groups

A number of attempts have been made to categorize types of youthful drug users (see, e.g., Zinberg, 1967; Keniston, 1967). There seems to be some general agreement that many youngsters experiment with drugs only two or three times. Their reasons for doing so are varied. Some seek "kicks," others succumb to peer pressure, and still others believe it to be sophisticated or daring. Keniston (1967) feels that the majority of college drug

16. As Yolles pointed out to a Senate subcommittee, there are potential hazards stemming from the use of marijuana, e.g., accidents due to muscular incoordination and distortion of time and space. Usage may also hinder the development of patterns of coping with reality during adolescence (*The New York Times*, March 7, 1968).

17. While many persons deliberately use these drugs to effect a "high," many students use them for such purposes as staying awake to study for exams. The results are sometimes disastrous, as in cases of hospitalization for exhaustion. Drugs of this family can also cause physical and psychological dependence from which withdrawal can be agonizing.

users are "seekers," that is, youth who are seeking truth and view drugs as a possible instrument in their search. Their use of drugs is part of a more general experimentation and seeking for relevance and meaning in life. Such students are occasional, but continuing, users of drugs and are not part of the "hippie"[18] subculture. Keniston believes this type of user tends to congregate at the "more selective, progressive, and academically demanding institutions." Typically, they major in humanities or psychology, are better-than-average students, come from upper-middle-class families, are uncertain of their life vocation, are highly introspective, and keenly aware of the contradictions in American culture. While not highly "alienated" from society, they have not yet decided it is worth joining. They struggle to experience life more intensely and to find a "rock bottom" that will serve as a basis upon which they can commit themselves socially and interpersonally and upon which they can build their inner identity. They make enormously high demands upon themselves, but often find their life experiences dull, although they show little tendency to project the inadequacies of their lives upon others. Rather, they seek self-understanding and often try deliberately through self-analysis to change their personalities. Drug use fits easily with the search for such experience.

Among a considerably smaller number of students, whom Keniston calls "heads," drug use becomes the central focus of college life. Some of these students seem capable of enduring the effects of drug use. Others seem unable to assimilate the experience or to recover from the disorganizing effects and lapse into a regressive state which, in rare instances, can be said to be psychotic. These are the users, as Keniston notes, who come to the attention of professionals. For that reason, the proportion of drug users who become regressed may be exaggerated.

Among "seekers," intensified drug use is often associated with reactive and situational depressions, e.g., romantic difficulties, realization of parental fallibilities, abandonment of religious values or vocational goals, etc. The motivations of "heads" are in many ways less complex. Keniston notes that these students are usually highly alienated from American society. They find in the "hippie" subculture a "provisional identity" that allows them to escape the demands of "Establishment America." For most young people, membership in the subculture is transient, after which they return to their families in the suburbs.[19] Keniston hypothesizes that regular drug use for some of these students may make dropping out of society unnecessary, since it provides an escape from pressures which they cannot or do not want to handle. It is therefore possible that the temporary regressive withdrawal from ordinary societal expectations and responsibilities is, for many

18. As Soskin (1967) notes, the word "hippie" has been applied indiscriminately to many types of "unconventional" youth. The term, as used herein, approximates Keniston's (1968) "culturally alienated" youth.

19. Annual parental income is over $15,000 (Keniston, 1967).

youngsters, a temporary or provisional maneuver in a turbulent transition to adulthood. But for a few, the picture is one of serious psychopathology. Drug use may either accelerate a regression upon which the individual is already embarked or, in some cases, a "bad trip" may topple a student whose equilibrium is fragile. Among this minority, drug usage sometimes appears to be a means of communicating a need for help.

Sociologists and psychologists, interviewed by *The New York Times* reporter Lukas (1968), agreed that drugs are only the most visible signs of the changing nature of American values, especially those relating to the Protestant Ethic and the Pioneer Spirit. Because these drugs are associated with passivity, introspection, mysticism, hedonism, and nihilism they are viewed as threats to these two values. On a deeper level, these drugs exert a powerful fascination for many middle-class Americans because they suggest that this society no longer holds to these values to which it still pays lip service. Upon being interviewed, Dr. Malcolm Bowers noted that for children who have known only comfort, the sacrifice inherent in the Protestant Ethic seems a senseless demand. For some, pleasure is sought in the here and now. Bowers feels the drug user "does not seek to impose his will on the environment, to go out and get what he wants from the world. He asks and expects the environment to take care of him, to feed him, to satiate him, to make him feel good." Psychologists have suggested that the adult generation really look at the drug culture of the young and analyze its meaning for our society, rather than simply continue to denounce it as an alien aberration. This Task Force feels, in fact, that this whole area of Psychedelphia's preoccupation with self-awareness, with or without drugs, is singularly important—not merely as a massive cultural shift but because it is found in a pace-setting segment of our society. For the Quietists of Psychedelphia who are concerned with the "purity" of their existentialist posture (since the pure experience is the source of all values) are committed to the absurd act, rather than to the practical act, and their lack of interest in the rational problem solving of the Square World has a parallel in the increasing refusal of intellectuals to become involved with our highly technological society. Eric Erikson reminds us:

The values of any new generation do not spring full blown from their heads; they are already there, inherent if not clearly articulated, in the older generation.

The much discussed generation gap is just another way of saying that the younger generation makes overt what the older generation represses (Lukas, 1968).

Social Involvement: The Alienated, Conformists, and Activists

The truth of Erikson's statement is reflected in today's young political activists whose rejection of the Protestant Ethic seems "clearly articulated" in the parental generation. Flacks (1967) found that the parents of activists tend to be of the professional upper-middle class and that their values deviate from those of the middle class in general.[20] Mention has already been made concerning the tendency toward social service and nurturant concern for others through the chosen professions and the activities of both parents—but especially of the women—in this class stratum. Compared to parents of nonprotesters, Flacks (1967) and Smith (1968) found that the activists' parents tend to be less authoritarian, more humanistic, and more rational and respectful of the child. Flacks notes that they place a greater stress on involvement in "intellectual and esthetic pursuits, humanitarian concerns, opportunities for self-expression, and tend to de-emphasize or positively disvalue personal achievement, conventional morality, and conventional religiosity." Evidence suggests that activists are closer to their parents' values than are nonactivists. Keniston (1968) concludes that many activists are concerned with *"living out expressed but unimplemented parental values"* and that they possess an unusual *"capacity for nurturant identification*—that is, for empathy and sympathy with the underdog, the oppressed, and the needy" (which may originate, in part, from an identification with the mother). Further, this empathy often follows the general modern trend toward *"internationalization of identity,"* leading to a peculiar responsiveness to world-historical events (italics in the original). In pursuing the role of protester, these youth reflect the adult-directed life style of the professional middle-class family, as delineated by Gans (1962).

Smith, Block, and Haan found that anti-Puritan humanistic values[21] discriminated groups of student activists, as well as students who participated extensively in protest activities *and* social service activities, from those students who belonged to conventional organizations, students who belonged to or participated in no organizations, and those who were high in social service but low on protest activities (e.g., Peace Corps participants). Use of the Kohlberg scale of moral development revealed that activists and those high in both activist and social service activities scored significantly higher on "The Morality of Self-Accepted Principles," whereas the other groups scored much higher on "Morality of Conventional Role Conformity" (Smith, 1968).

Commenting on the current scene Keniston (1968) writes: "One of the consequences of security, affluence, and education is a growing sense of personal involvement with those who are insecure, non-affluent and un-

20. However, Keniston (1968) feels the values of this class are more normative than deviant within this stratum. Interestingly, the grandparental generation of the activists tended to be better educated and to belong to higher status groups than that of nonactivists (Flacks, 1967).

21. E.g., "creative, imaginative; and free, unfettered, not hung up" were items which discriminated the two high protest groups from others, as measured by Q-sorts in which the respondents were asked to describe their "ideal selves" by sorting 63 adjectives into seven equal piles (see Smith, 1968).

educated." This description, however, is not highly applicable to those youth whom Keniston calls the "culturally alienated." While they share in common with the activists a rejection of the Protestant Ethic and other societal values, this rejection—together with an emphasis on "love" and "turning on"—inoculates them against personal involvement in long-range activities or sustained efforts to plan and execute demonstrations. These alienated students are highly apolitical, despite their opposition to war and their belief in interracial living. On those rare occasions in which they become involved in demonstrations, they generally prefer peripheral roles, avoid responsibilities, and are considered a "nuisance" by the activists. Often, these youth withdraw into their own "hippie" communities.

Although both groups are disenchanted with the American Dream, the activists seek to perfect the Dream in some respects, to change it in others. The alienated, however, either express disbelief that society can be changed or feel that it is not worth redemption. Both groups come from the same general social strata and tend to be highly talented. But their backgrounds are often quite different, both psychologically and ideologically. Unlike the activist, the alienated youth generally rejects his parents' values. He is likely to view his father as a man who has "sold out" to the pressures for success and status in society—a fate he wishes to avoid. Like the activists, the alienated youth expresses a special sympathy and identification with his mother. However, clinical data from a study by Keniston (1968) and his colleagues suggest that the alienated male student has ambivalent feelings toward his mother who is typically possessive, oversolicitous, and dominant. Generally, an unusually intense attachment existed between mother and son in the early years, but the mother of the alienated youth—unlike the activist's mother—never became an individuating force in her son's life.

The most striking characteristic of alienated youth is a far-reaching sense of distrust. As Keniston notes, this distrust extends beyond a low view of human nature. These youth believe that all appearances are untrustworthy and they show a great affinity for a pessimistic existentialist philosophy; they maintain that "passion, feeling, and awareness are the truest forces at man's disposal." Being highly introspective, their primary objective in life is to "attain and maintain openness to experience, contact with the world and spontaneity of feeling." Everything which might obstruct this goal is opposed. Attachment to a group is one such threat, since it is believed to entail the loss of individuality. Likewise, only disillusionment can result from intimacy. Although outwardly detached, the culturally alienated are inwardly highly, but ambivalently, involved with others. Many express strong feelings of anxiety or discomfort concerning sexual relationships, and every facet of friendship is likely to be scrutinized.

Despite the similarities between alienated and activist youth, Keniston feels that the activists are actually committed to many of the values which the alienated youth reject. The activists are much closer to the traditional American values of optimism, affiliation, and a faith in both human nature and the efficacy of human action.

Such generalizations obviously apply to "ideal types." Although Keniston has questioned whether it would be possible for the alienated or the activist to exchange roles if the culturally sanctioned expressions of either were repressed, there are growing indications that there is some interchanging of roles between the two groups.

Both groups represent minorities among our more affluent youth; however, Keniston postulates that in the future both groups will increase in size. Both types epitomize middle- and upper-middle-class parental emphases upon internal dynamics, individuation, self-actualization, and adult directedness—emphases which are becoming ever more dominant in these class strata. Further, urbanization, increased technology, mobility, "failure of community"[22] and other cultural factors implicated in the rise of these youth groups show no signs of declining in the foreseeable future. Concerning these nonconventional youth groups Smith (1968) writes:

How we view their defection from the values of order, control, rationality, foresight, and success depends very much on our own values. If . . . we take our stand firmly on the ground of the Protestant Ethic, we are likely to mistrust the new morality as a sign of the decadence that affluence and pampering brings in its wake. But if we are in more sympathetic touch with the new spirit, we may see it as an adaptive accommodation to a "post-industrial" society that no longer requires heroic sacrifice . . . at great psychic cost. We can hope that the trend may bring about a better balance in the human values that people can realize in society, a step toward the goal of "self-actualization" for more people.

At present, the adult world, and the institutions which it dominates, is seldom sympathethic to the voice of youth. For example, prior to the student revolts at some of our leading colleges, student protesters used various conventional means to inform officials of their complaints against academic procedures. When the administrators failed to respond, and showed few signs of being receptive to change, the students resorted to more dramatic forms of protest. Rather than share their power, or make joint efforts to arrive at a solution which the youth and their elders would find mutually agreeable, as Smith (1968) suggested, administrators relied on punitive action.

A group of Fellows at the Center for Advanced Study in the Behavioral

22. The "failure of community" reflects the present "absence of common experience, common interests, common values, and the sense of sharing a common human fate" (see Smith, 1968).

Sciences held several seminars at Stanford between December 1967 and April 1968 to study the problems related to campus protests. They concluded that less than 10 percent of the student body was actively involved in initiating activist demonstrations on campus. They concluded that the issue has often been the confrontation itself, rather than the causes or a meaningful outcome. They noted: "The history of student demonstrations shows that communication by crisis represents a crisis in communication" ("Student protests: A phenomenon for behavioral sciences research," 1968).

The struggle between students and administrators over academic issues is analagous to the way the adult world responds to social unrest among our youth. Many of the protests on campus, and elsewhere, revolve around broad social issues, such as war and poverty. Many youth are earnestly asking for change and for a chance to participate in change. But on these issues too, they most often experience punitive action and/or rejection. Such actions on the part of adults furthers the gap in communication and has done nothing to quell youthful protest. In fact, there are indications that future protests will reflect an increasingly prominent revolutionary component which may make resolution of the problems even more complex.

Most such confrontations occur with the alienated and the activists. Yet, it appears that these two groups are only extreme factions that communicate problems disturbing many of our young. Seemingly, many of the more conventional youth are content merely to imitate their parents. For example, college may be little more than the place in which one obtains the "credentials" for later success and status. Such youth deviate little from expected roles and behaviors and may view the dissent of the protesters with either abhorrence, amusement, or bewilderment. Like many of their adult counterparts, they seem oblivious to the poverty and injustices which so disturb our more sensitive youth.[23] Yet, these youth too must come to terms with the changing moralities of our day, with the problems of the draft, the pressures of academia, and so on. There are few indications that conventional youth experience any true communication with the adult world or that their participation in conventional youth groups (e.g., sororities and fraternities) offers them the needed preparation for adult life. Social interaction occurs largely among youth who share similar interests.

The problems of youth, their alienation from the adult world, their seeking, and their idealism find one communication channel, as Soskin

23. The relativity of our concepts of positive mental health has been noted for several years (see, e.g., Jahoda, 1958). For a discussion on the possibility that nonactivists may not be as "psychologically healthy" as activists, see Keniston, 1968 (pp. 317–18).

(1967) notes, which is "not preempted, monitored, and controlled by adults"—the world of music. In the past few years, the jukebox has become the "truthbox" which has helped to create "common attitudes" and "common understandings" among youth. Youthful folk singers write themes and lyrics that communicate the feelings and problems of adolescence and youth—"the honest embarrassment of first groping boy-girl relations, the feelings of estrangement from the adult society, the intense desire for family understanding, the frightening grotesquerie of loveless parental relations, the fear of the madness of adult warmongering." Instead of heeding the lyrics—"we're the young generation and we've got something to say"—adults usually respond with a demand to turn down the volume. The more disenchanted among our youth look to Camus, to Nietzsche, and to Sartre for a philosophy of life, to the oriental religions for spiritual meaning, and to drugs for expansion of consciousness. By taking art and drama into the streets, "hippies" seek to transform spectators into participants, to "jolt people out of their daily ruts, to make them feel, and feeling perchance to think" (ibid). The adult world—sometimes troubled, sometimes annoyed—has made little effort to effect meaningful communication with youth or to create for them any effective outlets for youthful idealism.

In summary, the material abundance of the American Dream neither guarantees our children or youth positive mental health, "happiness," nor adequate services. Some are now rejecting the values upon which the Dream was founded. Many parents who fervently pursued this Dream cannot understand the discontent of youth. As the editor of one college newspaper told reporter Dunbar (1968):

Most of our parents grew up in the Depression, and they were really hurting. They are concerned with money, status, and they're very insecure. Most of us, on the contrary, grew up in the most abundant society the world's ever seen. And to us, abundance and all the trappings isn't something to work for because you have it. You're used to it, it's nothing. So you start getting into human values because you've gone beyond the security thing. And our parents just can't understand that.

Similar feelings have been expressed by many affluent, highly talented, and sensitive youth. Such expressions are merely one signpost of the changing flux of values, of the longing for more meaningful human relations—one indication of the social crises of our times. In the following section, this Task Force addresses itself to the ways in which we might meet these crises which affect, in both similar and dissimilar ways, the children of our poor and the children of the American Dream.

Directions for Change

INTRODUCTION

The first part of this report has examined the well-being and effectiveness of American children and youth. Whether we consider the affluent or the poor, members of the successful "majority," or offspring of black and brown minorities, we find much that our society can ill afford to be complacent about. A number of recommendations for change in our social practices and institutional provisions have followed naturally from our analysis of youth's predicament.

In the second part of the report, we face more frontally the problem of institutional and societal change—how to get started with the radical changes that we see as required if every American child is to have a fair chance to realize his human potentiality. Our inquiry follows a logical path, one that Task Force VI pursued in its discussions. First, we examine some of the barriers to change, in our assumptions, in our institutional and professional practices, in our deficiencies of knowledge and skill. To balance the ledger, we turn to our resources of readiness for change; change efforts to be successful must be based on a realistic appraisal of our assets and liabilities. There follows a discussion of needed directions for change, priorities for planning in the fluid and developing society that it was our assignment to examine with respect to the promotion of the mental health of children and youth. The final sections of the report illustrate, in just enough concreteness to suggest their promise, a variety of innovations that point the way to what is possible for us to do for the mental health of children and youth in American communities and in the country at large.

This chapter was prepared for the Joint Commission on the Mental Health of Children by Ronald Lippitt, Ph.D.

115

Barriers to Change

Our collective inability, or refusal, to see clearly our crisis of social relations is our greatest barrier to change. This crisis is already upon us and is as serious as any external war crisis ever faced by this nation. The old patterns of child-rearing, family centeredness, and school, community, and church activities have disintegrated. Few new ways have been developed and those which have show no indication of widespread adoption. Consequently, enormous numbers of our children and youth are growing up without adequate internal structure and controls. They have not had the social, emotional, and intellectual guidance required to become independent, mentally healthy, and subsequently responsible, contributing adult citizens.

The crisis of our young is our own collective crisis. The rearing of our children and youth cannot be separated from the social processes of the society and the world. We have not yet had the foresight and wisdom to see that we have neglected, exploited, and despoiled our child and youth resources in the same way we have fouled and desecrated the air we breathe, the water we drink, and the land we inhabit.

Because of our overemphasis on controlling and developing the resources of the material world, we have seriously neglected both the study of human personality and the nature of productive social relationships. Upon ourselves and upon our children, we have imposed a tyranny of material preoccupation which has led to the disastrous social and emotional neglect of some children, and a serious overindulgence of others. The heavy penalty of this failure to get along with our fellow citizens, ourselves, and our children is manifested in many ways. We are just beginning to pay the penalty of individual and collective pain and national disorder. It seems clear at this point that personal and social disorganization will become worse before it can improve in the future. It is crucial that we mobilize our tremendous resources to evolve new patterns which will be based on a sound knowledge of man's physical, mental, social, and spiritual nature.

If our knowledge of agriculture and animal-rearing were as meager, or as poorly used, as our knowledge of child-rearing and social rehabilitation, we would still be using wooden plows and oxcarts on our farms. Knowledge alone, of course, is inadequate to the task. We must unleash the enormous reservoir of love and mutual care which is now fettered by our national fear and confusion. If we deny this tremendous reservoir of readiness and capacity to help each other, we are indeed in great peril.

Up to the present time, we have done almost nothing to change the social patterns that produce illegitimacy, delinquency, mental illness, family breakdown, and the dependency of "three-generations on welfare." Yet, when we wished to master the ocean, the Arctic, or space and lacked the knowledge and technology, we acted in our national tradition and mobilized the necessary scientific knowledge and technology. We have made no major commitment to acquire the social knowledge and technology needed to solve the crisis inherent in our child and youth development practices and in our own social relations. Our investments have been minor and piecemeal. Our major barrier, as well as our major challenge, is to analyze ourselves and subsequently to assess the means by which we can achieve collective commitment and action for change.

Invalid assumptions: Some of the barriers to creative improvement of our child and youth development practices arise from certain prevailing but incorrect assumptions about child-rearing and youth development. Five assumptions which block us are identified below:

1. The first commonly held but misleading assumption is that "clamping down" on and isolation of our young are necessary and beneficial disciplinary procedures. These techniques of repression no doubt help the adult society to cope with their fears and anxieties; however, there is no evidence that they result in either the development of internal self-control or the rehabilitation of deviant individuals. In spite of this, detention institutions which lack treatment programs are widespread and the reactive programs of "pick up" and "clamp down" are the most frequent means by which parents, schools, and communities deal with the troublesome and deviant behavior patterns of our young.

2. A second incorrect assumption is based on the idea that there is a single or major cause of any behavior or social problem, such as delinquency, school dropouts, "slum mentality," or welfare dependence. Efforts to solve these problems are often fated for failure because they are based on such simplistic notions as: "the real problem is the parents," "the life of a father is the issue," "employment opportunities would solve it," "just get them away from their parents," etc. It is indeed tempting to simplify problems by the "single cause assumption," but such incorrect thinking leads to incorrect feelings and actions and thus thwarts our attempts to be helpful to children and youth.

3. The third erroneous assumption is "give them the opportunities they need and those that deserve them will use them." We have painfully learned in the areas of unemployment, delinquency, birth control, drug addiction, and adult education that this assumption is not a valid basis for policy and program thinking for target populations who have experienced only repeated failure, frustration, mistreatment, and deprivation. Such persons often possess neither the readiness, trust, nor skill to utilize new opportunities. Thus, even though objectively available, new opportunities may be psychologically nonexistent.

4. Another misleading and almost fatal assumption is: "Youths are not old enough to know what is good for them; not mature enough to participate in the planning and operation of their own development and

education." It is unfortunate that the symptoms of discontent, alienation, and hostility among youth are pointed to as proof of the validity of this assumption. We fail to recognize these symptoms as evidence of our own failure when we operate upon this assumption. As we shall see later in this report, evidence indicates that youths respond with great responsibility and resourcefulness when given genuine opportunities for involvement. When the attitudes and opinions of youth are very different from our own, it is an easy defense to label them as immature and inappropriate. But we do so without testing, objectively, the validity of our assumptions.

5. A fifth misleading but commonly held assumption is: "I was professionally trained for child-rearing and youth work so my opinion should have the most weight." It is amazing how often our defensiveness against change is motivated by our own need to protect our status and influence. The children and youth of today differ a great deal from those of the period in which most of us received our education and training. Also, since that time, we have come to the end of the era of deference in the relationships between the generations. We must be ready to allow the young to test the merit of our ideas and values and to negotiate with them, rather than command them. To so use our adulthood as resourcefulness rather than authority will require a major shift of our assumptions and values.

Self-defeating institutional practices: The great investments in physical facilities, personnel, organizational structures, and set policies and procedures represent major investments in our present mode of operation. Certainly some of the major barriers to change result from our commitment to and investment in this institutionalization. The examples below illustrate such self-defeating institutional practices:

1. Deviant and neglected children and youth are typically dealt with in institutions where they live in depersonalized life situations. These children are isolated from their own families and experience only minimal relations with the institutional caretakers who function in parentlike roles. Essentially, these institutions are detention or custodial centers with minimal programs of emotional, social, and intellectual rehabilitation. The lack of professional or public evaluation of the outcomes of such practices results in the continuation of inadequacies in personnel, budget, programs, and facilities.

2. Another frequent method of social control designed to deal with alienated youth is the punitive cycle of restriction and retribution. In the school system, this cycle typically entails expulsion, isolation, or restriction of privileges. In the community, the police follow a similar pattern by relying on selective surveillance, aggressive clamp-downs, public accusations, and detention. As we know, this pattern of retribution creates a negative counterresistance which, from the viewpoint of the adult society, only justifies more retribution. Such a "program" of dealing with youth is certainly self-defeating.

3. Another self-defeating pattern is our attempt to end "dependency" by denying welfare support if the father is in the family and "able to work" or if the mother is trainable for employment. These policies have aggravated rather than solved the dependency problem and appear to create conditions which have a negative mental health impact on child-rearing practices and on youth development.

4. A frequently utilized self-defeating process is the uncritical and unskilled adoption of new fads in practice. This permits many professionals and institutions, when pushed to make efforts toward change in their tried and true professions, to respond virtuously: "We tried it, and it didn't work." Inappropriate and inept efforts to change and to adopt new practices are widespread barriers to innovation in the area of human services.

5. A closely related type of barrier might be called the defense of the "eyewash solution." Many welfare, education, and rehabilitation programs designed for children and youth adopt token solutions to problems with a show of pride and satisfaction. For example, some programs boast of a diagnostic facility in operation but have completely neglected treatment. Other programs focus on a very small and highly select percentage of their client population and express satisfaction with this tokenism. Other programs provide "consultation" as a substitute for remedial and treatment services. Others devote great energy and funds to program-planning but do little follow-through on implementation. Very frequently those involved in such programs are pressured to show results, no matter how superficial, in order to justify their efforts to legislators. All of these pressures to demonstrate cheap, quick results typically operate as barriers to creative sound program development and evaluation.

Our values and attitudes as child and youth workers: Many of the crucial barriers to change lie within ourselves, professionals and volunteers, as we carry out our functions of child-rearing, child care, youth development, and rehabilitation. Some of the most important breakthroughs will come when we are able to recognize and cope with these barriers to change.

1. One of the most difficult issues to be faced is the loss of adult influence if responsibility and power are shared with the young. It is difficult for many classroom teachers, school administrators, agency directors, and community leaders to recognize and accept a leadership structure within youth peer groups which is equal to or greater than the power exerted by adults. As one young black power leader said to us recently, in discussing his high school situation, "I don't know why they don't give us more say in how things are run around here. Don't they realize that not a single one of us has to learn anything from them?" Obviously, a mutuality of influence is imperative if we are to involve youth in programs which are designed for their productive growth. To accept this fact, many adults must effect a major shift in their attitudes.

2. Another barrier to change which stems from our own attitudes as professionals is our fear of losing status as a result of the increasing number of paraprofessionals and volunteers who are now entering our fields and working directly with our clients. Certainly one of the greatest hopes for significant breakthroughs in the improvement of child-rearing and development services lies in the recruiting and training of the great manpower resources of volunteers and indigenous paraprofessionals. Although this makes the professional's role as trainer and supervisor even more important, many professionals find it very threatening to give up some of their satisfactions of direct work with clients and to support volunteers in doing the kind of work for which they were trained professionally.

3. Not only are the traditional roles of professionals and volunteers changing, but many boundaries between agency programs are also being challenged. One barrier to change is the possessive and protective attitude which agency staffs have toward their own "program boundaries." Educators feel threatened by community agencies getting into the area of "tutorial programs," and community agencies feel threatened by school systems that are beginning to do "social work after school." One of the most difficult problems is to get the professionals from various community agencies to join together and plan and operate a joint program for delinquency prevention, sex education, identification of emotional disturbance, or any of the other various programs which require the coordination and even integration of the various community socialization and educational agencies.

4. The attitude of the professionals toward parents is another critical barrier to change. Typically, professionals regard themselves as substitutes for inadequate parents. This attitude prevents the development of collaboration between parents and professionals in regard to the rearing of children and also results in barriers to developing a positive parent education function. Parents feel rejected and devalued and are certainly not ready to learn in the context of such a negative relationship.

5. Many workers hold the attitude that "the rotten apple will spoil the barrel," and feel it is dangerous to mix deviant, deprived, or problem children with middle-class or "normal" children. This position blocks creative program development in many important innovative areas. There is a small but growing body of research which indicates that children of different social class backgrounds, or those who show differences in attitudes and values, have a great deal to offer each other if there is adequate program guidance. Thus, just as the track system is slowly yielding to educational research, so the segregation system in grouping practices is being challenged. But the attitudes of the professionals, parents, and children themselves must be worked through openly and creatively if the necessary attitude changes are to be effected.

Lack of skills and resources for change: Even when the intention and motivation to change exists, change may be blocked because the resources and skills required for the successful development or adoption of new patterns of work with children and youth are unavailable. The utilization of new program inventions and new research knowledge requires far more than good intentions and the right values.

1. One major barrier to change lies in the fact that our educational and social welfare systems and agencies have not yet developed effective self-renewal or research and development mechanisms. These research and development activities have been the major source of innovativeness and leadership in industry and agriculture. Only by allocating adequate budget and manpower, and by assigning a central place in the organizational structure to research and development activities, can we expect to achieve the vitally needed breakthrough in educational and social welfare practice.

2. A closely related blockage to change exists because very few programs in child-rearing and youth development have built in the evaluative feedback procedures required to provide the necessary data for program revision and efficient program functioning.

3. A third and most serious barrier to change in this area is the lack of sophisticated and ongoing training programs designed to prepare staffs for the successful adoption and utilization of new practices. It is often falsely assumed that new social practices can be adopted without an extensive reorientation and training of the staff. The typical result is low quality or unsuccessful adoption and utilization of new concepts and techniques. It is not possible in the field of human services to adopt new patterns of practice without intensive programs of conceptual and skill training and attitude reorientation.

4. As indicated above, many of the most important changes required in education and social welfare practice involve the coordinated efforts of individuals and groups with different skills and programs. This fact requires the development of new structures of interagency coordination which are now tragically lacking.

5. Finally, the lack of fiscal support for the development of our most precious national resource—our children and youth—is a national scandal. The lack of budget is a continuing barrier to research, innovation, dissemination, and training—all necessary functions if we are to break through our current patterns of "too little and too late."

SOURCES OF READINESS AND SUPPORT FOR CHANGE IN OUR CURRENT CHILD-REARING AND YOUTH DEVELOPMENT PATTERNS

In spite of the seriousness and the magnitude of our problem, the lack of needed manpower and resources, and the primitiveness of our techniques, there is reason to be optimistic about our ability to solve our problems of child and youth development.

To a greater degree than ever before, the public and the relevant professions are recognizing and facing the confrontations resulting from our failures to reach and communicate with youth, to challenge and support children to grow up in a changing world, and to involve the young in setting goals for their own growth and development. Many segments of society are pressing for new priorities on "solving the problems of youth," "educating children better," "paying for better teachers," and "giving the kids more say in things."

These pressures for new priorities are reflected in the great increase in federal funds and in new programs focused on the improvement of education, child care, youth participation, and strengthening of family life prior to the recent cutbacks that we can hope are temporary. The significant increase in research and development aimed at achieving a greater understanding of the growth and development of children and youth, and the accelerated invention of improved models of educating our young, are consequences of this trend. A second significant development is the new effort to store, organize, and retrieve the bodies of basic and applied knowledge so that it can be available for systematic use in program development. A third consequence of the new priorities is the beginning efforts to disseminate the new social inventions of improved educational practices and models of youth participation. Throughout the professions, the idea of disseminating new practices is becoming, for the first time, significant in terms of priority and responsibility.

Slowly but surely, we are beginning to see changes in the recruitment and training of young people into the critical professions where womanpower and manpower is so scarce and where training and performance is still so relatively inadequate.

But perhaps the most hopeful sign lies in the professional and volunteer programs across the country which are beginning to involve youths in helping youth. The results of these efforts indicate that when the young are given the invitation and opportunity to share with adults the responsibility for rearing and educating the younger children, they respond with enthusiasm, readiness to learn and to collaborate, and that they show great personal growth themselves. Obviously the young, in most cases, are eager and ready to collaborate if we give them a chance to be partners instead of puppets.

Another important indication of youths' readiness to participate is reflected in their creative initiative, both as groups and individuals, in developing growth opportunities for themselves. Finding exciting alternatives to unchallenging traditional educational programs is a new pattern among college youths. At the same time that rebellious disruption has spread over American campuses, more and more youths are beginning to express their discontentment through initiating constructive community service projects. But all rebellions, constructive or destructive, are pressure on the older generation to revise radically its patterns of relating to the young. The growing-up process has become more complex and the older generation—professionals, volunteers, parents—is needed more than ever before. If we, as adults, are able to grow with the young, we have a great opportunity to renew and develop our roles as sources of guidance, stimulation, and motivation in the complex growing-up process.

DIRECTIONS OF NEEDED CHANGE EFFORTS

Task Force VI spent considerable time analyzing present trends in child-rearing, child welfare work with youth, the nature of youth involvement, and reactions to our current societal situation. From these trends we made various attempts to project the future, based on the continuation of these trends. We also attempted to foresee the future as it might be creatively developed through major change efforts in our patterns of socialization. As we reflected on these prospects and potentialities, several assumptions emerged as guidelines upon which we could establish priorities for efforts to change the current unsatisfactory trends and thus create more satisfactory procedures and structures for building the future of our life with the young. These assumptions are stated briefly below, and are followed by a section which states more concretely the implications for directions of endeavor.

Some Assumptions

1. It will become increasingly necessary and desirable to involve the young from a very early age in the planning and implementation of their own educational growth experiences.
2. It will become increasingly necessary and desirable to establish opportunities for the young to participate actively and much more fully in the economic, political, and social activities of the community.
3. The changing occupational situation, with the great increase in the proportion of human service roles, means that we should be providing the young many more opportunities to learn interpersonal service skills and to try out such roles as part of the educational program.
4. With the increase in leisure time, a greater emphasis must be placed on training for the roles of spouse, parent, community volunteer worker, citizen, and intelligent consumer of recreational and cultural opportunities.
5. With the growing ecological pressures toward depersonalization and fragmentation of life, children and youth need to be given special education in areas of human relations, conflict resolution, self-awareness, and in the skills of giving and receiving help from others.

6. The revolutions in transportation, communication, and other sources of interdependence, mean that the child or youth must have extensive and intensive experiences with interaction and collaboration between himself and others who differ from him in many ways, e.g., cross-culturally, interracially, or in nationality, political orientation, religious belief, urban or nonurban background, and social class.

7. With the growing multiplicity and specialization of child-rearing and youth development programs the family and school must provide more supportive help to the child in his efforts to cope with and integrate the multiplicity of the inputs that shape his growing-up experience.

8. Because the rate of technological and social change is so great, and so complex, it is crucial that all educational objectives and designs focus on educating the young for creative change-ability.

9. Education for creative change-ability requires an increased individualization of educational experience and will require the participation of a much larger population of adults working in educational programs with children and youth. Manpower must be recruited and trained for these functions. Machine technology can be a very valuable supplement.

Implications for institutional and programmatic change efforts: Having the assumptions, above, about the future as the background for our thinking, the members of Task Force VI derived the major priorities for change effort which are summarized in the section below. Following the section below there are descriptions of existing or needed innovations which are intended to illustrate the types of effort required to effect these needed changes.

We have given first priority to two objectives: (1) achieving the attitudes, skills and mechanism of change-ability, and (2) involving youth in continuous partnership with us in the process of educational and social improvement.

Achieving the attitudes, skills, and mechanisms of change-ability: Faced with the many symptoms of blockage, hang-up, and wrong directions, man is finally beginning to face the confrontation of his own social situation. As awareness of the challenge and the responsibility develops and becomes clarified, a cluster of key concepts becomes more focal— "self-renewal," "learning to learn," "planned change," "change-ability," "change agent," and "feedback." All these ideas support the assumption that it is possible for individuals, groups, organizations, and nations to learn and to develop the problem-solving capability required to deal creatively and efficiently with the great range of complex problems with which we are now confronted and with those which will confront us in the future. It is the belief of Task Force VI that this orientation is both an appropriate and a crucial approach to the challenge of improving our child-rearing and youth development practices. The following are some of the elements involved in this capability.

1. Planning and policy making are typically the province of a small group of specialists or administrators; effective change must involve relevant populations in planning and decision making. One of the most difficult problems of planned change lies in the fact that there are no regular procedures for involving all the relevant populations in the retrieval and analysis of information about the present situation, in creating images of potentiality as the basis for short-range and long-range planning, and in the decisions to implement plans.

2. Another basic requirement for achieving and maintaining change-ability is a well-designed research and development mechanism. (All of these mechanisms will be illustrated in the case examples which follow in the next section.) The research function should include the scanning, retrieving, and interpreting of new knowledge developed elsewhere and the conducting of inquiries into the needs, readinesses, and potentialities for change within the particular school system, agency, or community. The development function should involve conducting a continuous flow of development projects to test the feasibility of significant new changes in practices and in demonstrating the validity of a change effort. Many organizations are discovering that if research and development are to have a major continuing impact for change, then each type of effort must involve a larger portion of direct workers with children and youth in some significant way so as to develop an understanding of and readiness for change. It is unfortunate that the concept of social invention has not become a significant idea. It is imperative that we help and promote the conception that new practices and models can be invented in this field of social practice, just as they are developed in the areas of physical technology and applied biology.

3. Intensive training and retraining are crucial elements of the self-renewal process. Little significant change can occur in child-rearing and youth development practices without confronting the values, attitudes, and skills of the practitioner. This requires changes in professional orientation and performance and thus an even more intensive retraining than is true in such fields as agriculture, medicine, and technology. The amount of and type of training, both preservice and inservice, currently provided in our educational and social welfare systems is woefully insufficient for stimulating or supporting significant changes in our programs and organizations.

4. Procedures for dissemination and adoption of new practice are a part of the self-renewal model. In most cases where new practices are developed or adopted within a school system, agency, or community, they are used by only a few practitioners. Usually there are no procedures for either disseminating new practices throughout the system, or for providing all participants the opportunities for high-quality adoption of the new practices. As we know, these procedures cannot be coercive; however, they must go far beyond mere provision of opportunity. In most agencies,

such as school systems, the mechanisms of dissemination are the most neglected aspect of the self-renewal process.

5. Procedures of evaluation and redirection are the fifth requirement for achieving and maintaining change-ability. In most institutions, evaluation is periodic rather than continuous, and is tied to supervision rather than to program development. Effective change must require every practitioner to be part of the evaluation team and to help clarify the objectives and criteria for progress. The assessment data will then become important and desired information which can be used to help review both goals and procedures and to provide stimulus for the redirection of effort. Evaluation must be expert and sophisticated. Simpleminded reviews may devalue a new program that has real merit.

Without these five ingredients of self-renewal, it is doubtful that any institution or program can achieve the flexibility and change-ability so crucially required to overcome the tragic lags in existing practice and the tragic insensitivity to the future and to our clients. We must strive to overcome such barriers if we are to move creatively toward the national building of our youth resources.

Involving youth in continuous partnership with us: The adult community must move forward by placing trust in the young. We must invite and support youth to become competent and committed collaborators in creating our mutual present and their future. What does this mean?

First of all, it means the genuine sharing of power, privilege, and responsibility. In the operation of schools, agencies, and communities, it means providing opportunities for sharing, planning, decision making, and action. Understandably youth have become discontented with the fact that their education is planned for them, rather than with them. In recent years one of the most eye-opening experiences for many teachers and administrators has been the positive response of youth who are given the opportunity to share in the teaching of younger pupils. They very rapidly become creative, competent, and highly committed members of the educational team. Several agencies are now experimenting with the youth as members of their boards of directors. For example, in Santa Cruz, California recently, a 17-year-old was appointed to the County Planning Commission. In the design for youth participation, presented later in this report, we suggest a variety of ways in which youth may become a significant part of the political, economic, and social structure of the community.

It is not easy to initiate this kind of collaboration with the young. Many of the important and powerful youth leaders have gone "underground." They distrust the efforts of adults to identify them and deal with them as leaders. They find it necessary to test the trustworthiness of the adult leadership. Much of youths' leadership power has been developed on the basis of mobilizing resistance to adult power or subverting its effectiveness.

Another test of the adult subculture's meaningful goodwill is whether it is willing to support and provide assistance to youth-initiated enterprises, such as the Real Great Society program which attracts dropouts, the less financially stable youth, etc. (see Kohler, 1968). As one professional said, "It's terribly hard to provide consultation to them in terms of the guidelines of their own enterprise instead of stepping in to give them leadership you feel they need." Like any other minority group, youth feel the need to prove what they can do on their own basis for establishing cooperative relationships. One of the most puzzling problems we must eventually face is a means by which youth may be provided appropriate representation in the political system of the community. In one way or another, we must break through the increasing cleavage between youth and adulthood to provide the young more meaningful connections with the serious affairs of society. Therefore, it becomes a critical part of our educational responsibility to provide youth with training for new partnership goals. One of the defensive, and often unconscious, maneuvers of many administrators and youth leaders is to offer responsibility to youth without providing parallel learning opportunities, and then, in turn, to point self-righteously to youths' failure to live up to their "responsibilities." This is a trap which young people often rush into because they lack the necessary perspective on the knowledges and skills required for competence. Their eagerness may contribute to this experience of failure. Therefore, several additional dimensions of change effort are required to support a solid base for successful youth involvement and collaboration. These requirements are identified briefly here. They have been illustrated and amplified in the case projects summarized by Kohler (1968).

Training the young for competent initiative and collaboration: In order to support responsible collaboration and creative initiative of the type mentioned above it is imperative that representatives of the older generation (e.g., parents, teachers, agency workers) put an early and continuing emphasis on training the child for such activities.

For example, during most of the early years of life the child's only occupational role is that of student or learner. Yet we almost completely neglect any training for this occupational role. We do very little to help the student develop a self-conception as learner, to practice the skills of learnership, or to develop pride in competent learnership. Because we neglect training for the occupational role of learner, we are responsible for much of the alienation which many of the young now feel toward the school and the learning process.

The failure to assist each child in coping with and integrating the daily variety of helping efforts and educational inputs is the second major deficiency of our educational program. Certainly from the first grade on every child should have the daily opportunity to conduct his own integrative value inquiry. He should be helped to articulate and clarify his own beliefs and decisions in relation to his manner of responding to the influence efforts of others. At the present time most children develop patterns either of conformity or rebellion. In neither case are children developing a positive problem-solving identity through participating creatively in their own learning process and in the development of their own values and initiative.

From an analysis of data, it seems evident to the members of Task Force VI that an effective way to train the young for responsible participation in their own learning process and in the development of the community is to recruit them as collaborators in the training of the young. This concept of learning through apprenticeship in teaching appears to be a basic innovation in recruiting youth's participation. We'll return to this model of the improvement of education in our next section.

Additional directions for change effort: Several additional types of change effort are required to effect the three types of priority efforts summarized above (i.e., achieving change-ability, recruiting youth as collaborators, and training children and youth for responsible collaboration).

To achieve these goals, community child and youth socialization agencies will need to develop procedures for communication, collaboration, and coordination. At the present time they compete ineffectively for the loyalty, time, and minds of some children and completely ignore and neglect others. The uncoordinated efforts of the school, the family, the leisure-time agency, the police, the churches, the mass media, and the peer groups create a medley of voices and efforts which do very little to promote the personal growth of children and youth.

It also appears that the political and economic leadership of the community needs to become involved in the development of youth, particularly, in the process of developing mature occupational and citizen roles. The last Joint Commission on Mental Illness and Health made a major contribution in "opening up the mental hospital" by making it an interdependent part of the community with outpatient programs, aftercare programs, follow-up support, and the utilization of volunteer and professional personnel from the community. Task Force VI believes that one of the most important outcomes of the Joint Commission on the Mental Health of Children could be the "opening up of the school system" to the community, which has many opportunities for learning and rich human resources for teaching. The resources and facilities for learning have been and are now very limited. All community citizens need to become involved in the development of the child and youth resources. No doubt this will require significant shifts in the allocation of economic resources and also drastic changes in legislative policies and programs.

The mass media is another promising vehicle of change. Significant efforts to influence values and behavioral models would benefit greatly by collaboration with communications personnel. Otherwise, there must be massive educational programs to inoculate the young against the influences of the mass media. Certainly these potent communication resources need to be involved in any major efforts to reevaluate and reconstruct our programs of educating the young.

Also, we must take parents into partnership in the improvement of child-rearing practices and youth development. All the professionals acknowledge that the parent has great impact on the development of the child. But no agency accepts responsibility for systematic and continuing programs of preservice and inservice parent education. This effort must become a major national priority. Again, the traditional didactic approach will not achieve the desired results (see Brim, *Education for Child Rearing*, 1959): learning that affects the practice is most likely to occur in the context of participation and responsibility (cf. Chilman, *Parents as Partners*, 1968).

One very special area of collaboration with parents is in the development of widespread day-care opportunities for preschool children. Task Force VI concurs with Professor Florence Ruderman's conclusion that "day care is needed on all levels of society—by the most normal families and by the middle class, as well as by others. It should be available to the entire society, just like our public schools, playgrounds, and libraries." The Task Force wishes to emphasize the necessity for the training and participation of the mother in nursery school programs.

Many economically disadvantaged mothers, like many middle-class mothers, will find that even if they do not *have* to work, they would prefer not to be tied down entirely to young children. Nursery schools, properly managed, would provide an excellent setting for providing good parent education, as well as a setting for meeting the psychological and physical development needs of children at one of the most critical periods of their development.

The development of major improvements of the types implied above will require new patterns of collaboration between federal, state, and local funding in the needed program efforts. Particularly this will require exploration as to the collaborative patterns between the public and private sectors, and new possibilities for the recruitment and collaboration of volunteers, paraprofessionals, and professionals. Until the traditional barriers between public and private, volunteer and professional, and federal and local efforts can be overcome, we will lack the motivation and the manpower to accomplish significant breakthroughs.

However, all our social forecasting and planning must consider the population explosion[1] and the volume of socialization services required.

---

1. The problems and suggestions relating to the population explosion were conceptualized by Dr. Joseph J. Downing, member of Task Force VI.

This level depends directly on the numbers of infants, children, and youth. We must not ignore the reproduction rate, which is well above that needed for a stable population. Our social and natural environments are being badly injured by the heavy demands resulting from a population excess.

Unless the growth of the population of this country is controlled at the replacement level in the very near future, the quality of life for all will greatly deteriorate. It is imperative, therefore, that individuals and families develop a sense of their responsibility in this respect. We recommend a high priority for a continuous national educational program aimed primarily at the teens and twenties of all social and economic levels. The objective is to produce acceptance of the need to limit reproduction, with emphasis on the quality of children produced and reared, rather than on the numbers.

The last direction for change to which we wish to call attention—legislation and policy—is perhaps the most promising means of effecting wide-scale social change. Regarding this issue, Judge Justine Wise Polier, member of Task Force VI, has the following comments:

The traditional concept that the primary role of law is to restrain or punish the criminal and protect or order property rights has yielded to a far more comprehensive concept. Through judicial interpretation of constitutional rights (as in Brown v. Board of Education) and through legislation with the resulting proliferation of administrative agencies, the law has come to touch the personal lives of all Americans to an ever increasing extent.

During the past three decades, legislation has become the most far-reaching mechanism through which our country has sought to meet recognized necessities for social change or, at least, express its goals. Such legislation may be enacted as temporary or fragmented measures as is the "war on poverty." It may provide only token help as through the housing program to date. It may slowly extend protections against some of the hazards of life as through the social security laws and their subsequent amendments.

When social legislation espouses policy positions, but fails to provide the means with which to achieve them, it encourages false hopes that invite disillusionment and that may intensify rather than resolve issues. When it narrows the gap between the American ideal of justice and practice, it becomes a constructive source of strength to individuals that are aided and to the body politic.

While the United States was far slower than many other countries to use legislation to meet social problems, it has enacted a vast volume of legislation for this purpose since depression days. However, thus far, legislation to prevent poverty, to substantially reduce its tragic effects in the lives of children, and to strengthen the mental health of children have been too fragmentary and limited in scope to prove effective. This country has failed to enact a family or children's allowance to assure a minimum standard of living for all children, and it has failed to enact legislation to provide comprehensive health services for its children. In both these areas the United States lags behind the procession of all Western countries. In both areas our legislation too largely presents promises for the future instead of serving as a transmitting agency for the support and services that children need.

Legislation, in America today, can provide a most effective channel through which our society can, if it will, steadily enlarge its commitment to establish rights under law that will guarantee the well-being and promise of its children.

These are some of the major dimensions for change-effort derived from this Task Force's diagnoses of the current situation and the directions required for future development. With these as the challenge, the Task Force spent much of its time projecting some concrete images of potentiality and seeking out current innovations which seem to represent directions for the future. The next section presents illustrations of these directions for the future.

ILLUSTRATIONS OF PROGRAM DEVELOPMENT FOR THE FUTURE

In the previous sections of this report, the members of Task Force VI briefly summarized their consensus on the diagnosis of the problems that most critically affect positive child and youth development and on the derived priority directions for change and improvement.

In this section, the Task Force illustrates how several of the change efforts might operate in the future. We wish to stress the fact that these models of program action are purely illustrative. We merely recommend that "something like this" should be developed, no doubt in many forms and varieties. Nevertheless, programs similar to these illustrative examples are already in operation. The 1950 and 1960 White House Conferences on Children and Youth provided an impetus to the development of youth participation programs. A survey of statewide programs of this type was conducted by the National Council of State Committees on Children and Youth for The Joint Commission on Mental Health of Children (see Clendenen *et al.*, 1968). The results indicate a vast difference in the state programs; however, the participants—both youth and adults—were enthusiastic about these programs, although they pointed to deficiencies such as inadequate funding. Another survey of 45 youth participation projects was conducted for the Joint Commission by The National Commission on Resources for Youth, Inc. (see Kohler, 1968). These projects represented cross-age, cross-cultural, and cross-economic groups and had at least one of the following among its aims: "Citizenship Training," "Personality Development," "Job Training," or "Academic Improvement." The success of these projects is encouraging; however, much greater efforts must be made if we are to successfully engage youth in such meaningful activities on a wide-scale basis. We have selected six illustrative models for action, each one of which focuses on one of the following priorities:

I.   The design for youth involvement and participation.
II.   The education of the young for participation and growth into adult roles—e.g., worker, parent, citizen, consumer.
III.   The coordination and integration of community socialization and educational services.
IV.   The recruiting and training of volunteers and paraprofessionals.
V.   The inservice training of parents.
VI.   Programs for the preschool child.
VII.   The training of professional child and youth workers.
VIII. The self-renewal model—guidelines for the development and maintenance of the illustrative programs described above.

I.   *The Design for Youth Involvement and Participation:*[2]

Task Force VI early developed general consensus that in contemporary America young people are hampered in finding a meaningful, satisfying, and productive role in life because of the lack of an adequate basis for the experience of community, binding individuals of different ages, generations, and social groups. Fragmentation of experience between family, work, school, and neighborhood is accompanied by discontinuities in the steps toward responsible adulthood and by ill-coordinated specialization on the part of youth-serving institutions and agencies. While the unsatisfactory state of affairs is most strikingly obvious as it applies to the children of the poor and to minority-group youth in the urban ghettos, the same problems in different guises affect all youth, all portions of society.

We have conceived the following illustrative model to help deal creatively with the crisis of trust between the generations, to provide youth with opportunities to participate more fully and influentially in all aspects of community life—local, state, and national—and to allow youth to share more fully in planning and decisions with regard to their own learning programs. A reciprocal purpose is to provide the adult community with the much needed key resources of youth.

Some assumptions

1. It is assumed that there are many segments of every community that have an interest in and commitment to the development and utilization of the resources of youths.

2. It is assumed that there are many functions of community life which would benefit greatly from the participation of youth, both in their collaboration with adult segments and in their actions as an autonomous source of initiative.

3. It is assumed that the majority of youth are motivated and able to

2. The major conceptualization and formulation of the youth participation model was contributed by John H. Niemeyer, member of Task Force VI.

contribute to community life and that they are ready to collaborate with the adult members of the community.

4. It is also assumed that there are a significant number of youths who would prefer to initiate their own developmental actions without adult leadership.

5. It is assumed that the development of youth as a resource deserves, and will require, more of the local and national budget than is now being allocated. But it is also assumed that the creative participation of youth in educational youth development programs will greatly reduce the drain on some parts of the community budget.

With these assumptions and purposes in mind the members of Task Force VI developed the following illustrative example of an organization and program for youth participation at the three levels of local community, state community, and national community. As we look at this example in retrospect, we realize that the organizational mechanisms that we envisaged may convey an unduly formalistic impression. Councils, representation, hierarchical organizations at local, state, and national levels— all this sounds formidable and obviously cannot be created full blown. And we have at least some doubts as to whether youth's need to be significantly involved in the business of society *can* be fulfilled best through such formal mechanisms. In spite of these misgivings, we illustrate the program as one that captured the imagination of the Task Force sufficiently to lead us to give it considerable discussion. We stand by the assumptions on which it is based; as for the model itself, we are much more tentative.

1. The development and operation of a youth participation and citizenship program at the local community level: We visualize a community organizational procedure that recruits and develops the involvement of two age sectors of the youth community, the 13 to 17 age sector and the 18 to 21 age sector. An elected youth council of youth leaders is to be created from the two age sectors. Half of the leaders on the council will be elected representatives from those agencies and organizations in the community that have youth clientele or constituency (e.g., the school system, youth-serving agencies, the churches, labor-sponsored groups). The other half of the youth council would be selected by a community-wide nomination and election procedure, organized separately from the two age sectors. Special efforts would be made in the nomination procedures to identify influential youth who are not "part of the establishment" of adult-organized programs. The political ward system might be used as voting units for such elections. This youth council would have continuing responsibility for identifying the organizations in the community which have the right to elect youth representatives to the council. The council would have the responsibility for developing its own constitution, rules, and procedures with the consultation and review described below.

As we look in on an imaginary youth council in operation, we find that it is engaged in two types of action. First, it is very involved in participating in and attempting to influence various adult-initiated functions of community life. These include political activities such as the operations of the city council, city planning commission, and the city human relations commission. The council has succeeded in getting representation on the planning commission and is pushing for action by the city council on direct election of youth members to the city council at the next election. It has been successful in getting representation on the Chamber of Commerce, and on the Council of Social Agencies, and is holding discussions with the Board of Education about appropriate representation.

In the second major type of activity the youth council is engaged in initiating, promoting, and supporting various activities initiated by youth themselves. They have established a clearinghouse for seeking and describing volunteer and paid job activities. A subcommittee of the council has responsibility for continually working with all types of employment, with special emphasis on a gradient of opportunities from occupational exploration for younger youths to part-time apprenticeships and full-time jobs for older youths. In collaboration with the school system, the council has organized a training program for child-care services. The training program certifies trainees as being prepared for various types of paid and volunteer services in relation to young children, i.e., baby-sitting, community recreational programs, family aid, helpers in Head Start and day-care centers, home-centered and school-centered tutorial programs, etc. The Executive Committee of seven members, elected from the council, is conducting a survey of the organizations and agencies in the community which do and do not have elected representation of youth on their policy-making boards. They are conducting interviews of youth serving in such capacities in an attempt to identify the most effective agency policies for youth participation and the types of training needs which should be taken into account in organizing training programs for those youth elected to such leadership positions. The Executive Committee is also planning to present, on the agenda of the next council meeting, two new proposals for the funding of developmental projects. One of these proposals will be addressed to the City Council and the other to the State Youth Commission which channels funds from the State Legislature and from federal funds, all of which are earmarked for promotion of youth participation and citizenship activities. The Executive Committee is also considering what to do about a proposed petition to the school board concerning more adequate representation of youth on the school board. Also on the next council agenda is the election of a representative to the State Youth Council.

A special Task Force of teen-agers and adults, initiated by the Youth Council, is planning a twice-a-year weekend laboratory on problems of intergenerational communication and collaboration. For each weekend 60 participants are accepted, half adult and half youths, from the larger number of applications. The weekend experience includes intergenerational sensitivity training and work on the diagnosis and the solution of problems of collaboration between the adult and youth sectors of the community. The last weekend lab had a very active and productive confrontation around interracial relations, and the issues of providing more adequate opportunities for employment and job training for racial and ethnic minorities in the community. The free and open communication initiated very healthy steps of action. More and more segments of the adult community are giving evidence of "hearing youths," and reciprocally, youth are demonstrating more and more initiative in taking responsibility for using problem-solving patterns other than those of destructive conflict. The Youth Council has provided a major context for the development of communication and reciprocal influence between those youth leaders who have been actively "antiestablishment" and those who have achieved their leadership in the context of active collaboration with the adult sectors of the community.

The funding of youth council programs, and the secretariat and office functions, are derived from several sources. At the local community level an annual budget as well as special project requests are presented to the city council. In addition, the council solicits and receives contributions from the private sector: agencies, businesses, and individuals. One local foundation is also an active contributor. At the state level, councils can apply for financial resources which come from both state and national sources, public and private. These funds are identified in the sections below. The council has responsibility for the stewardship of the funds. It is incorporated, makes annual reports to the public, and has an advisory panel of experts in the community.

Within the local political structure, the youth council is not subordinate to the city council. But there is an advisory panel of resource persons nominated by the Executive Committee of the council and approved by the City Council. This panel is chosen with an eye to providing resource expertness in the various areas of council activity and providing professional help in the areas of program evaluation and training activities.

No doubt, the major problems which this imaginary council faced in its own development and maintenance were distrust on the part of some sectors of the adult community about the council's competence to handle funds and program development responsibility; suspicion and testing of the council by those sectors of the youth community which suspect the council of having a conformist orientation to the adult establishment; and issues relating to the working relationship and influence patterns between the younger and older age groups participating in the membership of the council. Hopefully, in reality, all three of these problems would be openly faced. It is clear that such problems could be solved and that they should be because the payoff from such an enterprise would be so great to the community and to youth.

2. *The development and operation of the youth organization program at the state level*: We envision the youth participation program at the state level as operating somewhat like the following example:

Half of the State Youth Council is composed of elected representatives from local, community youth councils. The other half is selected by state level departments, associations, and agencies which have a youth constituency or are organized and run by youth. The two age sectors of youth are equally represented on the State Council just as they are on the local councils. Youth on this Council are representatives from such state groups as the State Education Association, the State Labor Council, the State Council of Churches, the State 4-H program, the State Association of Student Councils, etc.

One of the important functions of the State Council is carried out by the Task Force on Exchange of Information, which conducts a continuing survey of innovative practices in the youth participation programs of communities. As soon as a practice is identified, a field site visit is made to get description of the practice for documentation and dissemination. A newsletter describing the innovative practices is distributed four times a year along with data on how to secure additional information. The members of all youth councils are convened yearly at a state conference. Resource persons from other states actively participate in these work conferences which focus on the improvement and evaluation of programs of youth participation.

Another important function of the State Office and State Council is the providing of consultant help to the youth of any community who want to explore the development of a youth council or to improve the functions of an already existing council. An active program of interpretation and outreach to new communities around the state is maintained by teams of youths. These teams actively implement the State Council's policy of seeking opportunities to make presentations to student councils and other types of local groups of youths who might become the initiators of community programs.

The State Council also has an active program of contact and collaboration with the junior colleges and university campuses throughout the state to stimulate and maintain participation of the youth who have left their community base for a campus-community. Many significant youth-initiated programs have been sparked by collaboration between youth on campus and youth in the community.

The State Council secures the funding for its operation from an appropriation from the State Legislature, from contributions from companies and other organizations of the private sector throughout the state, and from matching federal funds. The State Youth Commission serves in an advisory capacity to the State Youth Council. This Commission has representatives from the professional, lay, political, and economic sectors of the state structure and from the sectors of HEW. A subcommittee of the State Youth Commission collaborates with the Executive Committee of the Youth Council in conducting a continuing evaluation of the Youth Council operation and helps with the yearly publication of the Annual Evaluation and Program Review. They also participate in the annual selection of outstanding projects of community youth councils to be nominated for state and national recognition.

3. The development and operation of the National Office of Youth Participation and Citizenship: To continue our imaginative illustrations, we move to a youth participation program on the national level. The National Office is established as a private-public corporate agency receiving support from several federal agencies as well as contributions from the private sector. The Board of Directors includes representatives from federal agencies, national youth-serving organizations, state and local youth councils as well as other outstanding public figures. Half of the Board of Directors is youth, elected by youth.

The National Office and Executive Committee maintain an active program of communication between states and active liaison with federal programs relevant to youth participation (e.g., Head Start, Neighborhood Youth Corps, Vista, Comprehensive Mental Health Programs, Model Cities Programs, Peach Corps, etc.). The National Office establishes and maintains a series of panels to review funding proposals for youth participation projects and proposals, and recruits applied research, documentation projects, evaluation programs, and innovations in new areas of youth participation and training. Most of the projects involve a matching of funds from local community and state level groups.

The National Office has developed a directory of consultants on the development of youth participation programs and intergenerational conflict resolution. They are a referral network distributed throughout the country. The National Office also conducts a very active program of influence and collaboration with the mass media. One very important aspect of this collaboration is the program of public recognition and awards to groups of youths throughout the country who contribute important services to the community and to their own growth and development.

In the actual implementation of such a National Agency, planners would, no doubt, face important initial problems such as patterns of funding and the question of federal political control, as well as the question of the representation and power of youth in national policy making. But one foundation has already been laid. The principle is recognized and accepted that the development of youth resources is a concern of the total national community—both the public and the private sectors. Also, there is a growing realization that youth participation in policy making and operations is just as relevant at the national level as at the state and local levels. But it will be important to prevent any one federal agency from having the primary sense of interest and responsibility, because the stimulating of youth involvement and participation is such a crucial aspect of federal programs in many agencies.

One of the major policy questions which should be worked on at the national level is whether it is possible to develop the concept of "national service credits" and "educational participations credits." The first idea has to do with the question of whether it is desirable and possible to develop the concept of universal service experience for all youth (Eberly, 1968). The second concept revolves around the question of whether it is feasible to develop the educational relevance of these experiences in such a way that participation in community service projects of various kinds can be accredited as relevant educational development experience. For more and more millions of young people, the part-time work experience, and training and participation as a volunteer, are playing a major part in the career of student and learner.

Concluding note

The development of a national and strongly financed program of youth participation is a priority recommendation of Task Force VI. The design described is now in the realm of social science fiction, but from our extensive discussions of it, we believe the elements described at the local, state, and national levels are feasible and adaptable. It is our urgent hope that work toward the development of such a program can begin immediately. The crisis in intergenerational alienation and the revolt of youth demands urgent concern and action.

II. *The Education of the Young for Participation and Growth into Adult Roles*:

Education for motivated commitment and competent participation in schooling must start early and continue throughout the life-span. One of our most serious failings revolves around the assumption that we can successfully provide the opportunities for participation and collaboration of youth without concomitantly providing the incentives. Continuous programs of education must be started early in order to foster the desire for responsible and competent participation. As the Task Force reviewed the program of learning activities provided in the typical school system, they identified a number of serious weaknesses in relation to training for motivated participation.

During the early school years the learning environment is primarily a feminine environment. The curriculum activity and classroom settings are more challenging to girls than boys. Thus, girls are generally more successful in school than boys, reap more rewards, and experience fewer failures.

Also, the school environment stimulates competition and exploitation between peers and between the younger and older pupils. Research indicates that a very frequent meaning of "helping each other" is "cheating." In such an environment there is a great deal of failure and an overemphasis on external criteria of success, such as grades and teacher evaluation.

A related weakness is that the school is typically a rigidly structured environment where children are classified by age level and by group ability. The restrictions on interaction between children of different age levels and different social backgrounds greatly reduce the opportunities for children to benefit from each other's resources. The school, as a learning environment, tends to be isolated from family and community resources. Few community adult resources are brought into the school to help with the educational program and, conversely, there is little utilization of family and community settings as sites for learning activities. Throughout the total school program there is remarkably little opportunity for children to participate in goal setting and in the management of their learning experiences.

At all age levels, the educational program is designed with a major emphasis on verbal cognitive learning and performance skills. The program design neglects value education and the development of value inquiry skills. It places very little emphasis on, and provides little training for, the relating of cognitive ideas to the actions taken in daily living or in preparation for the future. This verbal-cognition-centered curriculum is most frustrating for children from families of low socioeconomic and restricted educational background. But this curriculum, even for middle-class children, is almost devoid of any means which will prepare the young for coping with value conflicts, affective commitments, and action responsibilities.

A final observation is that the student is faced daily with a variety of teachers who have diverse educational philosophies, teaching techniques, and subject matter specialties which they attempt to promote. Few students receive any support and training in the task of integrating this variety of inputs into a meaningful self-identity and into a basis for self-initiated learning efforts.

There are many important innovations available. In its analysis of the educational situation, Task Force VI also identified the fact that many vital processes of change in our educational system are being stimulated by numerous new programs of educational research and development. But there is a very serious weakness in this whole flurry of national activity. Most significant innovations in educational practice are developed by a creative educator, or small team, in a particular school system. Typically, very little emphasis is placed on documentation or evaluation of the innovation, and there are no developed procedures or networks for the diffusion of significant innovation to other classrooms, school buildings, and school systems. So even where significant new educational approaches are developed, they seldom become a significant resource for very many educators and their students.

Illustrative priorities for development and/or dissemination: With our focus on training for motivated youth involvement and participation, Task Force VI emphasizes the need for the development and diffusion of the following types of illustrative educational activities in the elementary and secondary school programs.

1. Putting human relations into the curriculum: Most of the attitude toward learning, and motivation to learn or to reject learning, derives from social interaction with fellow students and with adults in teacher roles. In work contexts such as industry, there is a general recognition that the human relations within the work setting are important phenomena to study, to understand, and to learn how to improve. The school curriculum, from the first grade on, should include the study of human relations—of the phenomena of conflict, motivation, competition, cooperation, and the development of social supports for individual learning and achievement. Several existing innovations have demonstrated that first graders can study, with great profit, the issues of conflict and of conflict resolution; that young elementary school children can study and develop the group norms of support and encouragement in place of the current norms which inhibit and discourage motivation to learn and to be individualistically creative. Total elementary classrooms have conducted curriculum projects to study their use of time in the classroom, to evaluate the efficiency of their learning, and to study the extent to which they make use of the teacher, other adults, and older students as needed resources in the learning process. Such classroom projects have utilized the social science methods of the interview, observation, and the questionnaire to collect and assess data about the relevant human relations phenomena in the classroom.

At the secondary school level, the content of applied behavioral science is rarely in the curriculum. At an age level when there is high sensitivity to, and concern about, social relations and norms of group conformity the students should be receiving the technical training and conceptual tools which will allow them to become knowledgeable masters of their own social processes as work and learning groups, both in and outside of the school environment. Every high school student should be involved in studying the high school culture, the relations between the generations, and his own role as a learner and actor in both the school environment and in the larger community.

2. Learning through teaching: One of the most important recent innovations in educational theory and practice has been the development of cross-age teaching and learning projects. Older children and youths provide teaching services to younger children, with training and consultation from adult collaborators. The initial findings of a survey of some of these models was conducted for Task Force VI by the National Commission on Resources for Youth (see Kohler, 1968).

One rather consistent finding from these projects is that older children and youth—even near dropouts, dropouts, and others who are alienated by the learning process—respond with enthusiasm to the opportunity to collaborate with adults in being a teacher of the younger. These youth recognize the need for competence in this task and willingly accept training, become motivated or remotivated to their own learning activities as a student, and are receptive to teaching relationships with adults. A second discovery is that many youths who become involved in this type of apprenticeship develop an active interest in the occupational roles of teaching, social service, and other human service functions. This is the expanding area of occupational roles in the future.

Other discoveries from these early projects is that many young children are much more open to receiving help from older peers than from adults and that the older peers serve as models in the formation of attitudes toward work and learning in school. Such responses are particularly striking among older helpers and younger recipients in the most alienated and underprivileged learning environments.

As the result of these observations Task Force VI recommends that, from at least the third grade on through high school, the role of cross-age educational helper should be a continual part of every student's learning experience. Besides the great benefit of developing the motivations and skills of participation, and of educational motivation and achievement, the use of this type of educational manpower resource would help every teacher individualize her instruction in order to meet the varied needs of her pupils.

3. Collaboration in the planning and management of the learning environment: As we indicated in the description of the youth participation model, a crucial element in the planning and management of the learning environment is the involvement of youth. Besides planning, this includes decision making and the operation of their own learning situations. To do this successfully and responsibly requires training. We have identified several innovations in this area which seem worthy of development and dissemination.

In one important innovative program every student who is elected or selected for leadership function automatically becomes a member of a continuing leadership training program. This program includes weekly "leadership clinics" where youth analyze leadership problems, practice leadership skills, share in planning for leadership initiative, and learn the strategies of involving others more effectively in ongoing activities. In one instance, this leadership development program has become a part of the school curriculum and regular periods are devoted to this activity, with full recognition that this is a unique opportunity to learn some of the important content of the behavioral sciences.

Another very important innovation is one where a number of student and faculty committees have the responsibility for developing the goals, criteria, and the tools for evaluating the various aspects of the educational program. Becoming involved in thinking through "what we are trying to accomplish" and "what is the evidence that we are making progress" is one of the most effective procedures for developing competent collaboration and responsible initiative.

A third model for training for participation engages students who are in the process of becoming leaders to serve an apprenticeship with older students in leadership roles.

These are just three illustrations of the types of programs which schools and other agencies must provide in order to give youth an opportunity to develop the values, knowledge, and skills which will allow them to competently and successfully collaborate with adults and to take creative and responsible initiative, even though they may be frequently confronting adults' plans and expectations. We're not proposing training the young to "go along with adults." Rather, we would train the young to be more competent and responsible in their interactions with adults. Only in this manner can they more effectively influence their own educational situation.

4. Preparation for adult roles: Most children and youth are given very little opportunity, as part of their school curriculum, to observe, to identify with, and to have a program of developmental steps in learning the skills of such adult roles as effective citizen, productive worker, mature loving spouse, and intelligent parent. It is the consensus of Task Force VI members that learning about and training for these roles should become an integral part of the curricular design. One most important aspect of this recommendation is that the many relevant and significant existing innovations should be identified and made available for adoption and adaptation by all school systems and communities.

In the area of occupational orientation and preparation, one drastically needed development is a comprehensive linking of the school with the community through the development of an inventory of "placement situations" where students can observe and relate to adults engaged in all types of work. Volunteer work experiences of significant depth, duration, and variety need to be an integral part of the educational system in the upper elementary and early secondary school years, and should be succeeded by opportunities for in-school and out-of-school apprenticeships. The school system itself can provide many opportunities for work exploration, such as those described above where older students assist in the teaching of younger children. During all these explorations of occupational roles the students need to have a continuing "practicum seminar" which provides opportunities for them to relate their field experiences to their class work, to share and analyze personal experience, value problems, inquiries about the world of work, analysis of occupational trends, and the connections between the requirements of various types of occupational roles and academic training.

Perhaps the most serious omission in the school curriculum is the lack of preparation for marriage and for the parental role. One very interesting innovative program has boys and girls volunteering in pairs to act as aides in day-care center, kindergarten, and first grade. In their continuing practicum seminar, these children have opportunities to discuss the complementary roles and resources of males and females in the process of helping children grow.

Another significant innovative effort has senior high school students functioning as sex education counselors in the junior high. In addition, there is a continuing workshop seminar which provides the counselors opportunities to work through their own attitudes, values, knowledge, and skills so that they can be competent helpers of younger students. In the community, there are many needs for volunteer manpower resources which could provide opportunities for collaborative partnerships of boys and girls and for anticipatory explorations of child-care responsibility.

Providing significant opportunities to learn the role of active, committed citizenship implies the need for programs of training for school citizenship and for participation as a young citizen of the community. This idea has been developed more fully in the previous section on youth participation. The additional emphasis here concerns the need for a focus within the curriculum on training for social problem solving.

5. *Training for Social Problem Solving*: In almost any newspaper one can find illustrations where neighbors or fellow citizens avoid the confrontation and coping with a problem requiring corrective action. It is our observation that much of this avoidance, caution against risking action, and fearful turning away from confronting problems can be changed if individuals receive training in problem-solving skills and have successful experience with collective, collaborative action. This training must be provided for every child as a part of his weekly curriculum.

In one such curriculum, students work in teams of four to identify some problematic aspect of their environment which they would like to try to solve. In their laboratory course they study methods of action research and problem solving, carry through a diagnosis of their own particular problem-solving situation, develop a strategy for problem solving—with consultation from the faculty member and their peers—carry through action efforts, and evaluate the success of their efforts. The students also study the larger context of social problem solving in their community and society, critically analyze the adequacy of the existing social problem-solving efforts, and delineate the types of needed improvement. Continual efforts are made to help each student see himself as a problem-solving citizen, to develop in him conceptions of problem-solving potentiality and responsibility, and to provide him with the necessary tools and skills for realistic and effective problem solving. Such a focus on problem solving provides the student opportunities for integrating many aspects of curricular subject matter. But more importantly, this focus provides the youth with opportunities to develop personal identity as a being capable of taking initiative, of participating in contributing to collective efforts, and of involvement in creative coping with the social process.

These five areas for innovative effort identify a priority which Task Force VI believes must be promoted vigorously if we are to prepare and motivate young people to participate actively and successfully in their own programs of growth and development and to make a continuing and responsible contribution to their community. As such, these efforts provide a positive alternative to involvement in alienated and destructive counteraction.

III. *The Coordination and Integration of Community Socialization and Educational Services*:

Child-rearing, and the socialization and education of the young, is one of the major functions of the community. There are a variety of interest groups in the community that participate in this function, e.g., public schools, churches, recreation and leisure-time agencies, social control agencies, youth employment activities, the political socializers, therapeutic and remedial services, the various service groups with special child and youth projects, and, of course, the families and informal peer groups of which the young are a part. Most of the young, as they grow up, are exposed to a continuous barrage of the adult community's disconnected and uncoordinated attempts to guide and direct their development. The time and energy of some children and youth are competed for actively by a large variety of programs, while other young ones are relatively avoided and neglected. The particular input the young receive, or do not receive, is dysfunctional in terms of meeting their growth and educational needs. This fragmentation of helping efforts exists for individual children, for natural groupings of children within the neighborhood, and for family units. The typical splitting of age groups in programming fragments the natural neighborhood groupings, just as the typical splitting of family services results in a disregard of the family as a natural service unit. Doing something creative about this basically destructive and inefficient process requires effort at several levels. Examples of innovative changes and practices at four levels of effort are given below to illustrate the patterns of needed change.

1. At the level of the direct workers with the young: One innovative program utilizes a "regional team" composed of a police officer, a family social agency representative, a visiting teacher, an academic counselor, and a school administrator. Working out of a junior high school, this team meets each morning to review all student absenteeism and problem referrals from teachers and parents. The team endeavors to arrive at a collective decision in regard to the need for additional diagnosis and the appropriate actions which various members of the team should take in relation to the young ones who have been called to their attention. The team also provides consultation services to the elementary schools in their region.

Another very significant innovation is the "direct workers seminar," which involves, in regular weekly meetings, those adults who work with the same population of children, whether as volunteers or professionals (e.g., club worker, teacher, Scout master, big brother, church youth worker, etc.). The foci during these seminars are on the exchange of techniques of working with children and on the sharing of information about children and current program efforts. With the aid of the seminar leader, those involved develop a procedure for interviewing each other about specific educational processes. The procedure has, in practice, included dittoing the most interesting innovations for the purpose of developing individual notebooks. Those involved in this seminar exchanged invitations to observe each other and to aid in the evaluation and improvement of helping efforts. The volunteers and professionals, from both public and private programs, have expressed amazement and excitement in discovering how much their individual contributions mutually increase each worker's repertoire of program skills.

2. At the level of policy and program leaders: One of the most interesting innovations at the level of policy and program leadership involved a nomination procedure intended to identify key policy and program leadership in all sectors of the socialization community, both public and private. Once identified, these leaders were interviewed to determine what kinds of children and youth they hoped would result from their program efforts. The interviewees were asked to identify the major factors which they felt caused desirable and undesirable outcomes in child-youth development, and were asked to delineate their conception of the division of labor and responsibility within their own agency or organization as well as that of the other socialization and educational agencies in the community. This resulted in the discoveries that very diverse objectives existed in relation to desirable youth development outcomes, that very conflicting ideas were held about the causes of normal and deviant development, and that disparate ideas also existed concerning the division of labor and responsibility with the community. A seminar of the key policy and program leaders was convened to review and discuss the data, to identify issues of competition and neglect, to explore needs for collaboration on developmental projects, and the needs for pooling and coordinating resources (e.g., in the area of recruiting and training volunteers).

As a result of the sessions of this cross-community leadership seminar a "committee for continuing community leadership training" was developed. This committee sponsors two weekend laboratories yearly for the educational and socialization leaders from all segments and occupational levels of the community. These laboratories are financially self-supporting. A professional training staff, recruited from outside the community, is employed to work with the core of trainers who have been developed within the city. Each laboratory is oversubscribed in terms of applications for membership.

3. At the level of youth influentials: In both the direct worker and policy leaders seminar, the participants identified the significant influence of the dominant young people within the youth culture. The seminar members expressed their frustration concerning the charismatic antiadult youth leaders who disrupted or subverted the existing programs and were often able to provide their peers with more attractive, but "antisocial," alternative activities. Other young people were identified as independent but constructive leaders within the youth culture. The adults in both seminars nominated the most influential young people, both prosocial and antisocial, from the various community subcultures—racial, ethnic, social class, male, female, different age levels. A cross section of the most influential young nominees was invited to create a youth leaders' seminar with consultation from a young social scientist. The young leaders worked through considerable initial suspicion and intragroup hostility in weekend laboratories where conflicts were openly explored. The major task was determined to be the need to develop training sessions for teachers, parents, and other adult leaders in order to help them understand youth's point of view and to practice communicating with youth about important problems. As a consequence, they developed and operated a very exciting program of invitation sessions.

4. At the level of state and federal programs and legislation: Efforts at local comprehensive planning and coordination of services for children and youth are usually hindered by the divisive influence of "categorical programs" of funding which are maintained by state and federal legislation and divisions of program effort. These categorical programs reinforce the divisiveness already existing within the structure of the community organization of services. It is imperative that federal and state leadership experiment with the development of innovations in legislation and administration which will support, rather than inhibit, structures and mechanisms of collaborative planning and operation of community programs concerned with child and youth care education and socialization. Most of the current programs are divisive in a number of ways. For example, by imposing professional employment standards, present practices prevent the development and use of indigenous personnel. Through restricting the target population such programs fragment rational approaches to client systems, such as blocks, neighborhoods, and families. In addition, programs are divisive through such policies as ignoring the involvement of indigenous leadership in policy-making and program guidance; the channeling of funds within the community to separate and competitive channels; and the divisive separation of public and private sector efforts, and the work of professionals and volunteers. Task Force VI believes that major attention and energy should be devoted to developing new patterns of federal and state effort which will promote, support, and give guidance to creative coordination in the planning and delivery of services at the local community level.

IV. *The Recruiting and Training of Volunteers and Paraprofessionals:*
Our knowledge as to what is needed for the optimal development of each child is steadily increasing. It reveals the need for a variety of resources, both stimulative and supportive, which are supplemental to that provided by improved parenting. At the same time, the expanding need for diverse types of social services has far outstripped the production of professional manpower and the present limits of tax-supported funding resources. One of the most significant directions toward a solution of this problem is the systematic development of a vast pool of volunteer manpower resources and the development of a large body of paraprofessional helpers. The feasibility of this development is supported by the great and increasing amount of leisure time among much of our population and by the fact that important psychological needs are fulfilled by volunteer participation in human service activities. The recent recognition that volunteers and paraprofessionals can promote many significant functions previously regarded as sacrosanctly "professional" represents a major breakthrough; however, the trend is stymied by professionals' lack of training to function as trainers of volunteers, and sometimes by the fact that this trend is perceived as a threat to the professionals' role status. Task Force VI believes that the development and dissemination of new approaches to recruiting and training of volunteers and paraprofessionals in the area of child care and youth development is one of the most important developments for the future. A few illustrations of these directions for the future are identified below.

1. *The community volunteer bureau:* One of the most significant in-

novations is the total community volunteer manpower bureau which uses a variety of survey techniques to identify the skills, interests, and availability of community manpower resources. The bureau collaborates with all community agencies and programs in their efforts to obtain the needed manpower. This bureau also assumes leadership in helping agencies coordinate their volunteer training programs so that the most effective use can be made of professional trainers from the various agencies. In addition, the volunteer bureau serves as a clearinghouse for volunteer help. A limited example of this type of function has been adopted in a large school system. Here, one full-time central office person conducts a continuing inventory of the skills and interests of the schools' clientele—both parents and children. The relevant information is made available to principals and teachers in the various school buildings, and helps them orient and utilize parents as sources for special educational sessions.

2. *Leadership teams:* Typically, agencies have found it difficult to recruit indigenous adults as volunteers in socioeconomic-deprived areas where "imported" middle-class volunteers, often of a different race, have great difficulty relating to the children and youth with whom they must work. In one significant experiment in a ghetto area, leadership pairs and trios were created and trained. These teams were composed of one or two indigenous adults and one "imported" adult. Not only did they provide effective services to "deprived" children, but they participated in a mutual learning experience which served as a motivating force toward continuing volunteer service.

3. *Mobility from volunteer to paraprofessional:* In the school situation many children volunteer to be educational helpers to the younger students. Some of these volunteers become quite proficient as young educators and develop occupational interests in the area of teaching. They are provided opportunities for positions as part-time paraprofessional aides in manning the academic skills labs and working as part-time paid assistants to the teaching staff in classroom activities and extracurricular activity programs. A similar operating program recruits and uses parent volunteers, and, from the assessment of their work, recruits paraprofessional aids as more central members of the educational team. In another youth-serving agency, professionals spend a major part of their time training paraprofessionals and volunteers who carry on the direct work with the children and youth. There is a very extensive program of training and consultation. Almost all of the paraprofessionals have been recruited from the volunteer staff.

4. *Developing professional, paraprofessional, volunteer teams:* One school system has developed the concept of an "educational team" to work with large groups of pupils. This educational team consists of two professionals (i.e., teachers), three or four adult paraprofessional aides, and seven or eight adult and older youth volunteers. In the inservice training

program, this group has been trained as a team and has participated in daily team sessions in which their work is planned, coordinated, and evaluated. Full-time professional teachers find team work an exciting professional-growth experience. In addition, they feel that it is a far more significant way to provide differentiated and individualized instruction for their students.

Nationally, there are thousands of promising innovations in this crucial area of recruiting and use of volunteer and paraprofessional manpower. Task Force VI believes that priority should be assigned to the evaluation, documentation, and active dissemination of the most significant patterns in the development of such professional-paraprofessional-volunteer teams.

V. *The Inservice Training of Parents:*

Most scientists and professionals agree that the performance of parents is the most important set of influences upon the child during his early years. For most children the importance of this parental influence continues through adolescence. In spite of this general agreement about the importance of competent parent behavior there is a conspicuous lack of both preservice and inservice parent-training in our society. Of all the socialization agents, parents receive the most blame for inadequate performance but the least training and supplementary aid. Task Force VI believes that the development of both preservice and inservice parent-training is a top national priority. Central and state funding should provide the same impetus for research and innovation in parent education as that provided in the development of educational programs for children. The widespread diffusion of good parent education programs should have an enormous, rapid, and widespread impact on the problems of childhood, child mental health, antisocial behavior, and motivation to learn and to work. The brief illustrations below are examples of important directions for developmental work.

1. Community-wide family development council: In one instance a council has been developed of all the agencies which have programs relevant to family development and parent education. The school system is of course an important member of this council. The agencies pooled manpower resources to provide professional staff for the extensive program of training volunteer pairs (often a husband and wife team) who conduct an extensive program of parent education sessions. These pairs were recruited from all segments of the community and play an active role in the outreach efforts to attract parents to the training programs which are sponsored by all types of agencies and organizations. There is a program of public service recognition for the efforts of the volunteer pairs. The mass media collaborated in public recognition of significant inventions in parent and family practice which were identified and documented as part of the parent education program. Every effort is made to recognize and reward parenthood as one of the most important social practice roles which contributes to community and society. One section of this program focuses on teen-agers and young people before marriage and provides a wide variety of preparental laboratory experiences.

2. *The parent communications coordinator in the school:* One school system has recognized that collaboration of parents and teachers is necessary for the learning, motivation, and achievement of the young and that such congruence of efforts is the most important way to develop a truly educational community. To achieve such collaboration, each school building houses a parent communications agent whose major job is to develop teamwork between parents, teachers, and students. The coordinator does not function in a social service capacity but as a linkage between parents, teachers, and generations. The coordinator works closely with a steering committee of parents and teachers in the development of team-building activities which focus on communications skills, educational support of the child's work at home, and evaluative feedback to the teaching staff from parental observations at home. Emphasis is placed on the planning of joint parent-teacher conferences with particular children and on meeting with student leaders to work on problems of intergenerational collaboration. Another important area of activity has been the development of a census of parent resources designed so that parents can volunteer their expertness and teachers can be informed in order to initiate requests for parent collaboration in various educational activities.

3. *The intergenerational laboratory:* In one school system a team of human relations trainers were secured to conduct a weekend laboratory within the community. During Saturday and Sunday, parents, teachers, and students met in problem-solving groups to develop sensitivity and collaboration within the education community. Part of the time parents, teachers, and students met in heterogeneous groups. In the remaining time they clarified issues in their own homogeneous groups as well as planned intergroup communication systems. An evaluation of this program indicated that the intergenerational laboratory opens up important areas of conflict and communication.

4. *The family unit laboratory:* One agency has successfully innovated day-long family development laboratories for total family units. During part of the day, the parents and children of diverse age levels have separate group activities. These include a discussion of family life problems from their age-specific point of view, preparation of role-playing episodes designed for observation and discussion of problems, and the planning for feedback discussions within their own family units. During another part of the day each family unit meets separately for problem-solving discussions, with consultation as desired. During another period, families of comparable composition meet in family clusters to exchange innovations in family life

practice and to brainstorm ideas for possible improvements. The staff provides time periods for participants to observe demonstrations of family unit functioning, such as family decision making, methods of coping with typical crisis episodes, and also helps family members with problems. A variation on the family unit laboratories is the couples laboratory for husbands and wives. Children are not present at these sessions, and the focus is more on male-female role relations, openness of communication, division of labor, and collaboration in child-rearing and family management.

These are only a few examples of the many significant innovations in parent and family life education. Such programs have received very little community or nationwide support, evaluation, or dissemination.

The equally important area of preservice education has been referred to in discussing needed innovations in the secondary school curriculum. Comparable program development is needed in junior colleges, community colleges, and for those young people of the community who have dropped out of high school or who have moved into employment situations as single young adults. One very exciting innovation provided training sessions on interpersonal relations for engaged couples.

VI. *Programs for the Preschool Child:*

This Task Force does not believe that women who are on welfare should be made to go to work if they are employable, but it cannot adopt the moralistic view that "woman's place is in the home" and thus ignore the existing social and personal needs. The Task Force believes that nursery schools[3] must be recognized as a "public utility." These schools should be made available to *all* children on a number of bases, e.g., half day or less, full-day arrangements for the working mother, and round-the clock short- or long-term care during periods of family crisis or emergencies.

Sound psychological studies indicate that people need periods of relief from situations which require heavy emotional investment, and that periodic relief allows them to function more competently. It is hard to imagine any role which requires a heavier emotional investment than that of child-rearing. Because our nation has consistently refused to take this matter seriously, untrained and overburdened parents, their children, and the total nation suffer. More than 4 million preschoolers have mothers who work. Yet American women remain almost totally deprived of satisfactory child-care arrangements during their working hours. It has been estimated that 38,000 children under the age of six are left without any care while their mothers work and that twice as many are looked after by a brother or sister only slightly their senior.

3. The Universal Nursery Schools concept was primarily the contribution of Dr. Robert H. Alway and Dr. Robert L. Leon, members of Task Force VI.

The recent amendments to the Social Security Act, which require welfare mothers to enroll in job training or go to work, will force federal and state governments to set up some large-scale system of day care. There is a great danger, and likelihood, that this will lead to cheap custodial arrangements, since the goal is not to provide educational services for children, but to cut welfare costs. It is absolutely essential that nursery schools be expertly staffed and programmed—both as parent and child education centers. This argues against rushing into a nationwide compulsory program which could not be adequately staffed. The emphasis should be on a widespread distribution of well-planned "start-up demonstrations" with plans for snowballing the program by helping groups in communities to mobilize their efforts in this direction. Professional leadership can recruit, train, and supervise the potentially creative resources of paraprofessionals and volunteers in every community. This should include older youth who need this type of service opportunity for their own growth into parenthood roles.

As in our proposed design for a community-wide parent education council, it would seem imperative to develop a community-wide interagency mechanism for the leadership and coordination of child-care program development. Well-trained, well-supervised volunteers and paraprofessionals—old and young—are the basic resource which is needed, and which is plentifully available for such a crucial national effort.

VII. *The Training of Professional Child and Youth Workers:*

Currently, educators, social workers, therapists, health workers, and child care specialists are being trained in an era in which new research knowledge and the development of newly innovated practices are rapidly changing. Unfortunately the curriculum and the faculty of most professional schools are not closely linked with behavioral scientists and behavioral knowledge resources. Nor are they closely linked to the front-line agencies and organizations in those fields which are most active in innovating new models of practice. This means that the young professionals in training are unlikely to be specifically prepared for the job priorities they will encounter in the field. The challenge facing the professional school is to train for creative adaptability, an orientation toward continued professional learning, and general basic skills of practice. Also, as significant problems become more clearly delineated and sophisticated they become more complex. As a result, there is an increasing awareness of the need for interdisciplinary and interprofessional teams that can work in close collaboration. Training for this type of teamwork is seldom included in professional education. The newly conceived role of the professional as the leader of a team of paraprofessionals and volunteers is also a development primarily in the future, and one for which professionals are not adequately prepared. One of the major implications of this emerging role is that the training of professional workers must focus on the individual's ability to train others. Knowing how to do the job well is not an adequate preparation for training others in the attitudes, values, and skills required for competent job performance. The brief examples which follow characterize only a small sample of the priority innovations in this area of the development and maintenance of professional competence.

   1. *Undergraduate apprenticeship opportunities:* In our colleges today, undergraduates are demanding more and more involvement in and contact with the "real community," as contrasted to the campus. A program in one university provides an illustration of this trend—a trend which will certainly increase in the future. In this instance, one thousand undergraduates are engaged in a wide variety of "outreach projects" in a community. This project is part of the social science course program and is under the supervision of graduate students who undergo a continuous training program intended to prepare them for the leadership of the undergraduates. These experiences provide exciting preprofessional training, are effective recruiting experiences for students interested in applied social science professional careers, and provide a great fieldwork opportunity for the graduate students who are in professional training.

   2. *Interprofessional team experience:* In one graduate school a practicum on the professional skills of planned change serves graduate students from the schools of education, public health, mental health, social work, business administration, public administration, nursing, medicine, law, and journalism. As a part of this laboratory course, students work in cross-professional teams on field projects related to agency and community problems which require the pooling of cross-professional skills. Thus the students mutually contribute to their crucially important general education in applied behavioral science.

   3. *Integrating field experience and class work:* Task Force VI foresees that the future boundaries between campus and off-campus activities and those between classwork and fieldwork will become less sharply defined. In one innovative design, fieldwork is viewed as providing the springboard and guidance for classroom work in a weekly "integration seminar." In this design, fieldwork experiences are conceptualized and transformed into inquiry problems which require a literature search, the use of professors as expert informants, and the development of research problems.

   4. *The continuing job clinic:* Turning our attention from preservice professional training to inservice learning activities, one interesting illustration in a school system is the weekly teaching problems clinic where the inservice training consultant helps the staff members legitimize the open sharing of professional teaching dilemmas, the search for improved knowledge and skills, and the sharing of innovated practices between peers.

   5. *Training for trainership:* In one youth-serving agency the profes-

sionals participate in a workshop on the techniques of training volunteers. Subsequently, they hold a practicum session with their consultant where they review the training designs and techniques currently used in preparing volunteer groups.

6. *Training the staff unit or job family:* As evidenced by studies, inservice professional education is hampered by the professional's perception as to his colleague's evaluation of his work and performance. This, in turn, affects the professional's attitudes and performance. Therefore, one of the most significant areas of innovation in the training of professionals today is the focus on teams rather than on individuals. As an example, in one school system the inservice training groupings are composed of groups of colleagues who work together most closely in the same building. These job families make up a training group which focuses on skills relating to problem solving and sensitivity to interpersonal relations on the job.

7. *Training materials for continuing special education:* From the current trends, we predict that, in the future, a great wealth of training materials for continuing professional self-education will be available on video tapes, audio tapes, and record players with study guide materials. One set of materials which is currently available provides records and study guides so that individual professionals may work on their own at home, materials for self-initiated groups of colleagues, and provides a leadership guide for those who conduct inservice training programs.

These examples illustrate existing innovations in professional education which, if disseminated appropriately, would make a great difference in the quality of childhood education and youth development programs. Presently, existing innovations are improving the quality of programs in one restricted spot—in one agency, one community, or in one institution of higher education.

VIII. *The Self-Renewal Model—Guidelines for the Development and Maintenance of the Illustrative Programs Described Above:*

The most pervasive theme in the Task Force VI discussions has been that of adaptability to change, including the preparation and initiative to make contributions to change as the future unfolds.

We concluded that one of the greatest needs for education at all age levels—from the day-care center to the graduate school—is an emphasis on training for self-initiated learning and for competent change-ability or self-renewal. But we also concluded that the development of this type of competence is futile unless our outreach and dissemination procedures spread this competence to wider and wider circles of the total population through an extensive and high-quality program of diffusion of frontier knowledge and practice. Therefore, we return, at the end of this section on illustrative priorities, to the area of self-renewal. Below we illustrate briefly some of the dimensions of these ideas of self-renewal and spread.

1. *Long-range planning:* Modeling its design after the successful pro-

cedure of several corporations, one educational organization established a long-range planning mechanism which included an office of long-range planning. This office employed a full-time staff person to function as a secretariat for a long-range planning subcommittee of the board, a long-range planning interdepartmental committee of top staff members, and a consultant panel of several long-range planning specialists who were particularly knowledgeable in the area of social change. These groups met and worked both separately and jointly. In order to stimulate vigorous long-term perspectives, the director of long-range planning provided a continuous flow of information to the board and staff committees.

2. Mechanisms of research development and training: One large school system has recognized that it cannot and should not support basic research, except when it serves as a host site for university institute research teams. This school system's focus on research consists of continuous scanning and retrieving efforts in order to gain significant new knowledge relevant to the system's program missions. Twice a year the department of research and development organizes for the staff research retrieval and derivation conferences which focus on specific operating problems of the agency. For each selected problem a research retrieval paper is prepared summarizing the most relevant generalizations from new research. The staff spends two days, with scientist consultation, deriving implication statements for themselves from these research generalizations, moves from these implication statements to alternative action possibilities, and then selects the most feasible and preferred alternatives for the development of new action programs.

One creative socialization agency continuously maintains a program of developmental projects by identifying interested and competent task forces within the staff to test the feasibility of new ideas and to develop demonstrations. The remaining staff evaluates the possible adoption or adaptation of the new idea.

It is becoming ever more clear that it is neither desirable nor feasible to separate research and development from training activities within the educational and socialization agencies. If new practices are to be employed effectively by the agency, staff training and retraining must be a major part of the adoption process. Several educational systems have adopted the model of an "inside-outside training team," which is composed partly of trainers from other agencies and from university settings, and partly from competent training staff members within the organization. This model is based on the recognition that there is often more readiness to accept influence for change from outside consultants but a much greater probability that training will be focused on, and relevant to, the specific needs of the organization if key insiders have a significant hand in designing the training program.

3. Dissemination and utilization mechanisms: Basically the worth of any new idea rests in its dissemination and utilization. The development of one well-planned day-care center model is of little relevance to society unless the design is publicized and used appropriately in a multitude of settings. We can think of dissemination as both importing new practices from outside the community or agency and as spreading significant practices from one worker to another within the community or agency. One agency has developed a provocative design for importing new practices. First, the agency appoints a review and evaluation panel which secures documentation about innovative practices. The panel then has the responsibility for generating evaluation scales to rate the relevance, feasibility, adaptability, general applicability, and theoretical soundness of each new practice and subsequently to derive a set of recommendations concerning the exploration and potential adoption of particular new techniques.

One school system achieves the internal spread of new practices by conducting regular "sharing of practices" institutes. In these institutes innovative teachers serve as informants for groups of interested colleagues who previously have been provided with a group interview schedule designed to help them effectively use the innovator as an information source so that they can evaluate the desirability and feasibility of a particular practice. Provisions are also made for consultation from, and visitation to, the innovative practitioner.

4. Evaluative review: It is of little avail to have good objectives and good designs for implementation unless the entire staff is involved in a program of continuous evaluation and revision (i.e., renewal) of the ongoing efforts designed to meet the needs of children and youth. One small community developed a very creative model which provides for an annual review of the community's educational and youth development resources and programs. A series of task forces are responsible for collecting the relevant evaluation data through interviews, observations, and other techniques. In a full-day institute the reports are collated, reviewed, and compared with the data of the previous year. The results are used as a basis for discussing priorities essential to future efforts and goals, which in turn are to be evaluated and reviewed during the next year.

Another youth-serving organization uses the evaluative mechanism of the twice-a-year visiting committee which is composed of approximately five resource persons. This committee spends several days observing the program, reviewing documents, interviewing the staff, comparing their observations with their previous visit and conducting a feedback session with the staff, reviewing their observations, their diagnosis of needed changes, and devising their recommendations for desirable objectives.

We believe that the dimensions of self-renewal and continuity are vital to the design of any program of any educational and socialization agency. Only through such mechanisms can we cope with the tragic lag in our current efforts. The nature and complexity of our society are changing much too rapidly for us to permit ourselves the luxury of a slow rate of evolution in solving the problems which pertain to the mental health of our children and youth.

RECOMMENDATIONS AND STEPS TOWARD IMPLEMENTATIONS

Scattered through our analysis of the child welfare and youth development situation are recommendations for change and for development of new patterns. Recommendations, of course, can be well derived and valid and still never be useful. To be useful they must be addressed to the appropriate ears, and must convey not only policy ideas but also concrete images of appropriate and feasible steps of action.

1. Some of our recommendations are most appropriately designed for the attention of legislators and other federal and state policy makers.

2. Other recommendations are most appropriately the concern of professional leaders who are implementing the programs of educational and welfare policies.

3. Still other recommendations will perhaps be of greatest relevance and interest to the research and development specialists, and others.

4. Some of our recommendations are of greatest relevance to those professionals who are concerned about the development of new models of practice which will deal with priority needs.

5. Other readers, who may be primarily interested in the personal stimulation for reflection provided by these analyses of Task Force VI, can reflect on their own present role and practices and explore implications for new directions.

We have tried to call your attention to the recommendations relevant to different leadership stances.

References

THE POOR IN THE AFFLUENT SOCIETY

"A Look at Problems in Prenatal Service Programs." *Currents in Public Health* 5:1–4, May 1966.

ABLON, JOAN, ROSENTHAL, A. H., and MILLER, D. H. *An Overview of the Mental Health Problems of Indian Children.* Prepared for Task Force IV, The Joint Commission on Mental Health of Children, Inc., December 31, 1967. (Mimeo.) 88 pp.

ACHESON, R. M., AND FOWLER, G. B. "Sex, Socioeconomic Status, and Secular Increase in Stature: A Family Study." *British J. of Prev. and Soc. Med.,* 18:25–34, January 1964.

ACHESON, R. M., FOWLER, G. B., AND JANES, M. D. "Effect of Improved Care on the Predicted Adult Height of Undernourished Children," *Nature,* 194:735–36, May 26, 1962.

Action for Mental Health. The Final Report of the Joint Commission on Mental Illness and Health. New York: Basic Books, 1961, p. 175.

THE ADVISORY COUNCIL ON PUBLIC WELFARE, "Having the Power, We Have the Duty." Report to the Secretary of Health, Education, and Welfare, Washington, D.C., June 29, 1966.

ALBEE, G. W. "Manpower Myths and Realities. One Possible Answer: A New Mental Health Worker in a New Institution." Draft of a speech prepared for the Annual Meeting of the National Association for Mental Health, Palmer House, Chicago, November 16, 1967.

ALMOND, G. A., AND VERBA, SIDNEY. *The Civic Culture.* Princeton, N.J: Princeton University Press, 1963, pp. 89, 116, 188, 302–06.

ALSOP, STEWART. "A Conversation with Catfish," *The Saturday Evening Post,* February 24, 1968.

The American Federationist. "The Urban Crisis * an Analysis * an Answer." Amer. Federation of Labor and Congress of Industrial Organizations. Washington, D.C.: October 1967, pp. 1–4.

ANDERSON, E. H., AND LESSER, A. J. "Maternity Care in the United States: Gains and Gaps," *Amer. J. Nursing* 66:1539–44, July 1966.

ANDERSON, O. W. "Infant Mortality and Social Cultural Factors, Historical Trends and Current Patterns," in *Patients, Physicians and Illness*, E. G. Jaco (ed.). New York: The Free Press of Glencoe, 1958.

ARNOLD, M. R. " 'You Won't Find Many Are Dying from Hunger' But Malnutrition Problem Is Very Real, Even in Bountiful Iowa," *The National Observer*, August 7, 1967.

BAGDIKIAN, B. H. "It Has Come to This," *The Saturday Evening Post*, August 10, 1968, pp. 20–21.

BAKER, J. Q., AND WAGNER, N. N. "Social Class and Treatment in a Child Psychiatry Clinic," *Archives of Gen. Psychiat.*, 14:129–33, February 1966.

BAUM, O. E., FELZER, S. B., D'ZMURA, T. L., AND SHUMAKER, ELAINE. "Psychotherapy, Dropouts, and Lower Socioeconomic Patients," *Am. J. Ortho.*, 36:629–35, July 1966.

BEAN, L. L., MYERS, J. K., AND PEPPER, M. P. "Social Class and Schizophrenia: A Ten-Year Follow-up," in *Blue-Collar World: Studies of the American Worker*, Arthur B. Shostak and William Gomberg (eds.). Englewood Cliffs, N.J.: Prentice-Hall, Inc., 1964.

BEISER, MORTON. "Poverty, Social Disintegration and Personality," *J. Soc. Issues*, 21, No. 1:56–78, January 1965.

BENNETT, FAY. "The Condition of Farm Workers and Small Farmers in 1967." Report to the Board of Directors of National Sharecroppers Fund. (Mimeo.). 4 pp.

BRAGER, G. "Improving Services for Street-Corner Youth," in *Mental Health of the Poor*, Frank Riessman, Jerome Cohen, and Arthur Pearl (eds.). New York: The Free Press of Glencoe, 1964.

BRESLOW, LESTER. "New Partnerships in the Delivery of Services—A Public Health View of the Need," *Am. J. Pub. Health*, 57, No. 7:1094–99, July 1967.

BRILL, N. Q., AND STORROW, H. A. "Social Class and Psychiatric Treatment," *Archives of Gen. Psychiat*, 3:340, 1960.

BURCHINAL, L. G. *Rural Youth in Crisis*: Facts, Myths, and Social Change. Washington, D.C., U.S. Department of Health, Education, and Welfare, 1965.

BURGESS, M. E., AND PRICE, D. O. *An American Dependency Challenge*. Chicago: Amer. Pub. Welf. Assoc., 1963.

BURNHAM, DAVID. "Misconduct Laid to 27% of Police in 3 Cities' Slums," *The New York Times*, July 5, 1968.

CABAK, VERA, AND NAJDANVIC, R. "Effect of Undernutrition in Early Life on Physical and Mental Development," *Archives of Diseases of Children*, 40:532–34, October 1965.

CAPLOVITZ, DAVID. *The Poor Pay More*. New York: The Free Press of Glencoe, 1963.

Carnegie Quarterly, 14, Fall 1966.

The Challenge of Crime in a Free Society. A report by the President's Commission on Law Enforcement and Administration of Justice. Washington, D.C.: U.S. Government Printing Office, February 1967.

CHASE, H. C. "White-Nonwhite Mortality Differentials in the U. S." *Health, Education, and Welfare Indicators*, U.S. Department of Health, Education, and Welfare, June 1965, pp. 27–37.

CHEIN, ISIDOR, GERARD, D. L., LEE, R. S., AND ROSENFELD, EVA, with the collaboration of D. M. Wilner. *The Road to H*. New York: Basic Books, Inc., 1964.

CHILMAN, C. S. *Growing Up Poor*. Welf. Admin. Pub. No. 13, U.S. Department of Health, Education, and Welfare, Div. of Research. Washington, D.C., 1966.

CLARK, KENNETH. *Dark Ghetto: Dilemmas of Social Power*. New York: Harper & Row, 1965.

COHEN, W. J. "The Elimination of Poverty: A Primary Goal of Public Policy," in Poverty in Plenty, G. H. Dunne (ed.). New York: P. J. Kennedy and Sons, 1964.

COLE, N. J., BRANCH, C. H. H., AND ALLISON, R. B. "Some Relationships Between Social Class and the Practice of Dynamic Psychotherapy," *Am. J. Psychiat*, 118 (11):1004–1012, May 1962.

COLEMAN, JAMES, *et al.* "Equality of Educational Opportunities." U.S. Office of Education, Washington, D.C., 1966.

COLES, ROBERT. "Psychiatrists and the Poor," in *Poverty in the Affluent Society*, H. H. Meissner (ed.). New York: Harper & Row, 1966, pp. 181–90.

————. "The Easy Chair: Children of the American Ghetto," *Harper's Magazine*, September 1967, pp. 16–22.

COLL, B. D. "Deprivation in Childhood: Its Relation to the Cycle of Poverty," *Welfare in Review*, March 1965. 9 pp.

Comparative Study of Negro and White Dropouts in Selected Connecticut High Schools, State of Connecticut, Comm. on Civil Rights, Hartford, 1959, pp. 11–13.

CONGER, J. J., AND MILLER, W. C. (with the assistance of R. V. Rainey, C. R. Walsmith, and the Staff of the Behavior Research Project). *Personality, Social Class, and Delinquency*. New York: John Wiley & Sons, 1966.

CORNELY, D. A. "Urban Medical Blight," *J. of Pediatrics* 61:499–500, September 1962.

"Correction in the United States. A Survey for the President's Commission on Law Enforcement and Administration of Justice by the National Council on Crime and Delinquency." *Crime and Delinquency*, Vol. 13, No. 1: 64–65, 77, 82–86, 131, 252–53, January 1967.

COUNCIL OF ECONOMIC ADVISORS, *Economic Report of the President, 1967*. Washington, D.C.: U.S. Government Printing Office, 1967.

CRAVIOTO, JOAQUIN, DELICARDIE, E. R., AND BIRCH, H. G. "Nutrition and Neurointegrative Development: An Experimental and Ecologic Study," *Pediatrics,* 38:319–72 (Part II), August 1966.

CRAVIOTO, JOAQUIN, AND ROBES, BEATRIZ. "Evolution of Adaptive and Motor Behavior During Rehabilitation from Kwashiorkor," *Amer. J. of Ortho.*, 35:449–64, April 1965.

DAVID, MARTIN, *et al. Educational Achievement: Its Causes and Effects.* Ann Arbor: University of Michigan, Survey Research Center, 1961, p. 2.

DAYTON, N. A. "The Real Goal in the Education and Training of the Mentally Retarded in Residential Schools," *Mental Retardation*, 1, 1963, pp. 136–37, 182ff.

DELGADO, G., BRUMBACK, C. L., AND DEAVER, E. B. "Eating Patterns Among Migrant Families," *Pub. Health Reports*, 76:349–55, April 1961.

DEUTSCH, MARTIN. "The Disadvantaged Child and the Learning Process," in *Education in Depressed Areas*, A. H. Passow (ed.). New York: Bureau of Publications, Teachers College, Columbia University, 1963, pp. 163–79.

"Diphtheria in the United States—1963: Epidemiologic and Immunologic Challenges," *Clin. Pediatrics* 5:10A–23A, September 1966.

DOHRENWEND, B. P., AND DOHRENWEND, B. S. "The Problem of Validity in Field Studies of Psychological Disorder," *J. Abn. Psychol.*, Vol. 70, No. 1:52–69, 1965.

DONNELLY, J. F. *et al.* "Maternal, Fetal and Environmental Factors in Prematurity," *Am. J. of Obstetrics and Gynecology*, 88:918–31, April 1, 1964.

"Don't Get Sick," *The New Republic*, September 21, 1968, p. 13.

DUHL, L. J. (ed.). *The Urban Condition: People and Policy in the Metropolis.* New York and London: Basic Books, Inc., 1963.

DYBWAD, GUNNAR. "Trends and Issues in Mental Retardation," in *Children and Youth in the 1960s*. Survey Papers prepared for the 1960 White House Conference on Children and Youth © 1960 by the Golden Anniversary White House Conference on Children and Youth, Inc., pp. 263–73.

EICHORN, R. L., AND LUDWIG, E. G. "Poverty and Health," in *Poverty in the Affluent Society*, H. H. Meissner (ed.). New York: Harper & Row, 1966, pp. 172–80.

ELLISON, RALPH. "The Crisis of Optimism," in *The City in Crisis* (Ellison, Young, Gans, with an introduction by Bayard Rustin). A. Philip Randolph Educational Fund. © 1966 by Ralph Ellison, pp. 6–26.

ERIKSON, ERIC. "Identity and the Life Cycle," *Psychol. Issues*, 1 (1), 1959.

FARIS, ROBERT, AND DUNHAM, H. W. *Mental Disorders in Urban Areas.* Chicago: University of Chicago Press, 1939.

FERMAN, L. A., KORNBLUH, J. A., AND HABER, ALAN (eds.). *Poverty in America—A Book of Readings.* Ann Arbor: University of Michigan Press, 1965.

FILER, L. J., JR., AND MARTINEZ, G. A. "Intake of Selected Nutrients by Infants in the United States: An Evaluation of 4000 Representative Six-Month-Olds," *Clin. Pediatrics,* 3:633–45, November 1964.

Final report to the Secretary of Labor, United States Department of Labor on *OMAT Project P 3–63*. Washington, D.C.: Nat. Inst. of Labor Educ. Youth Employment Program, July 1965. 89 pp.

FITZPATRICK, J. P., GOULD, R. E., FERNANDEZ, MARTA, POLKA, JOSEPH, *et al. Mental Health Needs of Spanish-Speaking Children in the New York City Area.* Paper prepared for Task Force IV, The Joint Commission on Mental Health of Children, April 26, 1968. 158 pp.

FRIEND, J. G., AND HAGGARD, E. A. "Work Adjustment in Relation to Family Background," *Applied Psychol. Monog.* No. 16. Stanford, Calif.: Stanford University Press, 1948.

FURMAN, S., SWEAT, L., AND CROCETTI, G. "Social Class Factors in the Flow of Children to Outpatient Psychiatric Facilities," *Am. J. Pub. Health,* 55:385–92, March 1965.

GANS, H. J. *The Urban Villagers.* New York: The Free Press of Glencoe, 1962.

————. "The Case for Federal Help," in *The City in Crisis.* A. Philip Randolph Educational Fund, 1966, pp. 39–60.

GILBERTSON, W. E., AND MOOD, E. W. "Housing, the Residential Environment and Health—A Re-evaluation," *Am. J. Pub. Health,* 54:2009–2013, December 1964.

GLADWIN, THOMAS. "Social Competence and Clinical Practice," *Psychiatry: J. for the Study of Interpersonal Processes,* Vol. 30, No. 1:30–43, February 1967.

GOLENPAUL, DAN (ed.). *Information Please Almanac Atlas and Yearbook, 1967,* 21st ed. New York: Simon and Schuster. © November 1966 by Dan Golenpaul Associates, p. 597.

GORMAN, MIKE. "A National Program for Emotionally Disturbed Children." Speech delivered to the 20th anniversary meeting, Dade County Children's Psychiatric Center, Sheraton-Four Ambassadors Hotel, Miami, Florida, January 10, 1968.

GREENBLATT, M., LEVINSON, D. J., AND WILLIAMS, R. H. *The Patient and the Mental Hospital.* New York: The Free Press of Glencoe, 1957, chap. xxxvi.

GRIGGS, R. C., SUNSHINE, IRVING, NEWILL, V. A. NEWTON, B. W., BUCHANAN, STUART, AND RASCH, C. A. " Environmental Factors in Childhood Lead Poisoning," *J. Am. Med. Assoc.,* 187:703–707, March 1964.

GROOTENBOER, E. A. "The Relation of Housing to Behavior Disorder," *Am. J. Psychiat.,* 119:469–72, November 1962.

GRUENBERG, ERNEST. "Mental Disorders: Epidemiology." Reprinted from *International Encyclopedia of the Social Sciences.* New York: The Macmillian Co. and The Free Press of Glencoe. © 1968 by Crowell Collier and Macmillan, Inc., pp. 149–56.

HAASE, WILLIAM. "The Role of Socioeconomic Class in Examiner Bias," in *Mental Health of the Poor,* Frank Riessman, Jerome Cohen, and Arthur Pearl (eds.). New York: The Free Press of Glencoe, 1964.

HARRINGTON, MICHAEL. "The Technological Revolution: Human and Social Ecology." Paper presented to the Opening General Session of the 23rd National Conference on Higher Education, sponsored by the Amer.

Assoc. for Higher Education, Chicago, March 3, 1968. (Mimeo.) 6 pp.

HAUGHTON, J. G. "Nutritional Anemia of Infancy and Childhood," *Amer. J. of Pub. Health*, 53:1121–26, July 1963.

Health Care and the Negro Population. National Urban League, Inc., 1965. 2nd printing, 1966.

HEBER, R. *A Manual of Terminology and Classification in Mental Retardation*, 2nd ed. *Amer. J. of Mental Deficiency Monograph Supplement*, April, 1961.

———. "Research on Personality Disorders and Characteristics of the Mentally Retarded," in *Mental Retardation Abstracts*, Vol. I, 1964. U.S. Department of Health, Education, and Welfare, pp. 304–25.

HENRY, JULES. "White People's Time, Colored People's Time," *Trans-Action* 2: No. 3:31–34, 1965.

HERZOG, ELIZABETH, AND SUDIA, C. E. *Family Structure and Composition.* Prepared for the Institute on Research Toward Improving Race Relations of the NASW, August 13–16, 1967, Airlie House, Warrenton, Virginia.

HIGBEE, EDWARD. *Farms and Farmers in an Urban Age.* New York: The Twentieth Century Fund, 1963.

HOFF, WILBUR. "Why Health Programs Are Not Reaching the Unresponsive in Our Communities," *Pub. Health Reports*, 81:654–58, July 1966.

HOLLINGSHEAD, A. B., AND REDLICH, F. C. *Social Class and Mental Illness: A Community Study.* New York: John Wiley & Sons, 1958.

"How Do You Fight It?" *The New Republic*, September 3, 1966, pp. 6–7.

HUNDLEY, JAMES M. *et al.* "Height and Weight of First-Grade Children as a Potential Index of Nutritional Status," *Am. J. Pub. Health*, vol. 45, pp. 1454–61, 1955.

Hunger, U.S.A. A Report by the Citizens' Board of Inquiry into Hunger and Malnutrition in the United States. Washington, D.C.: New Community Press, 1968.

HUNT, R. "Occupational Status in the Disposition of Cases in a Child Guidance Clinic," *International J. Soc. Psychol.*, 8:199–210, 1962.

HUXLEY, MATTHEW. "So, Who Listens?" Paper presented at the Annual Meeting of the American Orthopsychiatric Association, New York, March 17–20, 1965. 14 pp.

INGALLS, T. H., TIBONI, E. A., AND WERRIN, MILTON. "Lead Poisoning in Philadelphia, 1955–1960," *Archives of Environmental Health*, 3:575–79, November 1961.

JACKSON, L. P. *Telling It Like It Is!* Washington, D.C.: Communicating Research on the Urban Poor (CROSS-TELL), Health and Welfare Council of the National Capital Area, October 1966, 16 pp. (B).

JACOBZINER, HAROLD. "Lead Poisoning in Childhood: Epidemiology, Manifestations, and Prevention," *Clin. Pediatrics*, 5:277–86, May 1966.

JACOBZINER, HAROLD, RICH, HERBERT, BLEIBERG, NINA, AND MERCHANT, ROLAND. "How Well Are Well Children?" *Am. J. Pub. Health and the Nation's Health*, 53:1937–52, December 1963.

JEFFERS, CAMILLE (with an introduction by Hylan Lewis). *Living Poor: A*

Participant Observer Study of Choices and Priorities. Ann Arbor: Ann Arbor Pub., 1967.

JOHNSTON, H. L. "Medical Needs and Responsibilities for Children of Migrants," in *Medical Responsibilities for the Displaced Child: Report of the Forty-third Ross Conference on Pediatric Research.* Ed. by Spencer G. Thompson. Columbus, Ohio: Ross Laboratories, 1963, pp. 27–30.

JOINT INFORMATION SERVICE OF THE AMERICAN PSYCHIATRIC ASSOCIATION AND THE NATIONAL ASSOCIATION FOR MENTAL HEALTH. *Fifteen Indices: An Aid in Reviewing State and Local Mental Health and Hospital Programs.* Washington, D.C., 1968, pp. 10, 12.

JONES, E. E., AND SCHENDEL, H. E. "Nutritional Status of Selected Negro Infants in Greenville County, South Carolina," *Amer. J. of Clinical Nutrition,* 18:407–12, June 1966.

KELLER, SUZANNE. "The Social World of the Urban Slum Child: Some Early Findings," *Am. J. Ortho.,* 33:823–31, October 1963.

KENNEDY, W. A., *et al. A Normative Sample of Intelligence and Achievement of Negro Elementary School Children in the Southeastern United States.* Mono. Soc. Res. Child Development 28, No. 6 (Ser. No. 90), 1963.

KIRK, S. A. *Early Education of the Mentally Retarded.* Urbana: The University of Illinois Press, 1958.

KNOBLOCK, HILDA, AND PASAMANICK, BENJAMIN. "Environmental Factors Affecting Human Development," *Pediatrics,* 26:210–18, 1960.

KOHLBERG, LAWRENCE. *The Modifiability of Mental Health in School Years.* Paper prepared for Task Force II, The Joint Commission on Mental Health of Children, Inc., 1968.

KOHN, M. L. "Social Class and Parent-child Relationships: An Interpretation," *Amer. J. Soc.,* 68:471–80, 1963.

KOZOL, JONATHAN. *Death at an Early Age: The Destruction of the Hearts and Minds of Negro Children in the Boston Public Schools.* Boston: Houghton Mifflin Co., 1967. © Jonathan Kozol, 1967.

LANGNER, T. S. "A Survey of Psychiatric Impairment in Urban Children." Unpublished MS. (A Preliminary Analysis, 1967.)

LANGNER, T. S., AND MICHAEL, S. T. *Life Stress and Mental Health.* The Midtown Manhattan Study. (Thomas A. C. Rennie Series in Soc. Psychiatry, Vol. II.) New York: The Free Press of Glencoe, 1963.

LARNER, JEREMY. "The New York School Crisis," in *Poverty in America,* L. A. Ferman, J. L. Kornbluh, and Alan Haber (eds.). Ann Arbor: The University of Michigan Press, 1966. © The University of Michigan Press, 1965, pp. 370–84.

LEE, P. R. "Health and Well-being," *The Annals of the Amer. Academy of Pol. & Soc. Science. Social Goals and Indicators for American Society,* Vol. II, September 1967, pp. 193–207.

LEWIN, KURT. "Self-Hatred Among Jews," in *Resolving Social Conflicts,* K. Lewin (Gertrude W. Lewin, ed.). New York: Harper, 1948, pp. 186–200.

LEWIS, HYLAN. "Child Rearing Concepts Among Low Income Families."

Child Rearing Proj., Health and Welfare Council of National Capital Area. Washington, D.C.: Washington Center for Metropolitan Studies, 1961.

————. "The Family: Resources for Change," in *The Moynihan Report and the Politics of Controversy*, L. Rainwater and W. L. Yancy (eds.). Cambridge: MIT Press, 1967a, pp. 314–343.

————. *Culture, Class, and Poverty*. Washington, D.C.: (CROSS-TELL) Health and Welfare Council of the National Capital Area, 1967b.

LIDDLE, G. P., AND ROCKWELL, R. E. "The Kid with Two Strikes Against Him." The City of New York, Dept. of Personnel, Municipal Cooperative Educ. and Work Program. (Adapted from *Safety Education Magazine*, December 1963). (Mimeo.) 4 pp.

LIEBOW, ELLIOT. *Tally's Corner*. Boston: Little, Brown & Co., 1966.

MACKENZIE, J. P. "Alabama Concedes a Point in Arguing for Welfare Curb," *The Washington Post*, April 25, 1968.

MALONE, CHARLES A. "Safety First: Comments on the Influence of External Danger in the Lives of Disorganized Families," *Am. J. Ortho.*, 36, No. 1:3–12, 1966.

————. "Some Observations on Children of Disorganized Families and Problems of Acting Out." *J. Child Psychiat.* 2:22–49, 1963.

Manpower Report of the President, U.S. Department of Labor, Washington, D.C.: U.S. Govt. Printing Office, April 1968.

MAYER, J. "The Nutritional Status of American Negroes," *Nutrition Review*, June, 1965, pp. 161–64.

MCDERMOTT, J. F., HARRISON, S. I., SCHRAGER, JULES, AND WILSON, PAUL. "Social Class and Mental Illness in Children: Observations of Blue-Collar Families," *Amer. J. Ortho.*, 35:500–508, 1965.

MCKINNEY, J. P., AND KEELE, R. "Effects of Increased Mothering on the Behavior of Severely Retarded Boys," *Am. J. Men. Deficiency*, 67:556–562, 1963.

MILBRATH, L. W. *Political Participation*. Chicago: Rand, McNally, 1965, pp. 64–72, chap. iii.

MILLER, S. M. "The American Lower Class: A Typological Approach," *Soc. Res.*, 31:1–22, 1964.

MILLER, S. M., AND REIN, MARTIN. "Poverty and Social Change," *Amer. Child*, National Committee on Employment of Youth, March 1964.

MILLER, S. M., REIN, MARTIN, ROBY, PAMELA, AND GROSS, BERTRAM M. "Poverty, Inequality, and Conflict," *Social Goals and Indicators for American Society*, Vol. II, *The Annals*, Vol. 373, September 1967, pp. 16–52.

MINUCHIN, SALVADOR, AND HALEY, JAY. *Broadening the Unit of Intervention*: *The Delivery of Services According to an Ecological Model*. Paper submitted to Task Force II of the Joint Commission on Mental Health of Children, Inc., 1967.

MINUCHIN, SALVADOR, MONTALVO, BRAULIO, GUERNEY, B. G., JR., ROSMAN, B. L., AND SCHUMER, FLORENCE. *Families of the Slums*: *An Explora-*

tion of Their Structure and Treatment. New York and London: Basic Books, Inc., 1967.

MISCHEL, W. "Father-Absence and Delay of Gratification: Cross-Cultural Comparisons," *J. Abnormal and Soc. Psych.*, 63:116–24, 1961.

MOOD, E. W. "Health and Housing Programs in Large Cities, U.S.A." Paper presented at the Annual Meeting of the Amer. Publ. Health Assoc., Chicago, October 19, 1965. 13 pp.

MOYNIHAN, D. P. *The Negro Family (the Case for National Action).* Washington, D.C.: U.S. Department of Labor, Office of Policy Planning and Research, 1965.

MYERS, JEROME, BEAN, L. L., AND PEPPER, M. P. "Social Class and Psychiatric Disorders: A Ten-Year Follow-Up," *J. Health and Human Behavior* 6:74–79, Summer, 1965.

NATIONAL COMMITEE AGAINST MENTAL ILLNESS, INC. *What Are the Facts About Mental Illness in the United States?* Washington, D.C.: 1966.

NIEMEYER, J. H. Prepared statement of John H. Niemeyer, President of Bank Street College of Educ., New York City, before the Subcommittee on Govt. Research, Committee on Govt. Operations, U.S. Senate, Washington, D.C., April 23, 1968, relative to Human Resources Development.

NORMAND, WILLIAM, FENSTERHEIM, HERBERT, TANNENBAUM, GERALD, AND SAGER, C. J. "The Acceptance of the Psychiatric Walk-in Clinic in a Highly Deprived Community," *Am. J. Psychiat.*, 120:533–39, December 1963.

O'CONNELL, D. J. "The Fourth National Conference on Indian Health." National Committee on Indian Health of the Association on American Indian Affairs, New York City, November 30 and December 1, 1967. (Mimeo.) 4 pp.

ORNATI, OSCAR. *Poverty amid Affluence.* A report on a research project carried out at the New School for Social Research. New York: Twentieth Century Fund, 1966, pp. 54, 60, 70–76, 79–80, 90–91, 113–15.

ORSHANSKY, MOLLIE. *Who's Who Among the Poor: A Democratic View of Poverty.* Washington, D.C.: U.S. Department of Health, Education, and Welfare, Soc. Sec. Admin., 1965.

———. "The Shape of Poverty in 1966." Reprinted from the *Social Security Bulletin.* Washington, D.C. Department of Health, Education, and Welfare, Soc. Sec. Admin., March 1968.

OVERALL, J. E., AND ARONSON, H. "Expectations of Psychotherapy in Patients of Lower Socioeconomic Class," *Amer. J. Ortho.*, Vol. 33:421–30, April 1963.

PAKTER, J., *et al.* "Out-of-Wedlock Births in New York City," *Am. J. Pub. Health,* 51:846–65, June 1961.

PARKER, SEYMOUR, AND KLEINER, R. J. *Mental Illness in the Urban Negro Community.* New York: The Free Press of Glencoe, 1966.

PAVENSTEDT, E. A. "A Comparison of the Child-Rearing Environment of Upper-Lower and Very Low-Lower Class Families," *Amer. J. Ortho.*, 35:89–98, 1965. (c) 1965 by the Amer. Ortho. Assoc., Inc.

PCMR Message. "The Retarded Victims of Deprivation." (An address by Whitney M. Young, Jr., Executive Director, National Urban League, to the 18th Annual Convention of the National Association for Retarded Children, Portland, Ore., Oct. 19, 1967.) The President's Committee on Mental Retardation, Washington, D.C.: January 1968 (7).

PECK, H. B., AND KAPLAN, S. R. "A Mental Health Program for the Urban Multiservice Center." November 15, 1967. (Mimeo.) 29 pp.

PETERSON, J. *The Comparative Abilities of White and Negro Children. Comp. Psychol. Monogr.,* 5:1–141, 1923.

PETTIGREW, T. A. *A Profile of the Negro American.* Princeton, N.J.: D. Van Nostrand Co., Inc., 1964.

PLENTY, RUTH. *Reading Ability and High School Dropouts.* Bureau of Publications, Teachers College, Columbia University, 1956.

POLIER, J. W. "The War vs. Poverty, the Role of Law and Mental Health," *Am. J. Ortho.,* 36:86–94, October 1966.

———. *The Rule of Law and the Role of Psychiatry.* Baltimore: Johns Hopkins Press, June 1968.

POLLACK, E. S. "Monitoring a Comprehensive Mental Health Program: Methodology and Data Requirements." Presented at the University of Wisconsin Post-Graduate Program in Medical Education, Madison, Wisconsin, June 1966.

Public Health Bulletin No. 19, U.S. Department of Health, Education, and Welfare, 1960.

Public Health Service Publication No. 1375, U.S. Department of Health, Education, and Welfare, *Mental Health in Appalachia.* "Problems and prospects in the central highlands." 1964.

REDLICH, F. C. "Discussion of Dr. H. Jack Geiger's Paper," in *Poverty and Mental Health,* Milton Greenblatt, P. E. Emery, and B. C. Glueck, Jr. (eds.). Psychiatric Research Report #21, Amer. Psychiatr. Assoc., January 1967, pp. 66–67.

REDLICH, F. C., HOLLINGSHEAD, A. B., ROBERTS, B. H., ROBINSON, H. A., FREEDMAN, L. Z., AND MYERS, J. F. "Social Structure and Psychiatric Disorders," *Am. J. Psychiat.,* 109 (10):729–34, April 1953.

REIFF, ROBERT, AND RIESSMAN, FRANK. *The Indigenous Nonprofessional.* A strategy of change in community action and community mental health programs, report No. 3 Nat. Inst. of Labor Educ. Mental Health Prog., November 1964.

Report of the National Advisory Commission on Civil Disorders. (Special introduction by Tom Wicker.) New York: Bantam Books, March 1968. © 1968 The New York Times Co.

RICHARDSON, S. A. "The Social Environment and Individual Functioning," in *Brain Damage in Children,* H. G. Birch (ed.). Baltimore: The Williams and Wilkins Co., 1964, pp. 100–117.

RIESSMAN, FRANK. "The Human Service Worker: A New Careers Movement," *Employment Serv. Rev.,* March–April, 1967, pp. 4–6.

RIESSMAN, FRANK, AND SCRIBNER, SYLVIA. "The Under-Utilization of Mental

Health Services by Workers and Low Income Groups: Causes and Cures," *Am. J. Psychiat.*, 121: 798–801, February 1965.

RIESSMAN, FRANK, COHEN, JEROME, PEARL, ARTHUR (eds.). *Mental Health of the Poor*. New York: The Free Press of Glencoe, 1964.

RODMAN, HYMAN. "The Lower-Class Value Stretch," in *Poverty in America— A Book of Readings*. L. A. Ferman, J. L. Kornbluh, and Alan Haber (eds.) Ann Arbor: University of Michigan Press, © 1965. 2nd Printing, 1966, pp. 270–85.

RODMAN, HYMAN, AND GRAMS, PAUL. "Juvenile Delinquency and the Family: A Review and Discussion," in *Task Force Report: Juvenile Delinquency and Youth Crime*. Washington, D.C.: U.S. Government Printing Office, 1967, pp. 188–221.

ROSEN, B. M., KRAMER, MORTON, AND REDICK, R. W. *Utilization of Psychiatric Facilities by Children: Current Status, Trends, Implications*. Biometry Branch, National Institute of Mental Health. Paper prepared for Task Force V, The Joint Commission on Mental Health of Children, Inc., 1968.

SCAMMON, R. M. "Electoral Participation," *Social Goals and Indicators for American Society*, Vol. I, *The Annals*, Vol. 371, May 1967. Table 4, p. 63.

SCHAFFER, L., AND MEYERS, J. K. "Psychotherapy and Social Stratification: An Empirical Study of Practice in a Psychiatric Out-Patient Clinic," *Psychiatry*, 17:83–94, 1954.

SCHNEIDERMAN, LEONARD. "Social Class, Diagnosis and Treatment," *Am. J. Ortho.*, 35:99–105, January 1965.

SCHORR, A. L. "How the Poor Are Housed," in *Poverty in America—A Book of Readings*, L. A. Ferman, J. A. Kornbluh, and Alan Haber (eds.). Ann Arbor: University of Michigan Press, 1965, pp. 215–34.

———. "Housing Policies and Poverty," in *Poverty in the Affluent Society*, H. H. Meissner (ed.). New York: Harper & Row. 1966a, pp. 151–64.

———. *Poor Kids*. New York, London: Basic Books, Inc. © Alvin Schorr, 1966b.

SCHORR, BURT. " 'Suicidal' Rural Gap in the Poverty War," *Wall Street Journal* (New York), February 20, 1968.

SCHRODER, CLARENCE. "Mental Disorders in Cities," *Am. J. Soc.*, July 1942, pp. 40–47.

SCHUEY, A. M. *The Testing of Negro Intelligence*. Lynchbury: Bell, 1958.

SCHULMAN, IRVING. "Iron Needs in Infancy," *Pediatrics*, 4:516–17, October 1962.

SEMPLE, R. B., JR. "Alabama Loses Welfare Appeal. 'Substitute Father' Rule is Voided by High Court," *The New York Times*, June 18, 1968.

SEXTON, PATRICIA. *Spanish Harlem: Anatomy of Poverty*. New York: Harper & Row, 1965.

SHAPIRO, S., JACOBZINER, H., DENSEN, M., AND WEINER, L. "Further Observations on Prematurity and Perinatal Mortality in a General Population and in the Population of a Prepaid Group Practice Medical Care Plan," *Am. J. Pub. Health,* 50:1304–17, September 1960.

SIEGEL, EARL. "Migrant Families: Health Problems of Children," *Clin. Pediatrics,* 5:635–40, October 1966.

SMITH, M. B. "Competence and Socialization," in *Socialization and Society,* J. A. Clausen (ed). Boston: Little, Brown and Co., 1968.

SODDY, KENNETH, AND AHRENFELDT, R. H. (eds.). *Mental Health in the Service of the Community.* (Vol. III of a Report of an International and Interprofessional Study Group convened by the World Federation for Mental Health.) Philadelphia: Tavistock Publications, J. B. Lippincott Co., 1967.

SOLOMON, FREDRIC. "On the Disabling Effects of Poverty upon Child Development." Paper prepared for the Committee on Minority Group Children, The Joint Commission on Mental Health of Children, Inc., 1968. 3 pp.

SOUTHERN CONFERENCE EDUCATIONAL FUND (SCEF). "There are 40 Million White People in the South." Louisville, Kentucky, 1968.

STAR, S. A., AND RUBY, A. M. "Number and Kinds of Children's Residential Institutions in the United States." Project on physical facilities for group care of children, Report #1. The Center for Urban Studies, University of Chicago, December 1965.

STRAUS, ROBERT. "Poverty as an Obstacle to Health Progress in Our Rural Areas," *Amer. J. Pub. Health,* 55:1772–79, November 1965.

STRINER, H. E. "Toward a Fundamental Program for the Training, Employment and Economic Equality of the American Indian." A reprint of a paper from *Federal Programs for the Development of Human Resources.* Submitted to the Subcommittee on Economic Progress of the Joint Economic Committee, Congress of the United States, Vol. I, Part II, Manpower and Education (Joint Committee Print, 90th Congress, 2nd Session). The W. E. Upjohn Institute for Employment Research, March 1968.

Summary of Vital Statistics. City of New York, Dept. of Health, 1960, Table 12, p. 10.

"Survey of Mental Health Establishments—Staffing of Patterns and Survey Methodology, October 1965." Nat. Inst. of Ment. Health, Bethesda, Maryland.

TARJAN, GEORGE. "The Role of Residential Care, Past, Present, and Future," in American Association on Mental Deficiency, Mental Retardation, Improving resident care for the retarded. (Proceedings: workshop attended by state administrators and superintendents of state institutions for the retarded held at the Sherman House, Chicago, Ill., December 2–4, 1965. Supported by National Institute of Mental Health, Pub. Health Service, U.S. Dept. of Health, Education, and Welfare.)

Task Force Report: Narcotics and Drug Abuse. Annotations and consultants papers. Task Force on Narcotics and Drug Abuse, The President's Commission on Law Enforcement and Administration of Justice. Washington, D.C.: U.S. Government Printing Office, 1967.

THOMSON, A. M. "Prematurity: Socio-economic and Nutritional Factors," *Biblio. Paed.*, 81:197–206, 1963.

TUCKMAN, J., AND LAVELL, M. "Social Status and Clinic Contact," *J. Clin. Psychol.*, 15:343–45, 1959.

U.S. BUREAU OF THE CENSUS. *Current Population Reports*, Series P–60, No. 53, "Income in 1966 of Families and Persons in the United States," Washington, D.C.: U.S. Government Printing Office, 1967, p. 28.

————. *Current Population Reports*, "Farm population," Series Census–ERS, P–27, April 2, 1968.

————. *Current Population Reports, Population Characteristics*, "Negro Population: March 1964," Series P–20, No. 137, May 1965.

————. *Current Population Reports, Population Characteristics*, "School Enrollments, October 1964," Series P–20, No. 148. Washington, D.C.: U.S. Government Printing Office, February 8, 1966.

————. *Statistical Abstract of the United States, 1964*, Table 88, p. 73.

————. *U.S. Census of Population*, special subject report, "Puerto Ricans in the United States," Series PC(2) 1D, 1960.

————. *U.S. Census of Population: 1960*, subject reports, "Inmates of Institutions," Final Report PC(2) 8A. Washington, D.C.: U.S. Government Printing Office, 1963.

————. *Vital and Health Statistics* [National Center for Health Statistics, Series 10, No. 28, May 1966.] "Characteristics of Patients of Selected Types of Medical Specialists and Practitioners. United States, July 1963–June 1964."

U.S. *Census of Housing, 1960*, Vol. A: *Metropolitan Housing*, Final Report, HC(2) 1:xii.

U.S. DEPARTMENT OF HEALTH, EDUCATION, AND WELFARE, Children's Bureau Pub. No. 435—1965. *America's Children and Youth in Institutions*: 1950–1960–1964. Washington, D.C., 1965.

————. *Programs for the Handicapped*. Washington, D.C., Jan. 12, 1968.

————. SOCIAL AND REHABILITATION SERVICE. "Advance Release of Statistics on Public Assistance and Appendix on Work Experience and Training Programs under Title V of Economic Opportunity Act, as Amended." December 1967.

————. WELFARE ADMIN., CHILDREN'S BUREAU, Statistical Series #78. *Statistics on Public Institutions for Delinquent Children*: 1963. (Prepared by Duplain R. Gant, Juvenile Delinquency Studies Branch, Div. of Research.) Washington, D.C., 1964.

U.S. DEPARTMENT OF LABOR, BUREAU OF LABOR STATISTICS, AND U.S. DEPARTMENT OF COMMERCE, BUREAU OF THE CENSUS. *Social and Economic Conditions of Negroes in the United States*. BLS Report No. 332, *Current Population Reports*, Series P–23, No. 24, Washington, D.C.: U.S. Government Printing Office, October 1967.

U.S. HOUSE OF REPRESENTATIVES, SUBCOMMITTEE ON THE WAR ON POVERTY PROGRAM. Hearings held in Washington, D.C., April 12, 13, 14, 15, and 30, 1965. 854 pp.

U.S. SENATE, SUBCOMMITTEE ON EMPLOYMENT, MANPOWER, AND POVERTY

OF THE COMMITTEE ON LABOR AND PUBLIC WELFARE IN THE UNITED STATES. *Juvenile Delinquency Prevention and Control Act.* (90th Congress, September 21, 26, 28, October 19, 20, 25, and 26, 1967.) Washington, D.C.: U.S. Government Printing Office, 1967, pp. 73, 94, 114, 223, 278.

U.S. SENATE, SUBCOMMITTEE ON EMPLOYMENT, MANPOWER, AND POVERTY OF THE COMMITTEE ON LABOR AND PUBLIC WELFARE. *Hunger and Malnutrition in America.* (90th Congress, 1st sess. on Hunger and Malnutrition in America, July 11 and 12, 1967.) Washington, D.C.: U.S. Government Printing Office, 1967.

U.S. SENATE, SUBCOMMITTEE ON EXECUTIVE REORGANIZATION OF THE COMMITTEE ON GOVERNMENT OPERATIONS. *Federal Role in Urban Affairs.* (89th Congress, 2nd sess., December 9 and 12, 1966, Part 12.) See pp. 2602ff. Statement of M. D. Thom, Exec. Dir. National Indian Youth Council.

VADAKIN, J. C. "Helping the Children," *New Republic,* December 23, 1967, pp. 15–18.

Vital Statistics of the United States, 1965, Vol. 2, Pt. A, Table 1–2–3. National Center for Health Statistics, 1965.

Welfare Law Bulletin, No. 11, January 1968, pp. 1–2.

WELLER, J. E. "Is There a Future for Yesterday's People?" *Saturday Review,* October 16, 1965, p. 33.

WERKMAN, S. L., SHIFMAN, LYDIA, AND SKELLY, THOMAS. "Psychological Bases of Excessive Intake and Iron Deficiency Anemia During Infancy," in Clinical Proceedings, Children's Hospital of the District of Columbia, Vol. XX, No. 7, July 1964a.

———. "Psychosocial Correlates of Iron Deficiency Anemia in Early Childhood," *Psychosomatic Medicine,* Vol. XXVI, No. 2:125–34, 1964b.

WHITE, J. M. "Surplus Food for Poor to Be Increased 40%," *The Washington Post,* June 11, 1968, p. A9.

WILKING, V. N., AND PAOLI, CESARINA. "The Hallucinatory Experience: An Attempt at a Psychodynamic Classification and Reconsideration of the Diagnostic Significance," *J. Am. Acad. of Child Psychiatry* 5:4321–40, 1966.

WILNER, D. M., WALKLEY, R. P., PINKERTON, T. C., AND TAYBACK, MATTHEW. *The Housing Environment and Family Life:* A Longitudinal Study of the Effects of Housing on Morbidity and Mental Health. Baltimore: Johns Hopkins Press, 1962.

WINDER, A. E., AND HERSKO, M. "The Effect of Social Class on the Length and Type of Psychotherapy in a Veterans Administration Mental Hygiene Clinic," *J. Clin. Psychol.,* 11:77–79, 1955.

WORTIS, HELEN. "Social Class and Premature Birth," *Social Casework,* November, 1964, 541–43.

YAMAMOTO, JOE, JAMES, Q. C., BLOOMBAUM, MILTON, AND HATTEM, JACK. "Racial Factors in Patient Selection," *Am. J. Psychiat.,* 124 (5):84–90, November 1967.

YOUNG ADULT INSTITUTE AND WORKSHOP, INC. "An exploration of the advisability of developing a research and demonstration project concerned with elevating the readiness for vocational rehabilitation of multiply-disabled young adults. Final report." (Supported in part by a research grant from the Voc. Rehab. Admin., Department of Health, Education, and Welfare, Washington, D.C., August 31, 1966.)

ZIGLER, EDWARD. "Research on Personality Structure in the Retardate," in *International Review of Research in Mental Retardation,* vol. 1, Norman Ellis (ed.). London-New York: Academic Press, 1966, pp. 77–108.

ZINBERG, N. E. Draft of a paper on Negro adolescents submitted to Task Force III, The Joint Commission on Mental Health of Children, Inc., 1968 (no title).

CHILDREN OF THE AMERICAN DREAM

AMERICAN SOCIAL HEALTH ASSOCIATION, *Today's VD Control Problem.* New York, N.Y.: American Social Health Association, January 1967. (This is a joint statement by The American Public Health Association, The American Social Health Association, The American Venereal Disease Association, and The Association of State and Territorial Health Officers with the cooperation of the American Medical Association.)

ARNOLD, MARTIN. "The Drug Scene: A Growing Number of America's Elite Are Quietly 'Turning On,'" *The New York Times,* January 10, 1968.

BARKER, R. G., AND WRIGHT, H. F. *One Boy's Day.* New York: Harper, 1951.

BEAN, L. L., MYERS, J. K., AND PEPPER, M. P. "Social Class and Schizophrenia: A Ten-Year Follow-up," in *Blue-Collar World: Studies of the American Worker,* Arthur B. Shostak and William Gomberg (eds.). Englewood Cliffs, N.J.: Prentice-Hall, Inc., 1964, pp. 363–70.

BOWMAN, C. C. "Mental Health in the Worker's World," in *Blue-Collar World: Studies of the American Worker,* Arthur B. Shostak and William Gomberg (eds.). Englewood Cliffs, N.J.: Prentice-Hall, Inc., 1964, pp. 371–81.

BRUYN, H., AND SEIDEN, R. H. "Student Suicide: Fact or Fancy?" *J. Amer. Coll. Hlth. Assoc.,* 1965, 14(2), pp. 69–77.

CHINOY, ELY. *Automobile Workers and the American Dream.* New York: Doubleday and Co., 1955.

DANSEREAU, H. K. "Work and the Teen-age Blue-Collarite," in *Blue-Collar World: Studies of the American Worker,* Arthur B. Shostak and William Gomberg (eds.). Englewood Cliffs, N.J.: Prentice-Hall, Inc., 1964, pp. 183–92.

DAVIDSON, BILL. " 'They Steal Just for the Hell of It,' " *Saturday Evening Post,* May 18, 1968, pp. 23–27.

DESCHIN, C. S. "Teenagers and Venereal Disease." A report of a study by the American Social Health Association in cooperation with the New York City Department of Health for the Venereal Disease Branch, Communicable Disease Center, Public Health Service, U.S. Department of Health, Education, and Welfare, 1961.

DUNBAR, ERNEST. "Campus Mood, Spring, '68," *Look*, April 2, 1968, pp. 23–27.

DUVAL, E. M. "Conceptions of Parenthood," *Am. J. Soc.*, 52:193–204, November 1946.

FARNSWORTH, D. L. *Mental Health in College and University*. Cambridge, Mass.: Harvard University Press, 1957.

FLACKS, RICHARD. "The Liberated Generation: An Exploration of the Roots of Student Protest," *The J. Soc. Issues*, Vol. XXIII, No. 3:52–75, July 1967.

GANS, H. J. *The Urban Villagers*. New York: The Free Press of Glencoe, 1962, ch. 11.

————. *The Levittowners*. New York: Pantheon Books, 1967.

GRUENBERG, ERNEST. "Mental Disorders: Epidemiology." Reprinted from *International Encyclopedia of the Social Sciences*. New York: The Macmillian Co. and The Free Press of Glencoe. © 1968 by Crowell Collier and Macmillan, Inc., pp. 149–156.

GURIN, GERALD, VEROFF, JOSEPH, AND FELD, SHEILA. *Americans View Their Mental Health*. New York: Basic Books, Inc., 1960, p. 227.

HANDEL, GERALD, AND RAINWATER, LEE. "Persistence and Change in Working-Class Life Style," in *Blue-Collar World: Studies of the American Worker*, Arthur B. Shostak and William Gomberg (eds.). Englewood Cliffs, N.J.: Prentice-Hall, Inc., 1964, pp. 36–41.

HARRISON, S. I., MCDERMOTT, J. F., WILSON, P. T., AND SCHRAGER, J. "Social Class and Mental Illness in Children," *Archives of Gen. Psychiat.*, 13:411–17, November 1965.

HAUSKNECHT, MURRAY. "The Blue-Collar Joiner," in *Blue-Collar World: Studies of the American Worker*, Arthur B. Shostak and William Gomberg (eds.). Englewood Cliffs, N.J.: Prentice-Hall, Inc., 1964, pp. 207–15.

HERZOG, ELIZABETH. *About the Poor: Some Facts and Some Fictions*. U.S. Department of Health, Education, and Welfare, Social and Rehabilitation Service, Children's Bureau, Publication #451. Washington, D.C.: U.S. Government Printing Office, 1967.

HOLLINGSHEAD, A. B., AND REDLICH, F. C. *Social Class and Mental Illness: A Community Study*. New York: John Wiley & Sons, Inc., 1958.

HYMAN, HERBERT H. "The Value Systems of Different Classes: A Social Psychological Contribution to the Analysis of Stratification," in *Class, Status and Power: A Reader in Social Stratification*, Reinhard Bendix and Seymour Martin Lipset (eds.). Glencoe, Ill.: The Free Press of Glencoe, 1953.

JAHODA, MARIE. *Current Concepts of Positive Mental Health*. New York: Basic Books, Inc., 1958.

THE JOINT INFORMATION SERVICE OF THE AMERICAN PSYCHIATRIC ASSOCIATION AND THE NATIONAL ASSOCIATION FOR MENTAL HEALTH. *Fifteen Indices: an Aid in Reviewing State and Local Mental Health and Hospital Programs*. Washington, D.C., 1968, p. 18.

KANTOR, MILDRED. "Some Consequences of Residential and Social Mobility for the Adjustment of Children," *Mobility and Mental Health,* Mildred Kantor (ed.). © 1965, Charles C. Thomas. (Reprint)

KENISTON, KENNETH. "Heads and Seekers: Student Drug Users." Paper presented at the Divisional Meeting of the American Psychiatric Association, New York City, November 17, 1967. 10 pp.

————. *Young Radicals: Notes on Committed Youth.* New York: Harcourt, Brace & World, Inc. A Harvest Book, 1968.

KIFNER, JOHN. "The Drug Scene: Marijuana, for Many Students, Has Become a Part of Growing Up," *The New York Times,* January 11, 1968.

KOHN, M. L. "Social Class and Parent-Child Relationships: An Interpretation," *Am. J. Soc.* Vol. 68, No. 4:471–80, January 1963.

KORNHAUSER, ARTHUR. "Toward an Assessment of the Mental Health of Factory Workers: A Detroit Study," in *Mental Health of the Poor,* Frank Riessman, Jerome Cohen, and Arthur Pearl (eds.). New York: The Free Press of Glencoe, 1964, pp. 49–56.

LANGNER, T. S. *et al. A Survey of Psychiatric Impairment in Urban Children* ("Progress Report"). (Unpublished MS, 1967).

LEGGETT, J. C. "Sources and Consequences of Working-Class Consciousness," in *Blue-Collar World: Studies of the American Worker*, Arthur B. Shostak and William Gomberg (eds.). Englewood Cliffs, N.J.: Prentice-Hall, Inc., 1964, pp. 235–47.

LUKAS, J. A. "The Drug Scene: Dependence Grows," *The New York Times,* January 8, 1968.

MILLER, D. R., AND SWANSON, G. E. *The Changing American Parent.* New York: John Wiley and Sons, Inc., 1958.

MILLER, S. M., AND MISHLER, E. G. "Social Class, Mental Illness, and American Psychiatry," *Milbank Memorial Fund Quarterly*, Vol. 37, April, 1959. See esp. pp. 189–91.

MILLER, S. M., AND RIESSMAN, FRANK. "The Working-Class Subculture: A New View," *Social Problems,* 1961. Reprinted in Frank Riessman, *The Culturally Deprived Child,* New York: Harper & Row, 1962.

MILLER, S. M., RIESSMAN, FRANK, AND SEAGULL, A. A. "Poverty and Self-Indulgence: A Critique of the Non-Deferred Gratification Pattern," in *Poverty in America—A Book of Readings,* Louis A. Ferman, Joyce L. Kornbluh, and Alan Haber (eds.). Ann Arbor: University of Michigan Press, 1966. © The University of Michigan Press, 1965, pp. 285–302.

PAFFENBARGER, R. S., AND ASNES, D. P. "Chronic Disease in Former College Students. III. Precursors of Suicide in Early and Middle Life," *Amer. J. Pub. Hlth.*, 1966, 56(7), 1026–36.

PARRISH, H. M. "Epidemiology of Suicide Among College Students," *Yale J. Biol. Med.,* 1957, 29, 585–95.

PENNINGTON, R. A. *Young Suicide.* Unpublished M.A. thesis, George Washington University, June 1968.

REIFF, ROBERT, AND SCRIBNER, SYLVIA. "Issues in the New National Mental Health Program Relating to Labor and Low Income Groups," in *Mental*

Health of the Poor, Frank Riessman, Jerome Cohen, and Arthur Pearl (eds.). New York: The Free Press of Glencoe, 1964, pp. 443–55.

SCHNEIDER, LOUIS, AND LYSGAARD, SVERRE. "The Deferred Gratification Pattern: A Preliminary Study," *Am. Soc. Review,* 18:142–49, April 1953.

SEIDEN, R. H. "Campus Tragedy: A Study of Student Suicide," *J. Abnorm. Psychol.,* 1966, 71(6), 389–99.

———. *Youthful Suicide.* Draft Report to Joint Commission on Mental Health of Children. Unpublished MS., November 1967.

SHNEIDMAN, E. S., AND FARBEROW, N. L. "Statistical Comparisons Between Attempted and Committed Suicides," in *The Cry for Help,* N. L. Farberow and E. S. Shneidman (eds.). New York: McGraw-Hill, 1961, pp. 19–47.

SHOSTAK, A. B., AND GOMBERG, WILLIAM (eds.). *Blue-Collar World: Studies of the American Worker.* Englewood Cliffs, N.J.: Prentice-Hall, Inc., 1964, pp. 121–92.

SMITH, M. BREWSTER. "Morality and Student Protest." Psi Chi Invited Address, American Psychological Association, San Francisco, Calif., August 31, 1968.

SOSKIN, W. F. "Hippie: Bastard Son of the Beat Generation." Paper prepared for the Joint Commission on Mental Health of Children, Inc., December, 1967.

SROLE, LEO, LANGER, T. S., MICHAEL, STANLEY, OPLER, MARVIN, AND RENNIE, THOMAS. *Mental Health in the Metropolis: The Midtown Manhattan Study.* New York: McGraw-Hill, Inc., 1962.

"Student Protests: A Phenomenon for Behavioral Sciences Research." Statement of a Group of Fellows at the Center for Advanced Study in the Behavioral Sciences, Stanford, Calif. *Science,* Vol. 161, No. 3836:20–23, July 5, 1968.

TEMBY, W. D. "Suicide," in *Emotional Problems of the Student,* G. B. Blaine and C. C. McArthur (eds.). New York: Appleton-Century-Crofts, 1961, pp. 133–152.

VINCET, C. E. *Unmarried Mothers.* New York: The Free Press of Glencoe, 1961.

WHITING, J. J. *Compilation and Analysis of Psychiatric and Related Services Relevant to Child Mental Health, in Relation to Manpower.* Paper prepared for the Joint Commission on Mental Health of Children, Inc., 1968.

ZINBERG, N. E. "Facts and Fancies About Drug Addiction," *The Public Interest,* Winter, 1967, pp. 75–89.

DIRECTIONS FOR CHANGE

BRIM, ORVILLE G. JR. *Education for Child Rearing.* New York: Russell Sage Foundation, 1959.

CHILMAN, CATHERINE. *Parents as Partners in Department Programs for Children and Youth.* A report to the Secretary of the Department of Health,

Education, and Welfare by the Task Force on Parent Participation. Washington, D.C.: U.S. Department of Health, Education, and Welfare, August 1968.

CLENDENEN, RICHARD, VOTAW, ROY, MCBRIDE, PARKER, AND CASSIDY, ROSA-LIND. *The Youth Participation Review.* A cooperative inquiry of the Joint Commission on Mental Health of Children, Inc., and the National Council of State Committees on Children and Youth. Paper prepared by the National Council on State Committees on Children and Youth for the Joint Commission on Mental Health of Children, Inc., June 13, 1968.

EBERLY, DONALD J. (ed.). *National Service: A Report of a Conference.* New York: Russell Sage Foundation, 1968.

KOHLER, MARY CONWAY. *Selected Youth Participation Projects.* Paper pre-pared by the National Commission on Resources for Youth, Inc., for Task Force VI of the Joint Commission on Mental Health of Children, Inc., June 13, 1968.

II

EXCERPTS FROM
THE REPORT OF THE COMMITTEE
ON CHILDREN OF MINORITY GROUPS

The major message of the Committee on Children of Minority Groups —the recommendations and Statement on Racism—is reprinted here from the Commission's Final Report Crisis in Child Mental Health: Challenge of the 1970's. *Much of the Committee's original study also appears in the Commission's Final Report under the chapter heading "Children of Minority Groups: A Special Mental Health Risk." The Committee's findings on poverty have not been published but are reflected in the material presented by Task Force VI in the first part of this book. Printed here for the first time are the opening remarks and the* entire *set of recommendations from the* Report of the Committee on Children of Minority Groups.

—EDITOR

COMMITTEE ON CHILDREN OF MINORITY GROUPS

Chairman: JOSEPH P. MALDONADO, A.C.W.S.
Executive Director, Economic
and Youth Opportunities Agency

INEZ CASIANO
Social Science Advisor to the
Secretary of Labor
Office of Policy Planning and Research
U.S. Department of Labor

PRICE M. COBBS, M.D.
Psychiatrist
Pacific Psychotherapy Associates

ADA E. DEER, M.S.W.
Coordinator of Indian Affairs
University of Minnesota

MRS. FRED R. HARRIS
President, Oklahomans for Indian
Opportunity

PATRICIA A. LEO
Special Assistant for Intergroup
Relations
The American Public Health
Association, Inc.

RUTH B. McKAY, PH.D.
Faculty Associate
Department of Psychiatry
Hillcrest Children's Center

ALEX P. MERCURE
State Program Director
Home Education Livelihood Program

DANIEL J. O'CONNELL, M.D.
Executive Secretary
National Committee on Indian
Affairs
Association on American Indian
Affairs

K. PATRICK OKURA
Administrative Director
Community Services Division
Nebraska Psychiatric Institute

CHESTER M. PIERCE, M.D.
Professor
Department of Psychiatry
University of Oklahoma Medical
Center

FREDRIC SOLOMON, M.D.
Associate Professor of Psychiatry
Howard University

PERCY H. STEELE, JR., A.C.S.W.
Executive Director
Bay Area Urban League, Inc.

WILLIAM WATERMAN
Director, Offenders Division
United Planning Organization

No nation can maintain the distinction of being democratic if it does not make allowances for cultural diversity. Such differences cannot be "just tolerated." They must be respected and encouraged so long as they have value for any segment of the citizenry. Thus, in a real sense, this opportunity to pursue autonomous goals is a measure of "democratic." No person can make his fullest contribution to the total society with a feeling of compromise about "who he is" because he is a minority group member.

—DAN W. DODSON

Preface

The mental health problems of many minority group children are extremely severe; anything that can be said of the majority group's needs can be multiplied several times for those in minority status. In today's social climate, we must accept responsibility for the severity of this problem and we must make a sincere and concerted effort to prevent continued damage to the mental health of the minority group children of America.

Comprehensive health planning exists on policy level. However, law (PL 89–749) is not presently being implemented. Further, there is evidence of resistance to committees composed of lay and professional, multi-racial, multi-ethnic, and multi-discipline members. This reflects the racial and professional biases that have been most serious barriers to effective planning and delivering of services to minority communities. To assure equality of treatment to all children, such professional biases must be eliminated.

This Committee, in considering the mental health needs of minority group children, is cognizant of the variations in life styles among the various minority groups which effect the potential success of all public policy and clinical services. The implications of these various life styles are reflected in the body of this report. However, the Committee also recognizes certain general trends which can be applied to all minority groups and has styled its recommendations around these general themes.

The recommendations of this multi-racial, multi-ethnic Committee are primarily of a preventive nature and call for drastic changes in the social, cultural, political, economic, legal, educational, and medical institutions of our society. We also recognize that family relationships are rapidly changing in America, particularly among minority groups. The historical ethnic and cultural differences in familial patterns are variables which have important implications for the planning and implementing of all programs dealing with minority groups.

183

In view of the fact that nearly all research data on minority problems have been gathered and interpreted by white social scientists, there may be serious limitations in its utility and in the applicability of such findings. This research implies that the problems lie with the minorities and it fails to recognize the crucial role of the majority in producing these problems. This Committee on minorities recognizes such assumptions as a barrier in the material reported in this paper. Furthermore, it must be emphasized that there is a pressing need to have minority members involve themselves in social science research, not because they are more likely to have greater access to truth but because they may provide new ways of evaluating our society. Corollary to this is the necessity of having both majority and minority scientists focus attention on behavior of the majority population rather than to continue the tradition of giving over excessive and near exclusive attention to the behavior of minority people. An immediate step toward the accomplishment of these objectives would be to include more minority social scientists at policy- and decision-making levels in the selection and administration of research.

The pages which follow set forth the recommendations of this Committee and the bases upon which these considerations have been formulated.

The Problem

RACISM

Racism is the number one public health problem facing America today. The conscious and unconscious attitudes of superiority which permit and demand that a majority oppress a minority are a clear and present danger to the mental health of all children and their parents. Traditionally, the criteria for defining public health problems are: (1) a problem that threatens a large number of people; (2) a problem that costs a large sum of money; (3) a problem that is impossible to treat on an individual and private basis; and (4) a problem that could cause chronic sustained disability.

This Committee believes that the racist attitude of Americans which causes and perpetuates tension is patently a most compelling health hazard. Its destructive effects severely cripple the growth and development of millions of our citizens, young and old alike. Yearly, it directly and indirectly causes more fatalities, disabilities and economic loss than any other single factor.

Over the last two decades, there has been a proliferation of scientific papers in the behavioral sciences attesting to damage to children, black and white, that can be directly traced to this endemic condition. Historically, minority groups of color have experienced the lash of racism. This is true whether we study the degradation of Indians, the subjugation of Mexican-Americans, the exploitation of the Puerto Ricans, the brutal relocation of the Japanese, the callous treatment of all Orientals, or the unresolved black question.

We must accept that the United States is not a white nation. The idealized image of the melting pot has, fortunately, never been realized. Our strength as a society rests in cultural pluralism. Biological evolution

185

demonstrates the survival value inhering in a range of physical types within the species. So does a nation profit when the unique cultural skills, styles, and genius of diverse peoples are valued as societal assets.

The country is now experiencing an acute crisis. The legitimate demands of the alienated and emerging groups of this country, if unmet, constitute a threat to our continued existence as a nation, as well as our potential role in the international sphere. Social scientists now have the predictive ability to forecast that the Mexican-Americans in the Southwest, the impoverished Appalachian residents, the newly assertive Indians, and the isolated urban dwellers—all have the same capacity for a violent resolution of our social crisis.

There are indications that the history of black people in the United States will be paralleled by other minority groups in America in the near future. Hope was generated by the 1954 and 1955 Supreme Court decisions.

During the late 1950's and early 1960's, hope sustained while the blacks petitioned for economic viability through nonviolent means. However, the failure to correct social and economic inequities and injustices following the 1964 Civil Rights Act and other socio-economic programs resulted in the mobilization of frustration and anger to the point of rebellion. Currently, the black population, filled with despair and ever aware of the failure of the actualization of bright promises, has become mindful of its need to unite in order to defend itself against the institution of repressive measures by the majority population. In a shorter order, the Mexican-American, the Puerto Rican, and the American Indian, without social intervention, may travel the same historical path.

The response to date by the mainstream culture has not been amelioration of grievances but punitive action. There have been few basic social or economic changes directed toward altering the value system of this society. There has been tragically little self-examination. The pathology of denial and lack of awareness has reached massive proportions. This indifference has robbed all Americans of the psychic energy so necessary for healthy functioning.

One of the realities of present-day America is that increasingly large segments of the minority population will be obliged to live in segregated communities, at least over the next couple of decades. In general, without massive intervention, this means that the majority of minority children between now and the end of the century will be growing up in mentally unhealthy atmospheres rampant with substandard housing, inferior education, and poor health care.

The country must outgrow its legacy of racism. There must be massive outpourings of resources, both financial and human, if the problems are to be resolved. A minority child must grow up seeing himself and his life as having positive value. The white child must be equipped to live as a member

of a multi-racial world. This will allow them both to grow up less handicapped by the effects of guilt, fear, anger, and anxiety.

The mutual distrust so prevalent in this country is leading to the polarization of Americans. The growth and viability of our society are dependent
on everyone achieving a full measure of growth and development. This is
true no less of the majority white than the minority group member. While
the financial cost of eradicating racism in all walks of national life will
obviously be immense, the result of making it possible for millions of wasted
human beings to contribute to our national production and creativity, the
development of millions of new consumers for our national product, the
improvement of our commercial relations with problems of other nations,
the cut in the present enormous costs of inadequate welfare programs
would seem to make it a relatively sound investment. The society can truly
find new strength and integrity by an acceptance of all diversity.

Manifestations of Racism Affecting the Mental Health of Minority Group Children

Definition of mental health: Mental health is the result of all factors
(social, psychological, and biological) that permit a person to be free of
crippling emotional states such as overwhelming fear, anger, envy and racist
projections. Such a person operates as a contributing member of his society
and feels himself to be both effective and efficient. He is capable of strong
and satisfying love and work relationships.

This operational definition of mental health is basic to the issues raised
by the Committee. The aim of this report is to promote and sustain the
mental health, as defined above, of the minority youth who will grow up
during the next decade.

Prejudicial treatment of minority group youth by social institutions:
The child growing up as a member of a minority group learns that his role
in relationship to most social institutions differs from that of other children.
He learns that members of his racial or ethnic group are most apt to live
in the least desirable section of town—in the inner city, the ghetto, the
barrio, the reservation, or the rural depressed areas. He discovers that
hunger, poor health, and demoralizing housing are the lot of those who live
in his neighborhood. The unemployment or underemployment of the adults
around him does little to stimulate his interest in preparing for a career.
Inadequate transportation and a paucity of recreational resources force him
to find what entertainment he can in his home environment. In an overcrowded classroom, his teacher treats him in accordance with her stereotyped notions of his minority group. Not only his textbooks, but television
and the movies suggest to him that the good life is mostly white middle or
upper class. Legal recourse, medical help, even adequate shopping facilities,
are not available in his neighborhood. Policemen become a visible mani-

festation of the enemy—the affluent world, the society that institutionalizes his degradation.

By the time he reaches adulthood, the minority group youth realizes that he is inescapably branded by white racists as inferior because of a racial or ethnic inheritance from which he cannot escape. With the opportunity channels of the greater society closed against him, he feels more secure competing for whatever status positions are available within his isolated environment. Demoralized by the self-concept he sees mirrored in the eyes of society and debilitated by an unhealthy environment, he is not likely to escape from a cage of poverty and bigotry unless the social conditions which bludgeoned him into that cage are changed.

Maladaptive life patterns: To survive discrimination and poverty, a life pattern which in itself perpetuates disadvantagement may be accepted. Motivation is stifled by a society which apparently prefers to support the poor with welfare payments which keep them at a level of bare subsistence rather than to allow minority groups an equal opportunity within the economic structure. The marginal activities of the ghetto, the reservation, the barrio, or the depressed rural sections are the only social settings in which many opportunities exist for enhancing self-esteem. Large families are at once a burden and a supportive group. Education may correlate with economic advancement, but the school institution tends to push out those children who cannot conform to the goals established by the school. Such life circumstances may be accepted in a pattern of ennui, hopelessness, and despair. A healthier adaptation may be rebellion.

Inadequate mental health services: Although living in circumstances which continually threaten their mental health, for minority group youth and the disadvantaged mental health services may be virtually inaccessible. Clinics are often located at a distance from the poverty neighborhood. Service is preceded by a lengthy intake process and predicated on a long-term treatment which may be inappropriate to the life style of the client. Mental health personnel are poorly equipped to understand the client's environment and feelings and may find communication beyond a superficial level to be impossible.

The disadvantaged are often reluctant to utilize what mental health services are available. Accustomed to the discomforts of ill health and unable to budget for medical care, the poor eschew preventive care and seek help only for emergencies. The poorly educated may not only ignore the first symptoms of mental illness but may hold unenlightened views of the nature of such illness.

Thus our social arrangements to cope with mental health are, like other institutions in this society, less available to minority group youth than to other youth.

Recommendations

The Committee identified racism as the number one public health problem. We believe that programs to eradicate racism should be initiated immediately because vast numbers of Americans appear ready to accept, either from egalitarian or humanistic motives or from simple self-interest, that the dangerous and destructive mechanisms of racism must be abandoned. However, racism will yield only to the strongest, clearest, and most diverse campaigns of information and education. Therefore, this Committee makes the following recommendations:

1. That the President of the United States ask all levels of government to mobilize their resources to combat racism; that he address a joint session of Congress with the goal of educating them to the racial problem and inspiring their support of programs aimed at alleviating ghetto conditions.

2. Specific efforts must be made to preserve and sustain many of the features of minority populations. These strengths are needed to assure the advantages of cultural diversity and healthy psychological development.

3. That the existing power structures on national, state, and community levels be committed to effect real change in the attitudes and behavior of people in their sphere of influence through a program launched and led by the President and backed by a committee of Governors.

4. That the President ascertain that each Cabinet department and independent Federal agency is making every effort to eradicate racism.

5. That the President call for government action related to the

Report of the National Advisory Commission on Civil Disorders; that members and staff of the Commission who are acquainted with the methodology and findings meet regionally with various public and private groups to acquaint them with the scope of the report and its recommendations.

6. That the leadership for planning and implementing the campaign against racism come from the top of all sectors of American society including government, business, education, religion, medicine, the communication industry, and the arts; that a multi-racial committee of nationally important leaders representing these sectors be immediately appointed to establish goals and policy.

7. The Committee recommends the creation of a National Foundation for the Social Sciences for the promoting and strengthening of these sciences as proposed in S. 836–90th Congress. It is further recommended that this Foundation support not only basic research in the social sciences but that it also promote social science research, development, and pilot studies aimed at developing ways of coping with and of solving the major social problems of our society.

8. The Committee recommends that the Federal government not only develop adequate programs in the health, education and welfare area but that it exercise surveillance of the effectiveness of these programs through the creating of a Council of Social Advisors to the President as proposed in S. 843–90th Congress.

9. That a new organization be established with adequate private and public support, to be called "The National Council Against Racism." The Council would have both scientific and change-promoting functions. It would serve as:

    a. a clearinghouse for valid and applicable data on effective racism-reducing programs and community organization efforts;

    b. a clearinghouse for valid data on the psychosocial strengths and disabilities of various racial and ethnic groups in the United States (including "majority" groups) as well as data on programs that capitalize on these strengths and lessen the disabilities;

    c. a research-promoting and idea-producing center;

    d. an agency that directly sponsors a variety of appropriate pilot projects and action programs;

    e. an organization energetically advocating the adoption of appropriate racism-reducing programs on Federal, State, local and private levels as well as providing consultation on the selection and implementation of such programs.

10. That the 1970 White House Conference on Children and Youth be devoted to examination of the problems of racism as they affect young children thus mobilizing hundreds of national organizations associated with the Conference.

11. Mental health professionals be vocal in declaring that: The issue of universal human dignity is deeply interwoven in our international and domestic crisis. Furthermore, there are psychological contradictions inherent in the concept of a two-fronted war; that is, a War on Poverty and an International War, presently typified in Vietnam. The bulk of our various national resources should be directed toward resolving the problem of racism and poverty.

12. That non-prejudicial attitudes, understanding, and the desire to make change be a prerequisite for public and private office and responsibility.

13. That the traditional networks of communications be drafted to provide exhaustive dissemination of whatever kinds of materials are required to eradicate the misinformation, the conscious and unconscious hostility, and the false fears that are corrupting the minds and hearts of so many Americans.

14. That every effort be exerted to eliminate prejudice from communication media, including comic books, television, films, and textbooks.

15. That school boards include representation of minority groups within the community.

16. That the study of minority groups be a required part of the training of all teachers and school administrators.

17. That the study of the heritage and contributions of all ethnic groups in America be included in the early education of all children.

18. That the concept of the mental health team be broadened to include many other skills necessary to combat racism; and this will require the development of such talent within the minority communities.

19. That each community assume responsibility for positive action in establishing and maintaining a society free from racism.

20. That housing integration efforts be directed at both cities and suburbs.

21. That innovative ways of implementing psychological change be explored by providing new methods of communication and interaction through which members of majority and minority groups affect a two-way exchange of tolerance, understanding, and respect, and that new television channels and radio stations be licensed with the prior stipulation that they discharge their responsibilities in this sphere.

22. That the recommendations regarding press coverage of riots in the Report of the National Advisory Commission on Civil Disorders be applied to non-violent events as well; that both sides of all controversies, confrontations, and other newsworthy material in race relations be carefully reported.

23. That prejudice in the individual be recognized as a psychological disability, damaging to the self and others and also limiting and reducing the quality and extent of the individual's interaction with his fellow men.

24. That a nationwide campaign against racism be launched featuring such slogans as "Racism is the number one public health problem" and seeking to instill such understandings as the following:

    a. America can no longer afford the material costs that stem directly from racism—the continuing physical decay of the inner cities; the rising bills for inadequate welfare payments; the property damage caused by riots and the subsequent programs of arson and looting; the loss of national income and taxes that could be produced by members of minorities if they had employment opportunities and equal access to capital; and the medical and mental hygiene cost to all public health services for repairing the human damage caused by ghetto life in the cities, on the reservations, or in the abandoned rural communities where automation has replaced human labor.

    b. America can no longer afford the spiritual and psychological costs attendant to the atmosphere of violence and counterviolence, rebellion and retaliation. We can no longer afford the feelings of guilt, fear, anxiety, and the other crippling emotions that affect both sides in a national atmosphere of hostility and aggression evoked by racial tension.

    c. America cannot afford the public image either at home or abroad of being a nation guilty of unfairness, intolerance, and disdain for human needs, contempt for human aspiration, and even blatant physical cruelty as shown on our television sets every summer and in the magazines and newspapers throughout the world. The sense of shame felt by Americans, particularly young Americans, as a result of being identified with such national and local action has become intolerable and is about to affect our national identity, our attitudes toward our laws and our leaders, and the very vigor of our national purpose and our will to maintain our national security.

    d. America will be enriched as its people better appreciate the strengths and contributions of minority groups.

25. That long-range programs of research, experimentation, and evaluation be conducted to determine the most effective communication practices for eradicating racism; however, the urgency of the danger to the children of America inherent in racism requires that we launch a campaign against racism now rather than waiting for the results of such studies.

26. In a very real sense the mental health of minority children depends on the education and research findings of mental health specialists, educators, and administrators of welfare programs. Thus there is no more important institution in our society, relative to the mental health of minority children, than the Department of Health, Education, and Welfare. Though the practices of this department on the whole have been undeniably and immeasurably positive, the Department must be evaluated critically in relationship to the mental health of the minority child.

For instance, despite the hundreds of qualified black physicians, sociologists, psychologists, social workers, and nurses, this Committee knows through the experience of its members only four blacks who have served the National Institute of Mental Health in a capacity of consultant, site visitor, study section member, or advisory councillor. We know of even less participation by qualified American Indians or Spanish-speaking Americans. Putatively, there are less than five intramural black professional staff at NIMH. Insofar as "credentials" are held by dozens of blacks who are professors in "white" institutions of higher learning, all of them would qualify for any of these services.

The lack of participation by minority members at critical levels in the use of the public funds which most influence the research, education, and service of the mental health aspects of our society not only reflects racism but prevents the intellectual input from the minority community. Such circumstances if connected might help preclude serious social disruption in our country.

27. Agencies such as NIMH, OEO, Children's Bureau, B.I.A., Office of Education, Labor Department, must discharge their responsibilities in planning and funding of services for children and youth of minority groups with a sense of urgency and daring. The vigorous recruitment for participation of professionals and non-professionals from the minorities must go beyond mere employment and consultation and must aim at the high-level planning as well as direct delivery service systems which are compatible with the cultural values and life styles of the recipient. Programs for mental health, community action, manpower, and youth development unencumbered by myths about low-income and minority populations (e.g., cultural deprivation, time orientation, disorganized families) will assure that the minority communities will be strengthened in their capacity to solve their own social problems.

Such programs will fail if they are encumbered by administrative timidity, *a priori* prescriptions, and fear of "high-risk" program ventures.

28. That the emphases on changing the attitudes and behavior of minority persons be broadened to that of changing the attitude and behavior of the white majority in the area of racism. New approaches to bring this about on a "wholesale" basis would need to be developed and the human and financial resources required be provided.

COORDINATED COMMUNITY ACTION TO IMPROVE THE MENTAL HEALTH OF MINORITY GROUP CHILDREN

Mental health services are not sufficient to resolve the emotional problems of children who live in inadequate housing, are failing in school, are physically ill, come from broken homes, and are constantly exposed to the harsh realities of discriminatory practices and poverty environments. Unless the overwhelming problems confronting minority group children can be ameliorated, efforts to improve and increase mental health services will be wasted. Americans have not assumed responsibility for the gross inequities that a large number of minority group children and their families face. The following recommendations are but a beginning.

Education:

1. That school curricula be made more relevant to the minority group child through such modifications as the following:

   a. The school systems of the United States should include in all general education more about cultural diversity and plurality of all groups as well as their historical antecedents.
   b. Supplementary textual material for specific cultures should be provided.
   c. Recognizing that drug abuse, including alcohol, is a national problem, special education programs to assist youth in avoiding psychopathological adaptations such as drug and alcohol addiction are strongly endorsed.
   d. Culturally specific curriculum materials and school programs to promote healthy psychological and social development in such areas as family life education and intercultural relationships should be developed. Such programs must reflect the standards of the community and the reality situations faced by the children. The curriculum should include some programs that lead to class discussions of prejudice and the appreciation of the differences among cultural and racial groups.
   e. Appropriately motivated teachers should be trained and encouraged to deal openly with the life stresses which destroy the minority group child's ability to participate in the calm atmosphere of the schoolroom. Although this may mean ventilation and comforting, we are not arguing for "therapy" in the classroom. However, the school experience should include various opportunities for students to reduce the gap between the educational process and their lives at home and in their natural surroundings.
   f. Such subjects as anthropology, social issues, social power systems, public agencies, and current advances in science, should be introduced in the elementary school.

2. That pre-school opportunities such as Head Start be available for all children from deprived environments. To insure that pre-school opportunities are available to all, they should be mandatory, even in states where public policy is opposed to them.

3. That technical and vocational education be tailored to the needs of the community, the projected employment opportunities, and the expansion of technological development.

a. Various audio-visual media should be developed to demonstrate how to get and keep a job, how to adjust to military service, how to travel on an airplane, how to obtain scholarships, how to keep house, how to insure welfare rights, how to seek legal redress of specific grievances, etc. Such materials should be distributed through schools, churches, settlement houses, and other community agencies and organizations. Television networks should also cooperate in disseminating such information.

b. "Career-mobiles" carrying individuals and materials to arouse interest in occupational opportunities could visit isolated minority neighborhoods.

c. "Successful People" programs would permit youth to observe role models who function in a wide variety of positions.

d. Minority youth should be enabled to visit industries and educational institutions as well as cultural sites.

4. That work experience programs allow junior and senior high school students to learn job skills while earning the modest sums of money that may enable them to remain in school.

5. That teaching procedures be restructured to better relate to the minority group child's language, life style, and culture.

a. Toys and games designed to train the child in such areas as demographic movement, use of a computer, problems in the use of credit, utilization of information channels, and advantages of credit should be available in schools and other sites.

b. Automated means of improving communication skills should be encouraged.

6. That the physical and psychological setting of the educational institution be reviewed in detail and revitalized.

a. Boarding school placement for American Indian children should be eliminated and quality education in local schools substituted.

b. To the extent that boarding school placement of Indian students will continue in the immedate future, it is crucial that the importance of the competent dormitory aides in the psychological development of the young child be recognized. The number, quality and training of these parent-substitutes need to be increased. The number of students supervised by each aide should be reduced to not more than 15.

c. To the extent that boarding school placement for Indian students is frequently used as a disposition for cases of psychological or behavioral disorders, social or family problems, it is crucial that responsibility for providing rehabilitative services be recognized and met, and that the passive custodial role of these institutions be restructured into an active therapeutic one.

d. In those areas where Indian boarding schools cannot soon be eliminated, either because of problems of geography or transportation or because of the need for residential placement for therapeutic considerations, the present large dormitory units should be replaced by smaller cottage-type communities which will offer greater privacy and a healthier setting for individual and group psychological development. Further, there is a clear need for developing active and ongoing communication between the family of the student and the boarding school. This communication should include orientation, regular progress reports, conferences over problems in their early stages, visits to the school by the parents and to the Indian community by school personnel.

e. An extensive effort should be made to institute the practice of placing Indian boarding school students in substitute families in the boarding school community. These families, whose close involvement in school activities should be sought, could provide for the student greater opportunity for enhanced development of social techniques, of a sense of personal responsibility, familial and cultural identity.

f. Experimental approaches to meeting the needs of the minority child should include changes in the age of entrance to school, length of the school day and the school year, and the type of school building.

g. A variety of approaches to educational integration should be tried on a wide scale and factors that effect success or failure should be determined.

h. Study space should be provided for inner city children in school basements, public buildings, churches, the stores of cooperating merchants, etc. Carrels equipped with automated teaching devices would be desirable.

i. The creative use of tutors, who may be peers and may or may not be paid, should be encouraged.

7. That motivation for school achievement be fostered among minority group children.

a. Career-mobiles, travel grants, domestic cultural exchanges, and similar programs would alleviate much of the socially reinforced narrowness of vision by which many majority and minority group youngsters limit their personal identities and interpersonal competencies. Not only must middle-class and lower-class youth, white and non-white, learn to include each other in their respective world views, but much work needs to be done to reduce the generation gap between middle-class adults and lower-class youngsters within the same minority group. This gap of mutual distrust and non-communication is a large factor behind the low aspiration level and sense of alienation found in so many of the adolescents of several minority groups in America today.

b. Numerous subsidized traveling grants should be arranged for minority children to provide them the sociological opportunity of extended travels. The majority group children should also be given the advantage of travel grants into minority areas.

c. Experimentation with material rewards for school achievement is recommended. Community groups should be involved in setting up such a system so personal relationships may develop.

d. Youth should be involved as early as possible in the decision-making process regarding problems that affect them and should be intimately involved in the implementation of those decisions.

8. That the quality of school personnel be improved.

a. Civil service and tenure systems of teacher employment should be modified so that meritorious service may be rewarded and maintained.

b. Many factors in the life and school career of minority group children mitigate against their taking hold of the learning atmosphere in the school. Therefore they are much less likely to recover from poor teaching than children from more favored families. All school policy-makers should deal realistically with the causes of poor morale and the avoidance of inner-city school systems by many of the best teachers who might otherwise be employed there. The remedies might include greatly increased financial incentives and administrative systems that emphasize flexibility and professionally rewarding interactions (as opposed to the current situation in which the administrative rigidity in schools serving minority groups is notorious).

c. Training for teachers should include field experience in minority group communities and continuing supervision by master teachers.

d. Instruction in mental health concepts should be an important part of the pre- and inservice training of teachers.

e. The employment of sub-professionals as members of the instructional team should be expanded; career lattices should enable the sub-professional to assume responsible roles within the school institution or enter the teaching ranks.

f. Members of the private and government sectors should be included in the planning and teaching. These people must be carefully trained and selected to work with minority youth. They might also be the agents for bringing special equipment into school systems.

g. Since personnel in the Bureau of Indian Affairs and the Public Health Service have such influence on the lives of the Indian people, mandatory continuing education on Indian history, culture, current and ongoing programs and problems is recommended. Material should be developed by these agencies to be made available to state and local bodies providing educational and other services to Indian communities. The goal of such a policy would be to increase the effectiveness of the professional by enabling him to employ the cultural perspective and value system of the group served in his efforts to enhance the process of identity-formation and the development of techniques for problem solving.

   h. That ways be speedily found to promote meaningful involvement in policy-making by the Indian community served by both the local and the boarding school.

9. That schools should be part of comprehensive human development centers including health and other public services. As a minimum, the following auxiliary services should be provided within schools that serve minority group children.

   a. Guidance and counseling programs should be meaningful to minority group children in the light of the pressures and experiences which they see daily.

   b. School community workers should be employed to bridge the communication gap between the school and minority group families.

   c. Follow-up services in school settings should make medical, psychological, and social work services available as needed to children and their families.

   d. Programs should be devised to insure that all children have a balanced diet.

   e. A means of providing new and attractive clothes for poor children, especially adolescents, will facilitate the development of a positive self-concept.

10. That research regarding the learning of minority group children be stimulated.

   a. Longitudinal studies to follow the progress of minority children in terms of their specific educational and social backgrounds should be instituted.

   b. Research in the effectiveness of various minority group children (e.g., peer learning, role playing, and simulation tasks) should be continued.

   c. New and more adequate ways of testing children should be determined.

Law Enforcement

1. As compared to the white child of the same age (and even the same economic status), the child of a racial or ethnic minority is much more likely to have negative experiences with the police which will leave permanent marks on his personality development and world-view. How the police are perceived by minority group youngsters will have a direct impact on the youth's view of the society at large, which too often is one of corruption and abuse of minorities. The importance of the policeman as a first-line contact and symbol of the total society to minority group children and youth cannot be overstated; initial impressions are often decisive in the formation of their attitudes and responses to other authority figures.

Police training and practices, therefore, should relate directly to the officers' need for an increased awareness of and responsiveness to the community's needs. Since community awareness is dependent to a great degree upon community involvement, it is recommended that an ongoing part of the policeman's role should be his actual participation in local community activities. The recommendations of the President's Advisory Commission on Civil Disorders pertaining to the police are heartily endorsed.

2. Recommended that policymakers be condemned for encouraging various repressive measures purporting to "control" civil disorders which are causing harm to the personalities of children. We note, for example, the reports of disorientation and psychosis resulting from an untested drug (Mace).[1]

Clinical Services for Minority Group Children

Minority group children have limited access to mental health services due to such barriers as language, finances, and transportation as well as the documented lack of mental health facilities in rural and urban low-income areas. Treatment is also hampered by the attitudes of minority groups toward seeking psychiatric help and toward what can be expected from such services. The problem is compounded by differing definitions of what constitutes mental health among minorities themselves and on the part of middle-class teachers, social workers, and mental health professionals. Therefore the Committee recommends the following:

1. That drastic reforms be undertaken in funding and administration so that the delivery of clinical and preventive services—both standard and innovative in nature—may begin to catch up with the tremendous backlog of need. The concept of administration incorporated into Federal law (P.L. 89–749) that both lay persons and mental health professionals function at the policy-making and decision-making level must be made truly operative. It must be recognized that the twin problems of inadequate funds and archaic administrative approaches take their toll on most programs purporting to serve the human needs of the poor. It must be recognized that the emotionally disturbed poor youngster, his family and, indeed, his country are the sufferers when novel ideas, effective personnel and costly proposals are so regularly crushed by policymakers and administrators whose primary orientation has become to look good and save money.

The fact that such policymakers and administrators are responding to a broader national orientation should be a source of national shame and a call to action, so that collaborative efforts to meet the needs of the poor

1. "Mace in the Face," *The New Republic,* April 7, 1968.

and the sick become a matter of highest, rather than lowest, national priority.

2. That clinics provide interpreters in areas where minority groups that speak other than English are concentrated—for example, Spanish interpreters in Mexican-American communities—and that the role of interpreter becomes the first ladder of opportunity for the training of community health technicians.

3. Because of the scarcity of psychiatrists, psychologists, and other mental health professionals, particularly from minority groups, who cannot meet the high costs of training, efforts should be made to reverse this situation through large scale financing. Furthermore, the human resources required to meet the needs of mental health facilities in minority communities must be provided in adequate proportions.

4. In order to reduce the apprehension with which mental health services are viewed, local non-professionals (community health technicians) be trained to function in a variety of roles which will enhance and extend mental health services to the community. The role of the trained community health technician must be envisioned within the concept of a team approach. This will allow full participation of both technicians and professional in action and policy-making roles.

5. That lattices of opportunity be constructed for community health technicians which will create lateral and upward technical and professional mobility and status. That is, testing materials, licensing procedures, and rigid qualifications based on traditional professional role definitions must be revised to include new careers. Furthermore in the interest of both continuity and efficient use of manpower, newly trained workers should become teachers and thereby fully participate in the policy-making and training process.

6. That special training and orientation be instituted for mental health professionals who deal extensively with minority-group clientele to enhance their understanding, knowledge, and sensitivity and to make them aware of social class biases.

7. That effective mental health clinics be made accessible to minority-group children by locating them in the centers of minority-group populations whenever possible; that, when central locations are not possible, transportation be made available.

8. That intensive studies be continued and expanded to determine the extent to which social class inequities in treatment are occurring and that such findings be published and corrective action taken.

9. That adequate funding be assured for innovative and long-range experimental programs as well as to include their proper evaluation. (a) In order to counteract risks of misinterpretation on the part of outside research professionals, it should be required that active community

members be part of the reviewing board. (b) Following successful screening of the experimental programs, the reviewing board should be active in channeling the positive results to the proper agencies in order to implement the programs on a widespread scale.

10. That the aspects of the life style of minority groups that tend to minimize or maximize tendencies toward mental health be identified and the latter become the basis of an educative program.

11. All clinical agencies that have minority-group members as potential patients, must especially provide preventive mental health education programs along the following guidelines.

I. *Personnel*

The traditional mental health professionals will supplement their usual roles with educational functions, but the major responsibility should be in the hands of non-medical mental health education specialists with a background of teaching, behavioral sciences, and mental health theory and practice. In addition, full use should be made of non-professional talents in the community, that by personality and background are acceptable to the minority group.

II. *Content*

A. Education for Mental Health
Positive material on sex, marriage, child-rearing, strengthening family patterns and ego development.
B. Education about Mental Illness
Recognition of signs of emotional disorders, which are often misunderstood and treated inappropriately. Changing of attitude toward mental illness and psychiatric services and knowledge about the availability of such services.
C. Special Education for Developing Minority Group Strengths
Developing health attitudes about one's own race, healthy habits of resistance to white racism, healthy habits of action to counteract tendencies to lassitude, despair and self-destruction.

III. *Methods and Materials*

Not only should use be made of traditional methods of communication (such as T.V., movies, books, pamphlets, lectures, etc.) but newer techniques (particularly of face to face confrontation of peers) should be explored and utilized.

It is most important that all materials used in such a program be prepared with an understanding of the present attitudes of the target group; this means that most existing material aimed at the white middle class is inappropriate.

Delivery of Services

1. That health, educational, and other public services be unified in experimental human development centers.

2. That a realistic program of welfare payments or child care allowances above the poverty level should be maintained to preserve the well-known strength of low-income parents vis-à-vis their small children and to help maintain the two-parent family.

3. That adequate financial aid and social services be available to all who need them; that a minimum level of assistance be established in the States; that need be the sole measure of entitlement; and that a national program standard be required that includes a Federal-State plan of financing for equitable cost sharing (Advisory Council on Public Welfare).

Housing

1. That the design of urban renewal and similar programs should give highest priority to the human needs involved and should minimize the risks of disrupting the family and the social constellation of community members by providing for community participation in every level of its development.

2. That a massive construction program be undertaken to assure adequate housing to all poor families.

3. That a small percentage of all federal monies allocated to cities be earmarked for beautification of the inner city, rural depressed areas, reservations, etc.

Community Participation

1. That control of the community by the community be promoted, especially in such areas as child care, school operation, urban renewal, police-community relations, and the operation of service centers.

Every effort should be made to strengthen the family life of all American families. One approach that would be especially relevant to the Indian reservation, the barrio, and the black ghetto would be to remove the sense of powerlessness over, and sense of lack of protection from, societal agents (policemen, school teachers, bill collectors, etc.). Obviously, this could only be the result of strong new efforts in grass-roots community organization for community control of local institutions.

The benefits to families of oppressed minorities of such a social achievement would be enormous. It is currently impossible for a non-white family to extend an umbrella of protection over its members in the way an average white family above the poverty level can. In most parts of the nation, non-white family members are being trained to avoid physical and verbal abuse, humiliation, unlawful search and seizure, and harassment by various authorities. This amounts to social "castration" and profoundly affects the fathers and young males in these families. A program for strengthening family life, therefore, must start with supporting the basic function of *protection* that the family must serve; and serious community organization efforts would have to produce social change to the extent that minority-group members could expect officials to serve and respect them, not humiliate them and to expect their local policemen to protect them, not harass them.

2. That community resources be developed through such activities as the following:

a. Involvement of parents in advisory subprofessional and volunteer capacities in programs providing services for children.
b. Provide training and job opportunities in para-professional capacities so that community members may develop special skills in such areas as recreation, mental health, medical care, teaching, and slum rebuilding; create career lattices leading to professional status.
c. That community development specialists institute classes on job skills required for community participation.

3. That the right to organize politically be protected zealously.

4. That all ethnic groups have recourse to experimenting with utilization of ombudsmen.

Manpower Training and Employment

1. Due to the close correlation existing between the psychological maladjustment of children and such problems as poor housing, lack of health care, poor education, inadequate and restrictive welfare benefits, and lack of employment opportunities, that gainful employment or a minimum income be guaranteed families in need.

2. That all manpower training programs, both in the public and private sectors, be coordinated and, if possible, consolidated at all levels.

3. That enforcement powers be exercised to eliminate discriminatory practices wherever they exist and that withholding of all federal grants-in-aid funds from activities which discriminate on grounds of race, color, religion, sex, and age also be exercised.

4. That labor unions include in their memberships, and especially

their apprenticeship programs, all potentially "qualifiable" minority group applicants.

5. That public sector at all operating levels, including federal, state, county, city, and municipality, revamp their departments, hiring practices, and policies to make available thousands of entry level jobs and opportunities for promotion.

6. That private sector, in spite of the profit motive, assume a major responsibility in providing thousands of jobs at the entry level, which would include on-the-job training, opportunities for the acquisition of basic education as part of the training, and adequate provisions for promotion.

7. That minority-group personnel, both sub-professional and professional, be recruited and trained in the areas of preventive medicine and mental health.

8. That location of business and industry in the slums, Indian reservations and other economic depressed areas be encouraged by giving financial incentives, guaranteeing insurances, obtaining support from banks and foundations, and establishing government offices. In order to qualify for this aid, a business or industry must substantiate that its operation will be consistent with the economic and social needs of the community and that employment practices will favor the advancement of personnel from that community.

9. That migration to the North be counteracted by providing opportunities in the rural South, reservations, etc., through fostering industrial development, setting up marketing co-ops, providing loans for developing truck farms, etc.

Community Parent-Child and Child-Rearing Facilities

The determination of the child's needs, as well as the adoption of appropriate measures of intervention should have, as its basic context, the family as the primary child-rearing institution.

However, the family is at present subject to the disintegrating effects of divorce, separation, illegitimacy and, even with the fullest support, may be unable to fulfill its role with regard to child development. Therefore, society and the family must collaborate in matters of child welfare. To the degree that the family is unable to carry out its functions with regard to child development, the community is responsible for supplementary or complementary services in a variety of degrees and forms appropriate to each concrete situation.

Programs must be varied, taking into account actual needs and problems of working mothers and minority-group children. A variety of care arrangements should be offered including homemaker services, centers providing a few hours of care, or facilities for an entire day. In all cases, parental involvement is crucial with the aim of maximizing adult potential in addition to enhancing child development.

The Committee, therefore, makes the following recommendations:

1. That comprehensive programs for parents and children including health, day care, recreation, and education facilities for children from birth on, be established.

2. That highest priority for placement in the all-day child care program be given to children in clinically or socially very disturbed homes, and second priority be given to children from homes where the parent unavoidably must be absent and efforts to find adequate regular child care inside the home or neighborhood seem to have failed.

3. That special attention (including both parental involvement and professional judgment) be paid to the following:

    a. The potential dangers of all-day programs as opposed to home-care.
    b. Proper timing of the phasing-in of the all-day child care program into the comprehensive program.
    c. The possible need to discontinue or limit the all-day program if staffing difficulties become severe once the program has become operative.
    d. The program and procedures of the child care staff.
    e. The training and composition of the child care staff.
    f. The maximum allowable rate of personnel turnover in the child care staff.
    g. The proper ratio of staff to children.

4. That the planning, development, operations, and evaluation of the program include participation from the populations to be served in all phases of the program and its administration having access to appropriate professional consultation. To be explicit, participation should be as follows:

    a. Policy and decision making board of directors composed of local population members.
    b. Advisory groups composed of the broader community.
    c. Employees operating at a variety of levels carrying out jobs that need to be done, depending upon the individual's interest and capabilities. (This would imply developing a career opportunities program so that community aides need not be locked into low-paying job levels.)
    d. The training program should also include institutes, workshops, etc., for the purpose of increasing the effectiveness of professionals serving the program toward the end of making them more responsive to

the particular needs, customs, and values of the people and community.

e. The establishment of parent and child care centers cannot be considered apart from programs to strengthen the community in all
areas (occupations, economic, income, etc.) enabling children to
develop healthy personalities within the style of their cultural group.
This is an extension of cultural pluralism, which the Committee
envisages as the best future for these United States.

APPENDIX

THE JOINT COMMISSION ON MENTAL HEALTH
OF CHILDREN, INC.

209

ELIZABETH M. BOGGS, Ph.D.
State College, Pennsylvania

THOMAS BRADLEY
Los Angeles, California

ORVILLE G. BRIM, Ph.D.
New York, New York

E. H. CHRISTOPHERSON, M.D.
San Diego, California

HENRY V. COBB, Ph.D.
Vermillion, South Dakota

ROBERT I. DAUGHERTY, M.D.
Lebanon, Oregon

ADA E. DEER, M.S.W.
Minneapolis, Minnesota

LEON EISENBERG, M.D.
Boston, Massachusetts

DANA L. FARNSWORTH, M.D.
Cambridge, Massachusetts

LORENE FISCHER, M.A.
Detroit, Michigan

V. REV. MSGR. ROBERT E. GALLAGHER
New York, New York
(Deceased October 6, 1968)

GEORGE E. GARDNER, M.D., Ph.D.
Boston, Massachusetts

MIKE GORMAN
Washington, D.C.

JAMES L. GROBE, M.D.
Phoenix, Arizona

NICHOLAS HOBBS, Ph.D.
Nashville, Tennessee

PHILIP A. HOLLAND
Fairbanks, Alaska

RABBI I. FRED HOLLANDER
New York, New York

EDWIN S. KESSLER, M.D.
Washington, D.C.

REV. LEO N. KISROW
Nashville, Tennessee

HYMAN S. LIPPMAN, M.D.
St. Paul, Minnesota

NORMAN V. LOURIE, A.C.S.W.
Harrisburg, Pennsylvania

REGINALD S. LOURIE, M.D.
Washington, D.C.

JOSEPH P. MALDONADO, A.C.S.W.
San Francisco, California

HARRIET MANDELBAUM
Brooklyn, New York

JOHN L. MILLER, Ph.D.
Great Neck, New York

MILDRED MITCHELL-BATEMAN, M.D.
Charleston, West Virginia

WILLIAM C. MORSE, Ph.D.
Ann Arbor, Michigan

JAMES M. NABRIT, JR., J.D., LL.D.
Washington, D.C.

JOHN J. NOONE, JR., Ed.D.
Washington, D.C.

JOSEPH D. NOSHPITZ, M.D.
Washington, D.C.

K. PATRICK OKURA
Omaha, Nebraska

ARNOLD PICKER
New York, New York

DANE G. PRUGH, M.D.
Denver, Colorado

KURT REICHERT, Ph.D.
New York, New York

JOSEPH H. REID, A.C.S.W.
New York, New York

EVEOLEEN N. REXFORD, M.D.
Boston, Massachusetts

JULIUS B. RICHMOND, M.D.
Syracuse, New York

MRS. WINTHROP ROCKEFELLER
Morrilton, Arkansas

ALAN O. ROSS, Ph.D.
Stony Brook, New York

CHARLES SCHLAIFER, F.A.P.A. (Hon.)
New York, New York

MEYER SONIS, M.D.
Pittsburgh, Pennsylvania

GEORGE TARJAN, M.D.
Los Angeles, California

PERCY H. STEELE, JR., A.C.S.W.
San Francisco, California

MARY ALICE WHITE, Ph.D.
New York, New York

ROBERT LEE STUBBLEFIELD, M.D.
Dallas, Texas

LEONARD WOODCOCK
Detroit, Michigan

STAFF OF THE COMMISSION

EXECUTIVE AND TECHNICAL STAFF

JOSEPH M. BOBBITT, Ph.D.
Executive Director

DOMINIC J. DERISO
Administrative Officer

CATHERINE S. CHILMAN, Ph.D.
Senior Writer

BEATRICE H. GUSTAFSON, M.A.
Senior Research Associate

RITA A. PENNINGTON, M.A.
Research Associate

BARBARA SOWDER, M.A.
Research Associate

ELIZABETH BOGAN, Executive Secretary
LORENA K. JONES, Secretary
ELEANOR M. JORDAN, Bookkeeper
SHEILA M. KELLEHER, Receptionist
EVELYN J. WOODS, Secretary

FORMER STAFF

EDWARD D. GREENWOOD, M.D.
Deputy Director

SIDNEY L. WERKMAN, M.D.
Deputy Director

ISRAEL GERVER
Senior Research Coordinator

RUTH M. BARTFELD, B.A.
Research Associate

CATHLEEN M. BLASKO

PAMALA M. BLOCHER

ROSLYN J. COHEN

ANNIE S. COPLAN, M.A.
Research Associate

STANLEY S. GOLDMAN, M.A.*
Research Associate

FLORENCE S. JACOBSON, B.S.
Research Associate

PEGGY LAMPL
Information Officer

ANNETTE G. MOSHMAN, M.S.
Librarian

FRANCES H. BUCHANAN

BERNICE S. GORDON

MARIA P. PEYSER

KAREN G. RICKER

JOHN SMITH

JAMES BETHEA

EUGENE D. DUGGER

ANN KELLEY

SHEP W. REIDINGER

RODNEY A. ROLLO

JOAN V. TODD

* Deceased.

Affiliate Organizations

American Academy of Child Psychiatry
American Academy of General Practice
American Academy of Pediatrics
American Association for Children's
  Residential Centers
American Association of Psychiatric
  Clinics for Children
American Association on Mental
  Deficiency
American College Health Association
American Humane Association
American Legion
American Medical Association
American Nurses Association
American Occupational Therapy
  Association
American Orthopsychiatric Association
American Parents Committee
American Personnel and Guidance
  Association
American Psychiatric Association
American Psychoanalytic Association
American Psychological Association
American Public Health Association
American Public Welfare Association
American Social Health Association
American Sociological Association
American Speech and Hearing
  Association
Association for Childhood Education
  International

Child Study Association of America
Council for Exceptional Children
Council of Jewish Federation & Welfare
  Funds, Inc.
Council of State Governments
Day Care and Child Development
  Council of America, Inc.
Family Service Association of America
Interprofessional Research Commission
  on Pupil Personnel Services
National Association for Mental Health
National Association for Retarded
  Children
National Association of Social Workers
National Association of State Mental
  Health Program Directors
National Conference of Catholic Charities
National Committee for Children and
  Youth
National Congress of Parents and
  Teachers
National Council on Crime and
  Delinquency
National Education Association
National League for Nursing
National Rehabilitation Association
National Society for Autistic Children
The Orton Society, Inc.
Planned Parenthood/World Population
United States National Student
  Association

Index